# Teaching in Primary Schools

Edited by
*Asher Cashdan and Lyn Overall*

CASSELL

**Cassell**

Wellington House
125 Strand
London WC2R 0BB

370 Lexington Avenue
New York
NY 10017–6550

First published 1998

**British Library Cataloguing-in-Publication Data**
A catalogue for this book is available from the British Library.

ISBN 0-304-70360-5 (hardback)
     0-304-70361-3 (paperback)

Typeset by BookEns Ltd, Royston, Herts.
Printed and bound in Great Britain by Redwood Books, Trowbridge, Wiltshire

# TEACHING IN PRIMARY SCHOOLS

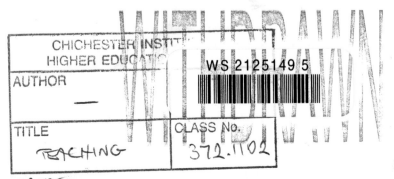

**Also available from Cassell:**

D. Coulby and S. Ward (eds): *The Primary Core National Curriculum, 2nd edition*
R. Crompton and P. Mann (eds): *IT Across the Primary Curriculum*
L. Poulson: *The English Curriculum in Schools*
E. Biggs and K. Shaw: *Maths Alive!*
K. Carlton and E. Parkinson: *Physical Sciences: A Primary Teacher's Guide*
A. Pollard and S. Tann: *Reflective Teaching in the Primary School, 3rd edition*
J. Glover and S. Ward: *Teaching Music in the Primary School*
J. Griffin and L. Bash (eds): *Computers in the Primary School*

# Contents

# Notes on Contributors

The contributors to the book all have strong Sheffield connections, either as permanent staff in the School of Education at Sheffield Hallam University or as professional educators in the area. Some of their specific interests and responsibilities are outlined briefly below.

**Di Bentley** is Director of the School of Education and well known for her work in science and teacher education. She has been a teacher and a Senior Inspector and worked with a National Curriculum development project.

**Susan Cameron** is the Senior Curriculum Adviser for Sheffield Local Education Authority and an Ofsted Registered Inspector. She has taught in primary and secondary schools in Liverpool, Clwyd and Cumbria and worked as a teacher trainer in Clwyd and Cumbria.

**Asher Cashdan** is Emeritus Professor of Education, with a background in developmental psychology, literacy and special needs.

**John Coldron** is a former PGCE primary course leader, active in research into equal opportunities, parents and education and teachers' thinking.

**Chris Glover** is a retired deputy headteacher and an experienced special needs educator and researcher.

**Alan Haigh** has been responsible for setting up and developing the School's partnership arrangements with primary schools.

**Joan Jones** is an experienced primary school teacher, with specialization in history.

**Jackie Marsh** has recent classroom experience and a particular interest in equal opportunities.

**Guy Merchant** has carried out research in literacy and is Head of the School's English Centre.

**Moira Monteith** is Head of the On-Line Education Unit in the School of Education.

**Margaret Noble** has been a primary school teacher and an LEA advisory teacher. She is subject leader for primary design and technology and has particular expertise in assessment.

**Lyn Overall** is course leader for the primary BA and BEd courses; she is an expert in literacy and in management studies.

**David Owen** has specialized in geography and outdoor education and has a background in both primary and secondary teaching.

**Angela Rees** has been Head of both primary and secondary initial teacher education and Director of the School of Education. She is currently Head of Continuing Professional Development as well as being an Ofsted Inspector.

**Alison Ryan** has been a primary school teacher and has expertise in archaeology and geography.

**Robin Smith** has a science and primary teaching background with a particular interest in the field of teachers' thinking.

**John Stirton** is responsible for work in special needs in the School.

**Brian Taylor** is an experienced primary teacher who is now Head of Wybourn Primary School, Sheffield.

**Pamela Thomas** is currently PGCE Primary Course Leader. She has a particular interest in personal, social and moral education as well as religious education.

**David Turner** is an educational historian who was until recently Head of Initial Teacher Training in the School.

# Acknowledgement

The idea for this book came from conversations with colleagues in the School of Education at Sheffield Hallam University, in particular John Coldron, Robin Smith and Angela Rees. However, as both they and a number of other colleagues eventually found themselves writing chapters, they hardly qualify for acknowledgement! But we would like to take the opportunity of thanking Di Bentley, the School Director, for supporting the project, and Fran Belbin, who came to the rescue on numerous occasions.

# Abbreviations

| | |
|---|---|
| ATM | Association of Teachers of Mathematics |
| CATE | Council for the Accreditation of Teacher Education |
| CLPE | Centre for Language in Primary Education |
| CMC | computer mediated communication |
| DfEE | Department for Education and Employment |
| GTC | General Teaching Council |
| HEI | higher education institute |
| ICT | information and communications technology |
| ILS | integrated learning system |
| IT | information technology |
| ITTE | IT in teacher training |
| KS | Key Stage |
| LEA | local education authority |
| MA | Mathematical Association |
| NCC | National Curriculum Council |
| NCET | National Council for Educational Technology (now BETCA: British Educational Communications and Technology Agency) |
| NPQ | National Professional Qualification |
| NPQH | National Professional Qualification for Headship |
| NPQSL | National Professional Qualification for Subject Leaders |
| Ofsted | Office for Standards in Education |
| PIN | Parents' Information Network |
| PoS | Programme of Study |
| QTS | Qualified Teacher Status |
| RE | religious education |
| SAT | standard assessment task/test |
| SCAA | Schools Curriculum and Assessment Authority (now QCA: Quality and Curriculum Authority) |
| SEN | Special Educational Needs |
| SENCO | Special Educational Needs Co-ordinator |
| TTA | Teacher Training Agency |
| WWW | World Wide Web |

# Introduction

## PRIMARY EDUCATION TODAY AND TOMORROW

There is probably no more exciting time than the present to be thinking about the future of primary education. Under the last government the introduction of the National Curriculum, Key Stage Assessment, league tables and Ofsted (Office for Standards in Education) inspection were among the huge changes imposed on teachers. The election of a Labour government in May 1997 has not slackened the pace of change or lessened the demands being made, but a spirit of consultation and collaboration is abroad and this book is partly a response to this. *Teaching in Primary Schools* is designed both for new and would-be teachers and for others also, such as parents and governors. This is not an academic textbook, but it *is* rigorous, and the ideas and principles raised here are designed to be readable, interesting and at times controversial. The book does not try to cover everything, but rather to propose key issues and principles that can be a starting point for further study.

The last few years have been very difficult for primary teachers. Their workload has been heavy and the pace of change has often been fast and furious. Much of this has been the result of the introduction of the National Curriculum. The notion of a National Curriculum which gives a broad view of subject knowledge and sets standards and levels is not unacceptable; in fact it is seen by many teachers as something positive and useful. However, as first presented it did seem to tear the heart out of the primary teacher's job. The promotion of subject knowledge as central to teaching was seen as naive. Often simplistic and unsophisticated models of how children learn seemed to have been used. In English, for example (rightly, in our view), there is an emphasis on the use of phonics in learning to read. However, the National Curriculum pays insufficient attention to the exact understanding of the way learners utilize this knowledge in making meanings from what they are attempting to read.

Further, the National Curriculum sidelined what many teachers thought of as their *raison d'être*: that was, to make a positive impact on the child's self-concept; to enable children to learn and to enjoy learning; to care for them and about them – not in a sentimental way but with a degree of altruism that needed to be celebrated rather than condemned. The impositions that were made were often bitterly resented. The workload, too, was huge. Many teachers simply left the profession. Those who remain are thankful that the review of the National Curriculum published in 1996 has given them a period of calm in which to rebuild and redefine. The report has slightly reduced the amount to be taught in most subjects and reintroduced an element of time to be spent as teachers decide. This has given a breathing space that will allow teachers time to rethink their role and to look forward to the needs of the next millennium.

Not that the pace of change has slowed that much: 1997 saw the introduction of the National Literacy Hour and the National Numeracy Hour on a widespread basis. Some teachers have welcomed these: 'Now I know what to teach.' Others have resented it as an imposition: 'They interfere with how I want to teach.' Yet others have used the changes to continue to teach what the child has to learn with sensitivity and care. Both 'hours' require high-quality whole-class teaching in which progression and continuity of instruction are given close attention. As with other good ideas, insufficient attention has been paid to the induction of serving teachers into understanding the underlying theories so that their practice can be thorough and effective. In more than one school, staff will not have their training for the literacy hour until the end of 1998. Neither of the 'hours' seems to have been properly resourced. For example, the literacy hour requires schools to equip themselves with sets of books for children to work on in groups; in many schools, this has left nothing in the budget for other necessities. However, to allow time for these developments in English and mathematics, schools are being given more flexibility in the delivery of subjects other than English, mathematics, science, information technology and RE.

Inspection of schools by Ofsted is also continuing to cause both pleasure and pain to teachers. In some schools, teachers have become adept at playing the inspection game. On the whole these schools have nothing to hide and much to be proud about, and there is little that the inspection will tell them of which they are not already well aware. In these schools, inspection, while not welcome, is not feared and may bring some well-earned public recognition. In other schools, teachers have not fully understood how to manage inspection and these schools have fared less well. Inspection has found very few schools to be 'failing'. Where this does happen, a combination of poor management with other adverse circumstances seems to apply.

What then of the school of the next century? If half the school population has a laptop computer by the year 2000, the virtual school could well begin then. The teacher would still be responsible for the intellectual and academic development of children but the methods and resources for this would be vastly expanded. The widespread introduction of information and communications technology (ICT) means that learning best done on a one-to-one basis becomes a reality and programmes could, for the first time, be tailored to match learning styles. The primary function of the school building is then the place where children go to be safe and cared for.

The job of the teacher will change. On the one hand, time will be spent setting up and monitoring individual progress and, on the other, an increased amount of time will need to be spent in providing very high-quality group work. To a greater extent than ever before, the teacher will be responsible for developing social abilities, teaching co-operation and collaboration in group work settings, helping children to understand and express their feelings, and developing children's sense of right and wrong. Children may be expected to spend more time studying beyond the school day, so it seems likely that the use of the school building could be considerably extended.

At present, homework clubs and the use of the building for coaching in academic subjects in the holidays are becoming more common. In future, the provision of quality activities beyond the school day both for school-aged children and for the community also seems to be likely.

The prospects for primary teaching and training seem brighter than they have been for some time. The acceptance by the new government of the latest Dearing Report into higher education is one aspect of this. It seems likely that in the twenty-first century we will continue to see teachers educated alongside other graduates. Despite the populist view to the contrary and Ofsted's best efforts to discredit the training of teachers, it found standards of training to be generally good. The report supports and drives forward the need for underlying understanding of educational theories by teachers. This means that teachers will be not merely good technicians delivering subject knowledge, but researchers as well. Another hopeful sign was the publication of the White Paper *Excellence in Schools*. Among a wide-ranging set of recommendations is that for the introduction of a General Teaching Council (GTC). A GTC that is independent of government could be a powerful force. The need for teachers to continue to develop their knowledge and skills throughout their service is also recognized in the White Paper. In the twenty-first century we look forward to seeing teaching as a fully recognized and revitalized profession, ready and able to play the leading role in the raising of educational standards.

## THE BOOK

Part 1 begins with **Angela Rees**' exposition of the new National Curriculum for Teacher Training. She brings her considerable experience of teacher education and school inspection to bear on this unique new development and concludes that it will prove a significant step forward as long as it is not allowed to stifle teachers' independence and creativity.

**Alan Haigh** surveys his experience of working with partnership schools. He sees much merit in the mentoring system's help for students and new teachers, though he insists that the resource demands this makes on primary schools in particular is difficult to accommodate, despite the spin-off from mentoring for the teachers themselves.

Part 2 begins with **David Turner**'s witty and penetrating account of the history of primary education in England, which he sees as a succession of unplanned developments of variable long-term value. He concludes his chapter with a fascinating historical catalogue of school buildings that could be drawn upon to enrich many a lesson.

Next comes **Jackie Marsh**'s analysis of diversity in the classroom and of how to work constructively and sensitively with pupils, parents and carers from a wide range of backgrounds and traditions.

**Asher Cashdan** explains how schooling can be much more about helping pupils to learn how to learn rather than about filling them up with facts. He also lays to rest some of the wilder fantasies currently prevalent about plunging educational standards, while agreeing that we certainly do need to raise our children's attainments.

**Robin Smith** and **John Coldron** continue the learning theme by showing new teachers how to improve their efforts by a continuous process of self-examination and reflection on the process of teaching.

Information and communications technology (now dubbed ICT) looks certain to revolutionize education in the next century; indeed, recent government statements have placed it alongside the three core curriculum subjects – English, maths and science – as the four areas on which all primary schools should concentrate their resources. In the first chapter of Part 3, **Moira Monteith** surveys the constantly changing area of ICT and offers the reader some immediately usable help and advice.

At the core of primary schooling there is still the learning of the traditional, as well as the newer school subjects. **David Owen** explains how the still new National Curriculum has already comprehensively changed the *content* of what is taught and now looks increasingly likely to lay down the *methods* of teaching also – a development that will want careful watching.

His chapter is followed by an appraisal of teaching in each of the three core curriculum subjects. **Guy Merchant** outlines developments in the teaching of literacy, including the new national strategy and the daily 'literacy hour', but stresses that there is far more to English than learning the mechanics of reading, however important that may be – and that we neglect a broader literacy at our pupils' peril.

**Susan Cameron** approaches mathematics as a subject that is as exciting and enjoyable as it is important. She makes use of both research and good classroom practice to show how to teach maths, and emphasizes the need for English schools to improve their work on number.

Science is no longer thought of as purely a body of factual knowledge, but rather as a set of more tentative explanations, where students construct their own meanings in their own, human, context. **Di Bentley**, herself an active writer and researcher in science education, provides a lucid exposition of constructivism together with guidelines for effective science teaching.

**Pamela Thomas**' special concern is with the school's role in the personal and social growth of its pupils. She shows how intellectual and character development go hand in hand. She also emphasizes the need for teachers to be supportive, but also firm, in their handling of the children for whom they are responsible.

A book of this scope could not reasonably offer a chapter on every school subject. Instead, **Alison Ryan** and **Joan Jones** agreed to set out some principles that apply to all primary subject teaching, particularly in project work. They then discuss in some detail their respective areas of geography and history, offering students (and teachers) a wealth of useful suggestions rooted in a firm grasp of both educational theory and tested practice.

The book's final part moves into the area of school relationships, both internal and with the outside community. The special needs Code of Practice makes heavy demands on class teachers. However, as **John Stirton** and **Chris Glover** explain, this is very much in the interest of teachers, parents and, of course, the pupils themselves. But help and support are available, and they point the reader to how and where this can be found.

Without adequate assessment, whether formal or informal, teaching would be meaningless. **Margaret Noble** explains how in fact all teaching has a built-in assessment component, though this has often not been consciously planned. She offers step-by-step guidance in articulating and developing quality practice.

**Lyn Overall** has in effect written two chapters. In the first section, she offers support in organizing pupils' learning, the bedrock on which good practice rests. The remainder of her chapter explores issues around behaviour, including the development of a positive policy to handle bullying.

The book concludes, deliberately, with a short chapter from a current practitioner. **Brian Taylor** runs his school with enormous commitment, energy and enthusiasm. When we look at his achievements in running a genuine community school, we can understand his occasional feelings of frustration at the bureaucracy with which he has to contend. Teachers who can emulate his approach, without being defeated by the pressures, will find themselves enjoying an immensely rewarding vocation.

*Lyn Overall*
*Asher Cashdan*
*October 1997*

# PART 1

# Becoming a teacher

# CHAPTER 1

# Learning to be a teacher – a national curriculum for teacher education

ANGELA REES

Just as children in the early stages of their learning ask many questions in order to make sense of new situations and experiences, so you will also have many unanswered questions as you embark on the exciting journey to becoming a teacher. For example, it is quite probable that you will have concerns about your ability to manage a class, how you will cope with teaching the whole National Curriculum or wonder how you can possibly learn everything that you need to know in the relatively short period of time of your initial teacher training course. Concerns such as these are quite natural. What should be remembered is that as a trainee teacher you are at the beginning of a journey that will be a career-long process.

During this time, among many other things, you will gain greater insights into the ways in which learning takes place as well as refining and developing your teaching skills. Hence it is desirable that from the outset you gain some understanding of the stages of professional development that you will encounter and how the framework for teacher education which is being developed by the government through the Teacher Training Agency will assist you in your progress from trainee to expert teacher. Thus while this chapter is aimed primarily at those who are embarking on the first stage of their professional journey, I hope that it will be of benefit to everyone in the profession who wishes to reflect on the content and process of becoming and developing as a teacher, within the context of an emerging national curriculum for teacher education.

Seeking answers to questions, such as what is the national curriculum for teacher education, why is it necessary, how when and where will it be implemented, and what are its implications for a trainee teacher, is highly pertinent to your understanding of this process. However, what may come as a surprise is that in spite of a recognition that the initial course of teacher training is, as its name suggests, but the first stage of a career-long learning process of professional development, until relatively recently the whole process of teacher education has lacked coherence and continuity. The reasons for this are complex and involve some understanding of the context in which teacher education has developed, without at this stage discussing the political and socio-economic factors.

As long ago as 1972, the report by the James Committee proposed three distinct cycles for teacher education to recognize stages of professional development in a teacher's career. Cycle 1 encompassed initial teacher education and recognized the need to create a more appropriate balance of time between learning in higher education and in schools. Cycle 2 introduced the concept of an induction programme for newly qualified teachers to replace the probationary year, with the provision of school-based tutors to help beginning teachers. Cycle 3 was to be a planned programme of in-service training for existing teachers.

This third cycle was considered essential since it was believed that no course of initial teacher training could provide a teacher with everything that would require them to keep abreast of changing requirements in schools. Unfortunately the James Report was never fully implemented on a national scale and, as David Hencke (1978) explains, radical and fundamental reform of the whole process of teacher education was blocked.

Since 1972 a variety of approaches to each of the three cycles or stages of teacher education have been developed within national guidelines, but are open to local interpretation. Hence until recently, different colleges of higher education and universities have been responsible for developing and delivering initial teacher training, within nationally prescribed guidelines, in the way they considered best so as to be able to award qualified teacher status to successful students – and they have done a very good job. The employer, whether this be the local education authority or the school, has been responsible for induction arrangements for newly qualified teachers. While the appointment of school-based tutors to support new teachers as envisaged by the James Report has never been fully implemented, the introduction of mentoring schemes in more recent years, whereby an experienced teacher is given responsibility for trainee teachers and very often also for newly qualified teachers in the school, is moving closer to this ideal.

For some years newly qualified teachers had to pass a 'probationary' year and were assessed by one of Her Majesty's Inspectors. Arrangements for this year were the responsibility of the local education authorities, which not only provided courses for the newly qualified teachers but also made time available for attendance. The removal of the requirement for a probationary year as a consequence of the James Report resulted in a more variable pattern of induction provision for newly qualified teachers. Irrespective of this particular change, it has however always been very much left to the individual teacher to decide whether or not to become involved in programmes of professional development offered by the local authority, college, university or other organization. While the majority of teachers see the need for this as a means of developing their professional skills, updating of subject knowledge or study of specific aspects of education, it has not been a professional requirement to engage in such activities.

One of the consequences – and some would suggest a strength of national guidelines, which allow for local interpretation – is the diversity and academic freedom which such a system permits. However, since 1979 this freedom has been constantly challenged and eroded as a result of increasing government intervention in teacher education. In particular there have been unprecedented changes to initial teacher training introduced by a succession of eight Secretaries of State for Education as part of their strategy to raise standards of pupils' achievement.

The establishment of the Council for the Accreditation of Teacher Education (CATE) in 1983 saw the beginning of changes which resulted between 1984 and 1993 in the publication of three government circulars for both primary and secondary initial teacher training. These prescribed the criteria to be met by all courses which lead to the award of qualified teacher status. It could be argued that as a consequence of these developments a national curriculum for initial teacher training was already in place.

But it was no surprise, following the implementation of the 1988 Education Reform Act by which the whole school system was reformed, that some of the changes to the content of initial teacher training over a period of time should be further adjusted to echo the new National Curriculum for schools.

In 1994 the government established the Teacher Training Agency – a non-departmental public body which is providing the catalyst for change. The Teacher Training Agency's ultimate aim is to raise pupils' achievement and improve their learning experiences. Fundamental to this is the improvement of the quality of teaching and teacher training and the promotion of teaching as a profession.

Hence the Teacher Training Agency has been given charge of resources, which include the allocation of numbers and funding for both initial and in-service training, together with responsibility for the recruitment of teachers and trainee teachers, initial teacher training, the induction of newly qualified teachers and the continuing professional development of serving teachers. Within its remit, one of the Teacher Training Agency's tasks has been to develop a national curriculum for initial teacher training, a task it considers to be most important and one which is being complemented by a framework for the continuing professional development of teachers.

This framework is being developed following a major review by the Teacher Training Agency in 1996 of the provision of continuing professional development, and is leading to the introduction of a series of National Professional Qualifications for Teachers. These will enable all teachers to have the opportunity to plan their professional development within an agreed national framework. One of the key features of the developing framework for the whole of teacher education is that it has been designed in consultation with teachers, headteachers, teacher trainers and representatives of professional organizations and subject associations, together with others both inside and outside education. Ultimately this will result in a new era in the development of teacher education and will I hope provide the much needed coherence and continuity.

28 June 1997 was a significant date for teacher education. On that day the Department for Education and the Environment published details of the new requirements for Initial Teacher Training (DfEE,1997b) that are to be implemented by all providers of initial teacher training in England. The requirements, based on the Teacher Training Agency's advice to the Secretary of State, are set out in four documents which describe the new criteria for all courses of initial teacher training in England, together with new standards for the award of qualified teacher status. They also set out the curricula for primary courses.

In a letter from the Department for Education and the Environment (DfEE, 1997b) to all providers of Initial Teacher Training and the Teacher Training Agency, it is specified that 'these new requirements are the first step in the Government's plans to work with the teacher training system to improve the standard of all new teachers'. It continues by endorsing its rationale for doing this, stating that:

> Raising the standards we expect of new teachers is crucial to raising the quality of education and pupil achievement across the system. Improving in particular the knowledge and competence of new primary teachers in the teaching of English and mathematics is critical to the Government's key policy aim of raising standards in literacy and numeracy and to achieving the new literacy and numeracy targets.

While this was the previous government's view, it is encouraging to note that the Labour government is clearly of the same opinion.

With such an explicit purpose to be implemented by all who train teachers, it is important that as a trainee teacher you also understand what knowledge, understanding and skills (National Curriculum for schools again!) you can expect to develop during your initial training. In the words of Anthea Millett (1997), chief executive of the Teacher Training Agency, this means that 'new teachers will be able to take control of their professional development from the earliest stage of their careers'.

At this stage a brief summary of the DfEE (1997c) document, *Teaching: High Status, High Standards* will assist your understanding of what is being required of you in a course of initial teacher training. In later chapters some of the issues which arise from aspects of the new curriculum for initial teacher training are addressed. As you read through the requirements, it is worth remembering that what is now being described has in recent years been incorporated in many courses of initial training. The difference is that the requirements are now spelled out in detail.

Hence the standards for the award of Qualified Teacher Status (QTS) set out more fully than ever before the core knowledge, understanding and skills which are considered to provide a foundation for effective teaching. The Department for Education and Employment (1997c) states that:

The **QTS standards** represent a full and detailed codification of requirements for new teachers. New teachers must not be admitted to the profession if they fall short of these clear standards. The standards are intended to ensure that, before taking over their own classroom for the first time, every new teacher will have proved his or her ability in a wide range of knowledge, understanding and skills including effective teaching and assessment methods, classroom management, discipline and subject knowledge. (p. 3)

The knowledge and understanding which you will be expected to demonstrate as a primary school trainee include the following. You will need to:

- understand the purposes, scope, structure, balance of the National Curriculum for your chosen age range plus religious education and be aware of its content

- understand how pupils' learning is affected by their physical, intellectual, emotional and social development

- have a secure knowledge of English, mathematics and science as prescribed in the Initial Teacher Training National Curriculum

- have a secure knowledge of your specialist subjects to A level standard in those aspects taught to Key Stage (KS) 1 and 2

- have a secure knowledge to at least level 7 of the National Curriculum of any non-core, non-specialist subject

- be able to cope securely with subject-related questions

- understand the progression of learning from pre-KS 1 to KS 3

- be aware of inspection evidence and research

- know pupils' most common mistakes

- have a knowledge of information technology

- be familiar with health and safety requirements.

Equally important is your ability to plan, teach and have effective class management skills, which demonstrate high expectations of all pupils in all subjects. These include:

- having secure knowledge and understanding of how and when to apply the teaching and assessment methods specified in the Initial Teacher Training National Curriculum for primary English, mathematics and science

- teaching to achieve progression in pupils' learning through identifying clear teaching objectives and content

- setting tasks for the whole class and individual and group work, including homework, which challenge and interest pupils

- setting appropriate and demanding expectations

- setting clear targets for pupils' learning, building on prior attainment

- identifying pupils who have special educational needs/are very able/are not yet fluent in English, and knowing where to get help in order to give positive and targeted support

- providing clear structures for lessons and for sequences of lessons

- making effective use of assessment information

- planning opportunities to contribute to pupils' personal, spiritual, moral and social development

- ensuring effective teaching of whole classes, groups and individuals

- monitoring and intervening when teaching, to ensure sound learning and discipline

- establishing a purposeful working atmosphere

- setting high expectations for pupils' behaviour and maintaining a good standard of discipline through well-focused teaching

- using teaching methods which sustain the momentum of pupils' work and keeping pupils on task

- being familiar with the Code of Practice on special educational needs

- ensuring that pupils acquire and consolidate knowledge, skills and understanding in each subject

- evaluating your own teaching critically.

Given that as a trainee teacher you could be observed teaching during an Ofsted inspection of a primary school, it is interesting to note the congruence between the standards to which you will be working in order to gain qualified teacher status and the inspection schedule used in inspections of primary schools. The criteria for inspection include the educational standards achieved by pupils at the school and the quality of teaching provided. Judgements made by the inspectors include the attainment and progress of all pupils, attitudes, behaviour and personal development of pupils, teaching, the curriculum and assessment, and pupils' spiritual, social, moral and cultural development. While the Ofsted Inspection framework was designed some time before the National Curriculum for Initial Teacher Training was developed, it is encouraging to find that the Teacher Training Agency has built upon this, rather than starting again.

Not surprisingly, the core curriculum for schools is very much emphasized in the National Curriculum for Initial Teacher Training, to reflect the requirements of the different key stages. Moreover, the Initial Teacher Training National Curricula for primary English and mathematics are consistent with both the national literacy and national numeracy projects. These curricula specify what is considered to be the essential core of knowledge, understanding and skills which all trainee primary teachers must be taught and be able to use in relation to English and mathematics. Clearly you need to learn these because they are what you are going to teach.

A similar curriculum is being developed for the teaching of science, and you will discover that some of the implications of teaching each of these subjects are considered in Chapters 9, 10 and 11. The curricula are considered to be a key element in the government's plans for raising pupil attainment in literacy and numeracy and making progress towards the new targets for the year 2000 described in the White Paper, *Excellence in Schools* (DfEE, 1997a) whereby 80 per cent of 11-year-olds should be achieving the expected standards in English and 75 per cent the expected standards in maths. For both English and maths the curricula specify the essential core knowledge, understanding and skills which all primary trainees must be taught, be able to use and be given opportunities to practise.

In the words of Geoffrey Parker (1997a), the first Chairman of the Teacher Training Agency, when writing to the Secretary of State for Education in June 1997, it is intended that 'they will ensure that trainees are taught how to teach reading, writing and number effectively, using methods that are known to work'.

The curriculum for primary English specifies that in order to gain qualified teacher status trainees must demonstrate that they know and understand how to secure pupils' progress in English. This means that as part of your course you will be taught the essential stages of development and progression in pupils' reading, writing, speaking and listening, since these are vital to your understanding of the high expectations that teachers should have of their pupils.

Moreover, you will be expected to teach effectively and to use appropriate methods of assessment. Consequently, your planning will include time dedicated to the explicit and systematic teaching of reading, writing (including grammar, spelling, punctuation and handwriting), speaking and listening appropriate to KS 1 and 2. In addition, you will be required to know how to identify and teach pupils whose difficulties in acquiring literacy skills arise out of a particular learning difficulty and to understand how to use information and communication technology (ICT) in order to foster the development of literacy skills.

As part of your initial training you will be taught how to recognize common errors of pupils in English, to understand how these arise, how they can be prevented and how to remedy them. In addition, you will be expected to understand how to evaluate and assess your teaching and pupils' learning in English, using formative, diagnostic and summative methods (see Chapter 15) and also to be able to recognize pupils' standards of attainment in English.

Fundamental to your ability to achieve these requirements is that by the end of your initial training you must demonstrate your own subject knowledge and understanding of English with respect to the nature and role of standard English and the spoken and written language systems of English, since these underpin effective teaching. In addition to the lexical, grammatical and textual aspects of English, you will be expected to know how to evaluate text and language critically and how to use the relevant technical terms.

The curriculum for primary maths, following the same pattern as that for primary English, describes the knowledge and understanding required by trainees to secure pupils' progress in mathematics at KS 1 and 2, effective teaching and learning methods and the knowledge and understanding in mathematics required by trainee primary teachers. This means that you will be taught the importance for pupils in nursery and reception classes to acquire the basic mathematical concepts necessary for later progression in mathematics. In order to ensure that pupils develop more powerful, abstract and precise understanding of mathematics, you will learn how their progress depends upon teaching which enables them to go beyond their concrete experiences, so that they can establish general concepts and develop the use of flexible and efficient mental and written procedures.

Hence it is necessary for you to understand the key stages of development and progression in pupils' understanding of mathematics. As in the teaching of English, you will be expected to appreciate the importance of engaging pupils' interest in and developing their enthusiasm for the subject. Effective teaching and assessment methods depend on your ability to understand how to teach, for example, the early stages of mathematics, accurate and rapid mental calculation, efficient standard and non-standard written and part-written methods of computation, the solving of numerical problems involving more than one operation, the appropriate and efficient use of calculators, the foundations of algebra, shape and space and measures, data handling, ways in which ICT can be used to support the teaching of mathematics, how to plan and pace individual mathematics lessons and sequences of lessons which include oral and interactive activities, and how to recognize the common errors and misconceptions of pupils in mathematics.

As with the English curriculum, you will be expected to understand how to evaluate and assess your own teaching and pupils' learning in mathematics, using formative, diagnostic and summative methods of assessment. Since it is essential that your own knowledge and understanding of mathematics is appropriate to the underpinning of your teaching at KS 1 and 2, during your initial training you will be expected to demonstrate your knowledge and understanding of number and algebra, mathematical reasoning and proof, measures, shape and space, and probability and statistics.

The final part of *Teaching: High Status, High Standards* relates to the revised requirements for all courses of initial teacher training. These show how it is intended that the standards of initial teacher training will be raised and provide details of trainee entry and selection requirements, course length and coverage, partnership requirements and quality assurance.

The emphasis on schools playing a central and active role in the training of teachers in partnership with higher education institutions is fundamental here. While this is a developing process, it is clear that schools now have a responsibility to be fully and actively involved in the planning and delivery of initial teacher training, as well as in the selection and final assessment of students. In Chapter 2, Alan Haigh provides useful insights as to how these arrangements have been and continue to be developed and the significance of their contribution to your training.

A further specific aspect within the requirements is the introduction from June 1998 of the Teacher Training Agency's *Career Entry Profile* (TTA, 1997a). Its purpose is to provide a summary of your strengths and priorities for further professional development in relation to the standards for the award of qualified teacher status, from initial training to your first teaching post. It is seen as a significant step in raising standards in teaching and is an important development in the induction procedures for newly qualified teachers in their first teaching appointment.

While at the end of your initial course of training you will feel confident and be competent in some areas, it is probable that you will need considerable support as a newly qualified teacher. Therefore the profile is intended to help those schools employing newly qualified teachers to deploy them effectively, to draw up an action plan for their induction and to provide targeted monitoring and support for them during that time.

Moreover, it is intended to help you to target and address your development needs by building upon your strengths in order to enable you to take responsibility for your own professional development. This is to be achieved by establishing the practice of target setting and review in order to provide a useful foundation for appraisal and for your future professional development. Hence it will start to be completed when you are nearing the end of your course of initial teacher training and decisions about awarding you qualified teacher status are being made – and will be further developed once you have completed your training and move into your first teaching post.

Following good practice, any weaknesses are not specified as such, but by writing down your strengths you will be enabled to identify areas for development. The *Career Entry Profile* (TTA, 1997a) comprises four sections:

- A summary of the newly qualified teacher's initial training, including any distinctive features

- The newly qualified teacher's strengths and priorities for further professional development during induction, as agreed between the provider and the newly qualified teacher

- The newly qualified teacher's own targets for the induction period

- Targets and an action plan for the induction period, as agreed between the school and the newly qualified teacher.

But the real significance and value of the *Career Entry Profile* lies not only in its contribution to bridging your development between initial training and induction into the profession, but in its development of your skills of reflection, evaluation and honesty with yourself about your abilities as a teacher. It is these skills which you should seek to develop throughout your career in order to improve learning about yourself and in particular about your skills as a teacher. Hence, throughout your career as you review your development, it is desirable that you continue to determine targets and devise action plans to achieve them.

So as you can see, the requirements for achieving qualified teacher status are now quite explicit, and provision is being made to ensure that once you are qualified, the beginnings of your career development needs are being addressed. Moreover, as indicated in *Excellence in Schools* (DfEE, 1997a), it is intended to establish a General Teaching Council in order to promote and raise the standing of the profession. Most significantly, the new standards for the award of qualified teacher status – the requirement for all who teach in the maintained sector of schooling – is now seen as the first National Professional Qualification in the framework of standards and qualifications being developed for all teachers.

Each of the consultation papers on the different standards provides the key elements of the framework and indicates that new standards are to be introduced for Advanced Skills teachers, special educational needs co-ordinators (SENCOs), together with qualifications such as the National Professional Qualification for Subject Leaders (NPQSL) and the National Professional Qualification for Headship (NPQH) (see TTA, 1997b). In addition, it is intended that training should be provided for serving headteachers. As a result of this framework, continuity and coherence between initial, induction and in-service education are being developed to assist in your development as a teacher.

However, while the notion of a national curriculum for teacher education may sound marvellous, a note of caution needs to be sounded. The teaching profession has to be careful lest only the prescribed professional development framework is perceived to be worthwhile. With the emphasis throughout each stage of development on training as opposed to education, it is worth remembering that a delicate balance needs to be maintained between enabling teachers to develop their own theoretical and practical framework for teaching, as opposed to telling trainees – and for that matter experienced teachers – what to do. The worry is that this balance may have begun to swing too far towards the 'practical' end.

With this word of caution in mind, it is none the less a significant achievement that a professional development framework for teachers is being developed. Based on clear, national, professional standards, it is being designed, according to the Teacher Training Agency (1996) to:

- establish clear expectations to help both schools and teachers at different points in the profession target and monitor their development and training effectively

- ensure the focus at every point is on improving pupil achievement

- provide a basis for professional recognition of the achievement of teachers

- help the Teacher Training Agency to ensure that high-quality, relevant provision is available to secure effective use of teachers' time and maximum benefits to their pupils.

This, together with the new standards for the award of Qualified Teacher Status, forms a national curriculum for teacher education. In the words of Geoffrey Parker (1997b), this will fulfil the Teacher Training Agency's expressed purpose, by encouraging

> progression up the professional ladder and securing teaching as an intellectually challenging profession that allows good teachers to enjoy career structures comparable to those in other professions.

## REFERENCES

DfEE (1997a) *Excellence in Schools*. London: DfEE.

DfEE (1997b) Letter to providers of Initial Teacher Training in England. London: TTA.

DfEE (1997c) *Teaching: High Status, High Standards* (Circular 10/97). London: DfEE.

Hencke, D. (1978) *Colleges in Crisis*. Harmondsworth: Penguin Books.

Millett, A. (1997) Bringing a new professionalism into teaching. *Education Journal*, March.

Parker, G. (1997a) Teacher recruitment – why we need the brightest and best, *Prep School*, Spring.

Parker, G. (1997b) Letter to David Blunkett, Secretary of State for Education.

TTA (1996) Letter to Chief Education Officers (and others), 29 November. London: TTA.

TTA (1997a) *Career Entry Profile for Newly Qualified Teachers*. London: TTA.

TTA (1997b) *Consultation Paper on Standards and a National Professional Qualification for Subject Leaders*. London: TTA.

TTA (1997c) *Training Curriculum and Standards for New Teachers*. London: TTA.

## SOME SUGGESTIONS FOR FURTHER READING

Beneath, N. and Carr, C. (eds) (1993) *Learning to Teach*. London: Routledge.
Calderhead, J. and Shorrock, S.B. (1997) *Understanding Teacher Education*. London: Falmer Press.
Craft, A. (1996) *Continuing Professional Development*. London: Routledge.

CHAPTER 2

# Partnership in primary school experience – or 'sitting by Nellie'

ALAN HAIGH

Since the late 1980s there has been a move to place students in school for greater lengths of time and to give more responsibility in the training of students to practising class teachers. Many of you reading this book will have been 'mentored' by a practising teacher during your school experience.

Is this a good idea? The answer is a qualified yes. It is common sense that learning alongside a competent practitioner in the workplace must have great benefits for the learner. Is it a new idea? No! The idea of a 'mentor' is as old as Aristotle. In nineteenth-century teacher education the principal mode of training was for the more able pupils to 'stay on' at school under the pupil-teacher scheme. Under this system the apprentice teacher worked alongside the practising teacher and later, when the forward-looking school boards established Pupil Teachers' Centres, the student teachers received further training after school. (The pursuit of improvement in standards is nothing new either – *plus ça change* ....) Could teacher training turn full circle in the twenty-first century?

In this chapter I would like to explore school/higher education partnerships and how these can best be developed in the interests of both the student teacher and the profession as a whole.

## TWO SCHOOLS OF THOUGHT

There have been – and still are – two distinct approaches to teacher education. On the one hand there is the 'technician–craft skill' model, on the other the 'academic–reflective practitioner' model. These differing philosophies have been mirrored over the last hundred years by the trend of putting the training of teachers either wholly in schools or making it almost completely college/university-based. How far are these two approaches mutually exclusive?

The technician approach identifies a set of skills or competences the beginner should achieve before being allowed to graduate as a qualified teacher. This is clearly specified in the government Circular 14/93 (DFE, 1993) as well as in Circular 10/97 (DfEE, 1997). The logic of this approach would move the initial education of teachers firmly towards a 'school-based' training model and perhaps even as far as fully 'school-centred' training, where the schools play the leading role in the partnership and take over the majority of the training. This was certainly the development envisaged by the authors of the 1994 Education Bill. Fortunately, or unfortunately, it is not the future envisaged by the vast majority of primary schools, which consider their role to be the education of children, and not the training of teachers. However, that is not to say that primary schools do not want to be involved in the training of the future members of their profession. On the contrary, my experience with over 150 partnership schools leads me to the opposite conclusion. However, they do not want to be seen as a cheap way of training teachers, and under present classroom conditions their contribution is forced to be somewhat limited.

The 'academic–reflective practitioner' approach does not view practice as less important, but sees theory not only in formal academic terms but also as being grounded in practice by a process of reflection and personal development. This approach obviously demands different skills from the mentor than just practical help and advice and is much more demanding in time and intellect of both learner and mentor.

On the one hand, the teacher mentor has to know the competence-based approach, with the emphasis on the student demonstrating the assessed skills delineated by the TTA. Teacher mentors need to be clear about their own practice and have shared expectations of planning and teaching with their higher education institution (HEI). The third partner in this relationship – the student – is obliged to model the practice and to evaluate him or herself against the expected competence. The HEI tutor is responsible for the agreement of the standards and expectations and involved in the learner's and mentor's preparation. Once this 'quality' is established, the role of the HEI is largely conducted at arm's length and the emphasis is more on assurance – that is, the monitoring and evaluation of the whole process. This system does not necessarily include reflective practice and could still deliver qualified teachers with top grades on the inspection criteria determined in the new *Framework for the Assessment of Quality and Standards in Initial Teacher Training* (TTA, 1997).

On the other hand, teacher mentors who see the value of developing a more reflective approach will need the knowledge and skills to be reflective practitioners themselves. Unfortunately, the term 'reflective practitioner' has many definitions and the Schön concept of reflection-in-action can at first be a little daunting for students and mentors alike. Dewey defined reflection as the 'consciously rational search for solutions to problems', and this seems to me a clear starting point. What is incontrovertible is that for teacher mentors to help different teachers they need to think about their own practice in order to articulate it. There is some evidence, as we will see below, that this has been a significant factor in the staff development of our teacher mentors.

My original question referred to mutual exclusivity – either one approach or the other. Most people involved in teaching will recognize that there is indeed a great deal of telling and guiding in the skills of the job, particularly at the beginning. However, one would also have to acknowledge that mature intelligent reflection will provide for the development of a more flexible, independent and creative teacher in the long term.

This argument parallels the present debate about teaching methods – that is, 'direct teaching' versus the 'child-centred discovery approach', where the contrast is between a pedagogy that emphasizes telling and explaining compared with one that involves children being more active: doing, discussing and making sense for themselves. Similarly, again, these two schools of thought are not mutually exclusive, but dependent upon the content and context of the teaching situation. In the same way, students and mentors have to decide when direct teaching and guiding is more appropriate and when it is time for reflection, reading and discovery.

## THE DEVELOPMENT OF THE STUDENT TEACHER AND THE ROLE OF THE MENTOR

Most teacher educators would recognize the stages outlined by Maynard and Furlong (1993, pp. 78–82):

- the apprenticeship model – learning to see

- the competency model – systematic training

- the reflective model – from teaching to learning

My own observations of student teacher development identify the initial stage as one of *survival*. During this stage learners are desperate to mimic, model, beg, borrow or steal any strategy that will help them survive in the classroom. (Unfortunately, some fall back on very rigid authoritarian models of practice which they themselves have experienced.) Often it is the case not that the learner does not ask questions; as some mentors point out, it is more a question of not knowing the questions to ask.

A lesson taught by an experienced teacher can appear deceptively simple, but the student teacher needs to 'learn to see'. The devil is in the detail, the behaviour strategies, the classroom management, the planning across the range of ability, the continuous assessment – all delivered with high expectations and lots of tender loving care! Student teachers have to recognize the detail in the planning and delivery of children's learning so they can practise the necessary skills. They also have to make the quantum leap from undergraduate language and thought to the language and concepts of young children, or they will fail to communicate successfully. At this stage the teacher mentor role is one of friend, supporter, instructor, guide, coach – also, just as with children, delivered positively, with lots of tender loving care.

The responsibility both of the students and of those involved in their preparation is to create guidelines of what to look for. These are tasks that demand that the student look and ask 'How do they do that?' Activities are also needed that allow students to practise in controlled and supervised conditions.

A good example is a task such as taking the register. It might seem simple enough and (as one of the mentor teachers pointed out) it is very good for establishing the student in the children's eyes as a teacher rather than another 'helper'. Other tasks involve giving clear instructions, routines for getting children's attention, practising clear, structured exposition, reading a story, ending and summarizing a lesson, and getting children to line up. Note that these are mainly whole class activities which the mentor can delegate to the student while team-teaching. If students have agreed to and prepared these teaching sequences, they not only begin to establish their credibility and authority, but they also begin to be regarded by the children more in a 'job-share' light: 'We have two teachers.' The survival stage is heavy on direct advice and the mentoring role is high on support.

As confidence grows, the student moves from sharing sequences, managing small groups and whole class 'story' to increased responsibility. There follows a stage of evolution analogous to that of a child beginning to walk unaided. The growth in independence begins a stage of striving to master the competence. A great deal of trial and error is involved, with lots of problem solving.

The student has first to recognize that things are not going right or can be improved upon. This may need teasing out by the mentor, as students will often recount that the lesson went well and the children enjoyed themselves. (Enjoyment is important but does not necessarily equate to learning!) Once the learner has adopted a more critical attitude there can follow analysis and suggestions for remediation.

Increasingly, the role of the mentor becomes one of adviser and facilitator, encouraging students to solve their own problems. The mentor needs to recognize when the student is ready to move into the 'mastery' phase and then to use more challenging strategies, which demand that students begin to solve problems themselves. The student will need to analyse, decide upon and implement a course of action. (Sometimes we need to learn the painful way, and the mentor may need to take a back seat.)

The vast majority of students are highly motivated and committed and this can lead to very ambitious plans. The mentor may have to stand by while the student plans half a dozen 'all-singing, all-dancing' integrated group activities for a class and watch from the sidelines as the situation descends into chaos, with the student teacher tearing around the room trying to be in three places at once. Practice is essential to gain control and mastery of any competence and teaching competences are no exception.

With this growth in mastery and confidence, students become more innovative. This would appear to be a further transition phase between the 'competence' and 'reflective' phases. The challenging now originates from the learner and not the mentor. The learner actively seeks challenge, such as addressing the needs of the less able and the more able; more practical open-ended problem-solving teaching situations; visits; class assemblies; extra-curricular activities, and so on.

The learner begins to become comfortable with his or her own practice. Teaching is seen as simple after all. You just have to get the children to shut up, listen to you and do as you say. You need to be clear about what you want them to learn and how they are going to go about it. The 'Yes, I can' inside you takes over and the panic retreats in its wake. Hopefully, all student teachers acquiring Qualified Teacher Status have reached this stage. In my opinion it is difficult to move to the reflective practitioner stage until you are comfortable with your practice.

It seems to me that the reflective practitioner stage is a much more philosophical phase, which is driven by the need not just to become competent but also to improve the quality of children's learning. The children are not only highly motivated but there is a cognitive match; the student teacher is aware of that match and how he or she will move those children on. The emphasis now seems to be not on the teacher's teaching skills, but more on the children's learning. This is a stage where theory and research do meet and inform practice.

It might be argued that this phase is more appropriate to the continuing professional development of teachers. Indeed, teacher mentors whom I have trained have claimed that their theory courses did not make sense until they had been teaching for several years, and they now wished they could attend the relevant sessions again.

Certainly this stage demands considerable academic and counselling skills from the mentor, not to mention time! Listening objectively with empathy and helping to refocus the learner's perspective in a non-threatening manner is a complex and demanding task. Without classroom release to reflect and review, this higher state of awareness is unlikely to be achieved. When the class teacher is continually faced with change from the outside, inner change is unlikely to happen.

The role of the mentor in enabling the student to learn through practice has been described in various ways in the literature, from what could be recognized as a job description, often seen as a contract between the HEI and the school, to lists of mentor skills. Fish (1995) refers to helpful behaviours that are useful in the mentoring process, placing the emphasis on the mentor giving up authority and allowing the learner to take responsibility.

There is a distinction between supervision and mentoring. A supervisor monitors the process and progress; a mentor is a good model and a critical friend who facilitates the process and establishes the progress. Supervision is an element of the mentoring process, but on its own it is insufficient to develop the growth of an independent reflective practitioner. Schön (1987) makes the point that 'when coach and student do their jobs well they act as on-line researchers!' A collaborative enquiry takes place, where both partners contribute to each other's understanding and the further development of their practice. Perhaps a little ambitious, but the point is well made that learners and mentors can and do learn from each other to the benefit of the children.

The notion of the teacher mentor's professional development, to which I have referred above, is supported by more than anecdotal evidence. In a questionnaire returned by 83 headteachers in the Sheffield Hallam primary partnership, when asked the question 'How does the partnership compare with the previous traditional system of placement?', only 3 ticked the 'not as good' box. In the comment section of this question the 'feel good factor' was consistently referred to; that is, schools appreciated the increased trust and professionalism developed between the partners in training. They further commented on the increased staff development of their teacher mentors.

Recent school experience evaluations from 120 Year 1 and 70 Year 2 BA students showed an overwhelming 90 per cent 'highly satisfactory' rating regarding the school and the help they had been given by their class teachers and mentors. Remarks like 'this was the best part of the course' and 'I have learned so much during my school experience' were very common. There is no doubt in my mind that the quality of school experience has improved considerably with the greater involvement of schools.

On the other hand, teachers have enjoyed the respect afforded them as professionals at a time when most of the observations made about them by the Chief Inspector and the press have been of a derogatory nature. This positive encouragement has had a hidden benefit for schools. Headteachers have noticed not just an improvement in teacher mentors' morale, but in many cases an effect on their practice too. At a recent primary teachers' conference, Meryl Thompson (1997) gave it as her view that primary partnership initiatives had been the single most effective measure in the drive for school improvement. One suspects that the government of the day had planned the changes with financial economies rather more in mind!

However, to return to my opening remarks concerning how far the circle will turn, I feel strongly that unless there are major resource increases, many schools will prove to have gone as far as they are prepared to go. They are not against involvement in quality assurance. Indeed, in our own partnership they are positively in favour of this. The idea of teacher mentors visiting students in other schools and being involved in the moderation and agreement of judgements is also an attractive one.

Since under the new *Framework for Inspection* (TTA, 1997) the mentors will be expected to grade the competence of final year students, then involvement in this process would seem to be a prudent measure on the part of the university partner. Indeed, the quality of the HEI's provision, and hence its future livelihood, will be judged by the accuracy and consistency of these final grades.

The schools are fast becoming the 'gatekeepers' in respect of the entrants to our profession and take this responsibility very seriously. But they see this as a responsibility *shared* with higher education institutions, which can then work to the benefit of the student, the school and the children.

## REFERENCES

DFE (1993) *The Initial Training of Primary School Teachers: New Criteria for Courses* (Circular 14/93). London: DFE.

DfEE (1997) *Teaching: High Status, High Standards* (Circular 10/97). London: DfEE.

Fish, D. (1995) *Quality Mentoring for Student Teachers.* London: David Fulton.

Maynard, T. and Furlong, J. (1993) Learning to teach and models of mentoring. In D. McIntyre, H. Hagger and M. Wilkin (eds) *Mentoring: Perspectives on School-based Teacher Education.* London: Kogan Page.

Schön, D.A. (1987) *Educating the Reflective Practitioner.* San Francisco: Jossey Bass.

Thompson, M. (1997) Presentation by the President of the Association of Teachers and Lecturers to the Annual Conference of the National Association of Primary Teachers. St Hugh's College, Oxford.

TTA (1997) *Framework for the Assessment of Quality and Standards in Initial Teacher Training.* London: Ofsted.

## SUGGESTIONS FOR FURTHER READING

Edwards, A. and Collison, J. (1996) *Mentoring and Developing Practice in Primary Schools: Supporting Student Teacher Learning in Schools.* Milton Keynes: The Open University Press.

Fish, D., *Quality Mentoring for Student Teachers*, as above.

Sushitzky, W. and Garner, B. (1995) It takes two to tango! Working with experienced others in the school. In J. Moyles (ed.) *Beginning Teaching: Beginning Learning in Primary Education.* Milton Keynes: The Open University Press.

PART 2

# The context of teaching

# CHAPTER 3

# The development of the English primary school

DAVID TURNER

The English primary school, like any other institution, is a product of its history. Some knowledge of that history and of key events in it will not only throw light on current practices and attitudes, but it will also assist in planning future directions and teaching. Some facts are well known; others may come as a surprise because of their origins. The physical layout of school buildings themselves is often a reflection of their educational purposes, so I have included a section on architecture as part of this chapter.

## ORIGINS AND STRUCTURE

Primary schools have not existed as long as some other schools such as grammar or infant schools. Not until 1944 were schools divided into primary and secondary phases, with a clear break at age 11. Before 1944, schools had been labelled 'elementary' and 'secondary' with a small proportion of scholarship pupils transferring to secondary school at age 11, while the rest remained in elementary school until age 14.

Why 11? At the beginning of the twentieth century the needs of the newly established state secondary (grammar) schools were seen as paramount. The concept of a ladder of educational opportunity linking the elementary school with the secondary school was also a key principle. Since grammar school pupils took their first public examinations at age 16, educationalists assumed that the mainly lower middle- or working-class pupils from the elementary schools would need five years to catch up and compete with the fee-paying middle-class pupils; hence the break at age 11.

Distinguished educators such as Sir William Hadow in his oft-quoted report of 1926 on *The Education of the Adolescent* suggested that the time was ripe for the use of the general terms 'primary' and 'secondary' to describe the first and second stages in education. He suggested too that 'there is a tide which begins to rise in the veins of youth at the age of eleven or twelve', and so both physically and psychologically this was a good time to transfer. No one questioned this, so 11 remains the critical age and was enshrined in law as almost sacred.

We all know from our own experience that puberty, if that is what he meant, does not simply manifest itself at age 11, and that in any case boys and girls develop at different rates. There have been attempts to change this division at 11, with a small minority of middle schools flourishing in the 1970s and 1980s catering for age ranges 8–12, 9–13 and 10–14. However, the Education Act of 1988 and the National Curriculum, with its Key Stage 1 at 7 and Key Stage 2 at 11, reverted to the former clear divide, sounding the death-knell of the middle school.

In reality, the middle schools never had any logical rationale, for they were pragmatic and administrative excuses for various forms of secondary comprehensive reorganization, expedient for the sake of the secondary sector – a thread that runs through the history of the primary school. Eleven is a useful age to transfer, but one consequence of this has been the continuation of differences between the state schools and those in the private sector, where pupils attend preparatory schools from 8–13 and public schools from 13–18, so eliminating the divide at 11. There are people who prefer to reinforce these differences, rather than bridge the divide.

## THE INFANT SCHOOL (1819–1839)

The concept of the infant school, which forms the first phase of primary schooling, has a long and honourable history which is worth noting. The first infant school in England was established in Westminster in 1819 by James Buchanan who had been sought out because of his teaching experience at New Lanark in Scotland where Robert Owen, factory entrepreneur and philanthropist, had established his famous school in 1816. Within a decade, infant school mania had spread throughout the country and by 1839 about 3,000 such schools had been opened, catering for 90,000 children and supported by voluntary subscriptions from the well-off. These schools had many aims, including the prevention of juvenile delinquency and the development of God-fearing workers. Owen's own purpose had been to develop the children's potential with a view to producing a harmonious society (he also inspired the formation of the Co-operative Movement).

These early infant schools also absorbed many new ideas in child-centred education from the European continent, from Rousseau, Pestalozzi and later Froebel, which brought a liveliness to infant education lacking in other schools. This thread of child-centred education developed and emerged in the modern primary school, though currently it is not always welcome in government circles. In the infant school there was an emphasis on education through play, music, dance, lively pictures and even enjoyment. In the 1820s textbooks extolling the virtues of infant education abounded and as the state began to make meagre contributions towards education from 1833 the infant school was firmly incorporated in that model. Today, we would view those early infant schools as prototype nursery schools. However, that tradition continues, and even the National Curriculum recognizes the special needs of the very young child, a valuable legacy from the past, reinforced by twentieth-century nursery school pioneers such as Maria Montessori, Margaret McMillan and the child psychologist Susan Isaacs.

There was some confusion in the very early days about the right age to start schooling and Owen claimed that some of his infants started school before they were 3 years old. The legal age for starting compulsory schooling in England is 5, almost unique throughout the world. This also came about by accident during the debates on the 1870 Education Act, when a Member of Parliament suggested a starting age of 5. This was never changed or even queried, since members were too busy trying to decide on such issues as whether education should be compulsory, what role religion should play, and when children should leave school, none of which were resolved! But they left us with 5 as the starting age for full-time education, now reinforced by the imposition of Key Stage 1. The debate, begun in 1819, as to whether infants need a distinct and separate education or even separate schools, will no doubt continue – especially as so many infant schools are now being incorporated into junior schools to save the salary of a headteacher, indirectly reducing the chances of headships for women.

A final little-known fact is that without the infant pioneers of the 1820s the concept of the playground and playtime would never have emerged so early and become so embedded in our system. Owen and his English disciple Samuel Wilderspin had regarded the playground, fitted out with swings, maypoles and other equipment as well as with room for marching, skipping and games, as an essential part of their philosophy of education. When the government established the first Inspectors of Schools in 1839, the plans they produced for setting up schools included playgrounds for infants, and so began a tradition that continues today.

## RELIGION, THE CHURCHES AND VOLUNTARY SCHOOLS (1800–1870)

To those brought up on the *laissez-faire* ideas of the eighteenth century, the idea of state provision of education was anathema, so voluntary efforts were encouraged – the Lady Bountiful principle. As factory acts increasingly abolished child labour there appeared to be more and more children roaming the streets and fields without adequate provision. Fears for their property and the prospects of revolution prompted the nation's rulers to turn to the churches to advance the cause of education.

The Church had played a major part in the provision of education for the ruling classes since the foundation of monastic and cathedral schools in the Middle Ages, and it controlled entry to the ancient universities. Now it took up the cause of the education of the poor. From the early 1800s a system of monitorial schools developed – using a model akin to the factory production line, whereby a few cheaply trained teachers could control and teach large numbers of children through monitors who each taught a small group a specific task. Has this method any affinity with the modern practice of asking more able children to help the others in their group?

Both the Church of England, in the guise of the National Society, and the other denominations (for example, the British and Foreign Schools Society) began a period of rapid expansion, setting up many schools with voluntary contributions. Thus by 1833 the state was persuaded to step in and make a small contribution to their running, which in reality amounted to no more than the former annual cost of the Prince Regent's stables in Brighton.

Luckily for us this proved to be the thin end of the wedge and all schools are now generously supported by the government of the day. The system of voluntary schools continued to grow until 1870, when the cost of building schools in the expanding industrial towns was beyond the purse of even Lady Bountiful. What is this to do with us? Well, there are still a large number of voluntary schools run by the churches (mainly the Church of England and the Roman Catholic Church) especially in small villages. You must know one near you, and some are still in their original buildings (see below, p. 33).

Although the churches could no longer afford to build and maintain schools, they ensured that Parliament in all subsequent education acts maintained special privileges for church schools. Even the old church training colleges are still encouraged to provide denominational teacher training, though most students and teachers and their pupils do not attend any church, in spite of the fact that parents seem to want religious education to continue.

The upshot of this for teachers is that religious education is compulsory, together with a daily act of worship. Paradoxically, this is also the only subject that pupils and teachers may opt out of. Most do not, pupils because parents believe it may improve their children, teachers because it would inconvenience colleagues in primary schools to opt out of teaching it.

So here is a real legacy from the past, which raises a number of issues for teachers and also poses the question of why should other faiths not run their own schools at the state's expense.

Religious education (RE) is part of the National Curriculum, though strangely it is neither a core nor a foundation subject. In fact, the Secretary of State rather forgot about RE when he was introducing the 1988 Education Act, until the powerful Church lobby and Conservative backbenchers raised the matter; hence the anomaly continues. Teachers cannot even teach the subject as they wish, since a group of local people has to approve an agreed syllabus for the region which all then have to follow. The oddest point is that the religious impositions originally designed for church schools actually apply to all state schools, unique I believe throughout the world. I am sure the debate will continue: join in, but remember that the churches have had long experience in this field and are unlikely to give up easily.

## THE ELEMENTARY SCHOOL TRADITION (1870-1902)

The new schools, called board schools, which spread after the 1870 Act, while they advanced education for the masses, left us with a few less valuable traditions. The very word 'elementary' poses a problem today. It was so named because the schools were supposed to deal with only the most basic aspects of the curriculum and their pupils left at the earliest possible opportunity without any qualifications. In the 1890s pupils were able to leave school as early as age 11 and it was not until 1918 that the leaving age was fixed at 14. Before that, pupils could even attend part time, working in factories or on farms for the other half of the week. Many of the teachers at these schools were unqualified; others merely served apprenticeships as pupil-teachers in the schools they attended.

After 1918 the leaving age was fixed at 14. Additionally in 1918, fees in such schools were abolished, whereas secondary schools continued to charge fees, except for scholarship pupils, until 1944. The elementary teachers were also on a lower pay scale than their secondary counterparts. The primary schools which were the heirs of the elementary schools, sometimes remaining in the same buildings after 1944, were tainted with this label of inferiority, a stigma encouraged by ignorance and prejudice on the part of the public, many of whom should have known better.

It is only a few years since the Secretary of State for Education visited a school in the home counties to present an award to a primary teacher who had been named as outstanding teacher of the year, and made the revealing comment that he supposed she would now be looking for promotion to the secondary school! So do not be surprised if you come across this attitude, a point of view hardened by history. There is still a view that the younger the child the easier the task and the fewer resources that are needed. Examine your non-teaching time (if any) or that of primary teachers you know, the breadth of curriculum covered and the per capita income, and compare this with the situation in the secondary school, then blame history and prejudice for this state of affairs. What are you going to do to redress the balance?

## THE CURRICULUM, PAYMENT BY RESULTS, SATS AND LEAGUE TABLES

The National Curriculum of 1988 established virtually the same curriculum in primary as in secondary schools, with a new emphasis on science and technology added to the existing focus on language and number. Some might see this as the culmination of the struggle begun in the elementary schools for recognition and status. The mid-nineteenth-century voluntary schools had had a very limited curriculum, often characterized as the three Rs (reading, writing and 'rithmetic) with of course the compulsory fourth R – religious education, then more commonly called 'scripture'. Some useful subjects were added, such as 'housewifery' for girls (sewing, patching and darning) and occasionally manual work for boys (shoe repairing). Indeed, the future Bishop of Manchester told Parliament in 1866 that this was all the working-class child needed.

To ensure that schools kept to this narrow regime after 1862, inspectors tested all the children annually, and if they fell below the appropriate level (called standards, so that classes were organized in standards: 1, 2 and so on up to standard 7) or even were absent on the day of testing, money was deducted from the school's funding and the teachers' already meagre salaries were reduced. Although this system of 'payment by results' had died out by the 1890s it still weighs heavily in the collective memory of the profession. Teachers resorted to all manner of scams to outwit the dreaded inspectors, none of whom had ever taught in an elementary school, being 'gentlemen' from Oxford or Cambridge and frequently clergy. Could our standard assessment tests (SATs), Ofsted and league tables have anything in common with this discredited system, whose main aim was allegedly to raise standards, or if not at least to save money?

It was the development of the board schools from 1870 to 1902 that helped to broaden the curriculum and lay the foundations for some of the present-day work in primary schools. The big city schools, funded in part by local rates, reflected the pride of the growing conurbations. The boards encouraged an extension of the curriculum beyond the elementary, the teachers too were better trained and wanted to extend their new knowledge, and a new breed of more enlightened inspectors encouraged these moves. After 1880, when education became compulsory, the second generation of parents demanded more of schools and this raising of parental aspirations continues to this day. Subject areas such as science, geography, history and English literature became common, especially the rote learning of famous poems, Tennyson and the like.

At the turn of the century, the country was so shocked by the poor physical condition of the men who had volunteered to fight in the Boer War that attention in schools turned from the curriculum towards welfare, in the belief that physically deficient children could not take full advantage of the new opportunities in education. So there was provision for medical and dental inspection, free school meals and the introduction of PE into the curriculum. Schools now took on an added pastoral dimension, which was particularly crucial for the younger children and continued the infant school tradition.

The two world wars accelerated this trend, since in both wars food and other shortages meant the introduction of rationing, with an increase in the provision of school meals. During World War 2 the expansion of school provision for nursery age children was so great that it has still not been equalled. The effects of wartime bombing, the evacuation of children to safe areas in the country and the sharing of premises by more than one school all focused attention on the pastoral role. This element reinforced the image of the school as a caring institution – a key feature of the primary school today. The call up of so many male teachers into the armed forces also reinforced and perhaps even helped to create the imbalance between men and women teachers in primary schools which is still increasing. Ironically, it was not until after World War 2 that we saw the disappearance of the rigid rule that women teachers had to leave the profession on marriage!

It was in the 1920s after World War 1 that not only the curriculum but also the methods used in the junior departments of elementary schools began to blossom and innovation became rife in some schools. During this period, especially in the 1930s, the terms 'junior school' and 'primary education' came into common use.

Project or topic work was regarded as a welcome method, which enabled the teacher to focus upon an area of study using a multi-subject or integrated approach. This was very much in contrast to the narrow single subject approach of the secondary school. The Dalton plan, which spread from the United States to England in the 1920s, though now long faded from memory, was very much favoured in elementary schools in the interwar period. It placed emphasis on allowing children to programme their own studies according to individual needs, together with a growing recognition of their importance as citizens with democratic rights, very much in the vein of the American educationalist, John Dewey. Perhaps it laid the foundations for our present-day emphasis on meeting the differentiated needs of pupils and allowing flexibility in the timetable. It also reflected the developing interest in child psychology, including the theories of Jean Piaget (see Chapter 5), whose first work appeared in English in 1926, together with those of Susan Isaacs, both of whom were beginning to examine the mental growth of children.

Throughout the first half of the twentieth century, the Board of Education (now the Department for Education and Employment – DfEE) issued an annual book of 'suggestions for teachers' which was a way of spreading good practice from the centre, usually through inspectors. A glance at some of the suggestions from the 1905 edition compared with those issued just before World War 2 in 1939 illustrates the progress that had been made.

The study of English had grown to English language and literature, there was less emphasis on formal grammar, and oral expression and drama were included. Arithmetic had turned into mathematics by 1939 and there was less interest in speed and accuracy in computation and more emphasis on the need to understand the basic processes. Science was replacing 'observation and nature study'. Drawing had become art and craft, in which 'the free expression of young children's drawing and painting should be recognized as of greater importance than imitative accuracy'. Singing had become music and though history and geography remained, they no longer consisted of dates of kings and queens or lists of capes and bays.

All this was conclusive proof that a widened, more challenging curriculum approach had penetrated official circles. An interesting question which teachers and government inspectors are raising today is whether or not this widening of the curriculum has gone too far. Is there a need to return to the more formal curriculum of a hundred years ago? If you are concerned about this, you might try to get hold of some old school textbooks or question older generations of teachers, parents and grandparents and ask how far they benefited from a narrower curriculum.

After the 1944 Education Act, the primary schools, as they then became, were able to focus on developments appropriate to their own age range, rather than see themselves as merely a preparation factory for secondary schools. Shortages of buildings, teachers and resources after World War 2 in 1945 meant that many of these new developments did not come to fruition until the mid-1950s.

There was one further factor that hindered progress, and that was the continuous need to prepare pupils for the eleven-plus selection examination for secondary school. In many primary schools the whole curriculum was distorted for this sole purpose. There was much pressure from parents, especially from the middle and aspiring working classes, to secure maximum success in the examination. Unofficial league tables grew up in each locality, teachers made extra income from eleven-plus coaching, children were promised bicycles if they succeeded and congratulatory messages were printed in local papers to the successful few. Timetable space in primary schools was given over to intelligence tests and to reworking old eleven-plus examination papers.

This reinforced the principle of streaming, which already existed in many schools. This practice had been strongly recommended by the second Hadow report of 1931 on the primary school and forcefully advocated by respected educational psychologist Sir Cyril Burt, and many now advocate its return. As a result, streaming became a standard form of organization in all schools above the infant level for decades after 1930. Although some of Burt's findings and methods have since been challenged and the concept of streaming questioned in the latter part of this century, it seems firmly embedded in the system, especially at secondary level and sometimes in primary schools too, in the guise of 'setting', particularly after Key Stage 1.

Only after 1965, with the increased change to the secondary comprehensive school (primary schools had always been comprehensive, but no politicians or parents had made a fuss about this!), was the eleven-plus dropped and primary schools freed to pursue their own destiny. Today, with hindsight, some think they went too far in creating 'subject-free' timetables, and you may like to discuss this with older teachers whom you meet.

At the same time, the primary school was regarded as an example to the whole world. In the 1960s coachloads of American teachers came over here to summer schools to learn about the English primary school, often with an emphasis on the infant school. It was no accident that Bridget, Lady Plowden, produced her long-awaited very weighty report on primary education in 1967. This report followed naturally upon two enquiries into secondary education as well as the Robbins Report (Committee on Higher Education, 1963) and completed the government's survey of the wide spectrum of education, reaffirming the status of primary education within the national system.

The whole nation, myself included, eagerly took the Plowden Report to their hearts. The government, the Inspectorate, the teacher training colleges, and teachers in the schools, all supported the Report. A few began to repent in the so-called Black Papers, which began to emerge after 1968. However, at the time it had almost universal support and was regarded almost as the Bible of the progressive primary school movement.

It was a very thorough report, which cost a lot of money by the standards of the time and it celebrated what were seen as the successes of the primary school: a child-centred focus, activity through group work, and recognition of the vital importance of the home–school link. It also drew attention to the profound influence of socio-economic factors and encouraged the identification by local education authorities of educationally deprived areas. It suggested there was a need for a change in the age of transfer and advocated more part-time nursery places and the setting up of a new category of staff, teachers' aides, who possessed limited training.

Today some of these views are decidedly out of fashion with politicians of all shades, some educationalists and even members of the Royal Family. But many teachers I know have a lingering sympathy for the Report's message and the status and public recognition it gave to primary school practice. Today it is alleged to have led to poor standards in schools and diverted attention from the need for rigorous whole-class teaching. I am not sure, if you read it carefully, that this is really true, but try glancing at it yourself or talk to older teachers about it. Be warned: even Lady Plowden recanted from some of its messages! It serves as a useful warning to those of you who are likely to be carried away by current fads and fashions, that they may be on the scrapheap in a few years, only to be revived yet again a few years later. This is one lesson we can learn from history. My advice is to pick and choose from the ragbag of information and practice that is available to you from the past – take what suits you best and works well with the pupils.

## BUILDINGS

The environment will have a major impact on the way you and your pupils work, and it is through the school buildings that you are most closely in contact with the past. All buildings were designed for a past age and different teaching ideologies and may well pose problems for us. You will need to accept these limitations and if possible turn them to positive advantage. There follows a brief description and commentary on the types of school building in which you might find yourself working.

### Early nineteenth century

These small, often stone buildings were usually church schools and are most frequently found in small country villages. Some may now be part of the suburbs of large towns or cities that expanded into the surrounding countryside. Few of these old schools remain. They are generally attractive from the outside but have been subjected to many changes internally. There are some rare specimens from the 1800s but most date from the 1850s. They are usually single-storey buildings which may have incorporated the headteacher's house and included a small bell tower. The classrooms are usually adequate, especially in small villages, since they once accommodated huge numbers of children (80 was not uncommon before 1900). This material can enrich history lessons.

## Board schools (1870–1902)

These were usually substantial buildings, often designed by leading architects in the large towns and cities, with at least two storeys. There are usually high windows to prevent pupils from looking out. Corridors and classroom walls beneath these windows were often covered with particularly repulsive green, brown or cream tiles, much favoured in old-fashioned Edwardian public lavatories. Such schools may have a large internal hall with classrooms along each side. Originally there were tall, folding wood and glass screens between classrooms, but many of these have since been removed. The ceilings were very high and may cause echoes today. Quite a number of these buildings are still in use because they are sturdy and spacious, and have plenty of character, but they are expensive to heat and repair.

Outside you will see separate entrances for boys, girls and infants. A plaque usually records the date of the school building. If you are fortunate enough to work in such a building your National Curriculum work on Victorian schools will be greatly enhanced. These schools are usually surrounded by separate playgrounds, but the ornamental wrought iron railings which once graced them were all removed at the beginning of World War 2 to provide material for the munitions factories.

## Council schools (from 1902 to 1939)

These schools were generally smaller than the board schools and exhibit a wide variety of styles. They are on one level more often than not. The open-air education movement in the first decade of this century indirectly influenced subsequent school buildings. For this reason many interwar schools have lots of windows (some French), quadrangles and E-shaped designs to trap the sun. Purpose-built halls, dining-rooms with stages and space for physical education reflected the widening curriculum and activities in schools. Such schools tend to be rather draughty places and were often over-provided with long corridors, but they were well built and can be usefully adapted. In addition to hard surface playgrounds, grass playing fields began to make an appearance.

## Early post-war (1948 onwards)

The post-war population bulge of 1947 led to a desperate shortage of schools. Prefabricated buildings seemed to be the answer to this problem and so the Nissen hut style prevailed in many areas. These were characterized by flat roofs, an over-indulgence in asbestos and some rather dangerous heating systems with cast iron coal-burning stoves in the centre. They served a useful purpose at the time, but many have now collapsed or been pulled down. You are unlucky if you work in such a classroom, but you may find that many of the prefab huts, long past their 'sell-by' date, have been drafted into other schools to cope with a shift in population. Such prefabs had a variety of names, including Terrapins, mobiles, Portakabins and York-ons.

## The swinging sixties and seventies

This was an era when powerful LEAs, led by London, employed their own architects and competed with one another to build showcase schools, primary and secondary, incorporating the latest educational ideas. The schools looked attractive at the time, after the style of the Festival of Britain in 1951. There was lots of glass, bright, cheerful, flexible classrooms, pleasant halls and stages for multiple use, landscaped gardens, attractive playgrounds, imaginative and stimulating designs and unusual shapes. However, the extensive use of new materials, flat roofs and poor-quality concrete has led to crumbling and dangerous facades and leaking roofs, and the original bright, cheerful aspect is often no longer evident. They reflected the child-centred or maybe architect-centred approach and were not a good investment.

In the latter period, fewer schools were built or needed; the government enforced ever tighter financial restrictions as well as limiting the permitted square footage per pupil, so out went the fancy extras – definitely no adventure playgrounds or inside gardens. The fashion for integrated learning and multiple use of facilities led to the open plan school, that is the removal of as many internal walls as was safe and possible so that several classes, even the whole year group, could share common facilities. Consequently there was no need for corridors, thus saving money. Cloakrooms and toilets were often incorporated into classrooms. There were multi-purpose spaces for drama, physical education, worship and dining. Other resources were grouped centrally – science, art, maths and so on.

This open plan fad was also popular in the USA, but teachers soon reacted to this incursion into their own private classroom space, and shunned public gaze by erecting walls of cupboards, bookcases and potted plants. The experiment was not a success, noise levels were often high and tensions arose between teachers, yet it is almost impossible today to convert these spaces into separate classrooms, so take care! Ironically, after this failed experiment in schools, offices, town halls and hospitals are developing open plan work areas, with much the same impact and likely success.

## Recent developments (1980s and 1990s)

You will be very lucky if you teach in a school built in the last twenty years. Because the population is declining and resources are limited, very few schools have been built, except on new housing estates. A few schools incorporate community facilities such as libraries and nurseries. Many schools provide a special room for parents. If you happen to be in a new school or even an older one, think about it: How does it meet your needs and those of the children? Is technology catered for, and especially IT? Have you ever thought how you would like your ideal school or classroom to be? How would it reflect your educational aims? Why not ask the children to design their own school or classroom? Can you adapt your classroom? Could pupils make suggestions for improvement at minimum cost? Why be a prisoner of history and your building?

## CONCLUSION

Although we may not always be aware of it, every time we take a decision or try to move in a new direction we are constrained or encouraged by what has gone before. Nothing exists that does not have a history; therefore whether we want to progress, regress, rest on our laurels or simply be aware of what has happened, to draw inspiration from our predecessors and not waste time re-creating the wheel, or to avoid their mistakes, we need to know something of history. There is an additional bonus for you as teachers. Some of your historical knowledge can be put to good use with the children by recreating a Victorian schoolroom – it can be an exciting learning experience. Ask how children managed during two world wars, bring in their mums, dads, aunts and uncles, granddads and grandmas to talk about their schooling; they will love it and so will you.

## REFERENCES

Committee on Higher Education (1963) *Higher Education (The Robbins Report)*. London: HMSO.

Hadow, W. H. (1926) *The Education of the Adolescent* (Report of the Consultative Committee on Education). London: HMSO.

Hadow, W. H. (1931) *Report of the Consultative Committee on the Primary School*. London: HMSO.

Plowden, B. (1967) *Children and Their Primary Schools*. London: HMSO.

## SOME SUGGESTIONS FOR FURTHER READING

There are many books in college libraries which tell you the facts about the history of education, but to get a real flavour of the times browse through some of the old reports by Hadow, Plowden or Newsom. They are a mine of surprising information. Or see if you can find any old textbooks, or read any school log-books which were (and still are) compulsory for every school to keep, and date from 1862.

# CHAPTER 4

# Schools, pupils and parents: contexts for learning

JACKIE MARSH

Each school is unique, individual and serves particular communities. If we are to be successful teachers in schools, we need to understand the ways in which schools are different from each other and be able to adjust our approaches to the work we do accordingly. It would not be possible to outline all the different types of schools we could find ourselves teaching in, nor would that be profitable. Rather, what we need to do is underpin our teaching with those key principles which will facilitate the development of every child we teach and ensure that we have a good, mutually beneficial relationship with the parents and communities we serve. We need to be able to deal with diversity in the classroom. This includes meeting the needs of all ability levels, but it is much wider than that. We need to provide a classroom environment and curriculum which reflects and incorporates the experiences that children bring with them to school and does not ask them to cast off home and community along with their coats when they enter the classroom.

This chapter explores some of the key principles involved in responding to diversity in the classroom. In the first section, we explore the way in which culture and society can affect how we learn. We then move on to look at the implications this has for the content and delivery of the curriculum. The final section of the chapter examines the complexities involved in building up relationships and establishing clear lines of communication with different groups of parents. The intention of the chapter is not to provide teachers with a 'rough guide' to teaching in inner-city, suburban, semi-rural and rural schools but to promote the role that reflection and sensitivity can play in building meaningful contexts for learning.

## WORKING WITH CHILDREN

Most teachers are drawn from a narrow socio-economic band. The majority of teachers trained in our institutions come from white, middle-class communities. The beliefs, attitudes and values of teachers are based upon their own life experiences. If these are very different from the experiences of the children they work with, how can they ensure that they provide an inclusive curriculum that reflects the children's realities? One way of doing this is to examine the assumptions we make about children and their families. I want to begin by looking at the kinds of assumptions we can make about children and how these assumptions can affect our work.

We are each a unique product of our upbringing, and our behaviour, attitudes and beliefs are affected by the situation and culture in which we grew up. This influence of socio-cultural factors also affects how we learn. For example, some of us prefer to learn new things by being allowed to explore for ourselves, while others like to see a demonstration of the principle being taught before trying it themselves. Some of these learning styles are individual, others occur as a result of the norms of our culture. Kendall (1996) explores this issue fully and outlines a number of ways in which cultural norms affect the way in which children learn. Some children may have been encouraged to explore new situations and materials throughout their early life, while other children may have been taught that they must not touch items which do not belong to them. This will affect how they use materials and resources when they first come to school.

Certain children may have been brought up to believe that asking questions of adults, without first being invited to do so, is not permissible, and so may be reluctant to ask their teachers if they are unclear about something. Kendall refers to Longstreet, who identified six ways in which children's behaviour may influence their learning, each of which is likely to be affected by cultural norms:

1. The child's manner of participating in activities - whether she or he watches from the sidelines or gets enthusiastically involved.

2. The attention she or he gives to activities - attending to one task at a time or doing several things at once.

3. The ways in which she or he processes information - asking many questions as the teacher is talking or taking information in, thinking about it, and coming back later with questions.

4. The manner in which the child presents his or her thoughts to others - teaching another child how to complete a task by telling her or him about it or by demonstrating the activity.

5. The ways in which she or he asks questions - carefully, fearing that there might be a risk to admitting ignorance, or with abandon, believing that the way to discover something is to ask.

6. The kinds of questions the child asks - intimate ones, like 'Why are you so skinny?' or careful and circumscribed ones, like 'Do you think that flower is pretty?'

(Kendall, 1996, p. 36)

We need to be aware of the ways in which culture can influence learning styles and ensure that we adapt our teaching in a way that bridges these gaps. Some working-class children, both black and white, are used to commands that are straightforward in nature, such as 'Pick up the book from the floor'. However, many Western middle-class cultures tend to couch commands in different forms, using statements or questions, such as 'Excuse me, the book is on the floor', or, 'Would you like to pick up the book?' For some children this may be genuinely confusing, as they think they may have an option, not realising that the teacher wants them to pick up the book. As Vernon-Feagans (1996, p. 26) states:

> Children who did not interpret these utterances in the way the teacher intended, and just looked up at her in a puzzled way, might find that the teacher inferred a negative motivation on their part, or at the very least poor language comprehension by the children.

So as we can see, children have different styles of learning and interacting with adults and some of these are based upon cultural norms. A further example of this is the adoption of particular learning strategies by some Chinese children. Chinese children may attend a Chinese community school at the weekend where they learn to read and write Chinese. The Chinese script is very different from English in that characters represent whole words, not single letters or groups of letters. For these children, learning to read in English could be facilitated by a 'whole word recognition' approach; that is, learning whole words as a single unit rather than breaking them down into their constituent parts. This will build upon the learning strategies they are used to, rather than attempting to use a programme that is very much based on the teaching of phonics. Once children have started to read in English in this way, they will be ready to develop phonological awareness.

So as teachers we need to be aware of the ways in which children's previous experiences have affected their preferred methods of learning and be responsive to this. I would not like to suggest a deterministic approach to the effects that socio-economic status and culture can have on us; rather, I want to point out that each child may have had particular influences which can have implications for their education. Not all children will feel at ease with the culture and pedagogy of your classroom. We must be careful not to over-generalize and make erroneous assumptions; just because some Chinese children prefer to learn to read in one particular way does not mean that every Chinese child will do so. Simply because some Muslim children who are learning to read the Qur'an in the local mosque memorize whole chunks of texts at a time when learning to read Arabic does not mean that they need to transfer this method to learning to read in English. It is much more fruitful to assess each child's learning style as an individual and provide appropriate experiences for her or him in order to facilitate development.

It is not only learning styles that are affected by socio-cultural factors.

Behaviour is also, and this can lead to misunderstandings in the classroom. For example, Kendall (1996) points out that some families teach children that it is polite to avert their eyes when an adult is talking to them. The children can then run into difficulties in a school, if such behaviour is seen as a sign of evasion and non-compliance with a teacher's instructions or reprimands. This can cause confusion for the child and a possibility of being labelled as defiant by the teacher.

It is important to be aware of our own expectations of behaviour and attitude in the classroom and make sure that they do not disadvantage certain groups of children. In a recent Ofsted report by David Gillborn and Caroline Gipps (1996), it was pointed out that in some of the schools visited, African-Caribbean boys were more likely than their white counterparts to be reprimanded and even excluded by teachers. This is a finding that is supported by national statistics on exclusions. How much of this is due to misunderstandings relating to differing cultural experiences is unclear, but it is evidence that racism can 'operate 'in ways which are more subtle and widespread than the crude, often violent, attitudes usually associated with notions of discrimination and prejudice' (p. 56).

It is clear, then, that we must move away from making assumptions about children and their families. We may think that we are recognizing certain patterns that belong to a particular cultural group, but we can never be sure of this. We are all unique individuals and react to the same situations in different ways. To look at the ways in which teacher's assumptions can affect the experiences of school that some children have, we need only listen to the voices of people who have felt alienated from the methods and materials used in schools in this country. What follows are interviews with three different people. At the end of each extract, I pose a series of questions that directly address us as teachers.

*Kelly*

> I was brought up in a white, working-class community and started school in the early sixties. My father had left us and my grandmother was bringing us up. My mum was never at home, she worked all the time. I remember being read stories by the teacher about a character called Milly Molly Mandy. She seemed to have a perfect life, a mother, father, a tablecloth on the table .... The teacher talked to us about the stories and assumed that we all had similar experiences, asking us about how our dads reacted to that, or this .... I began to get the feeling that my background was not quite normal. I told my friends that my father had died in the war, I was too ashamed to tell the truth. The image of the family presented to us was always one of a happy, nuclear unit, living in a home that had things like an indoor toilet and a garden. None of it related to my experience and I never felt able to join in class discussions. Maybe things are better now ... there are certainly more children who have parents who are separated.

*Questions to consider:*

- Did the teacher provide an appropriate range of stories for this class?

- If commercially produced stories which reflected this child's circumstances were not available, what could the teacher have done to ensure that the child felt included, not excluded, from the ethos built up in the classroom surrounding the concept of 'family'?

- Was the teacher wise to ask the whole class questions about what their fathers did?

- How could the teacher have encouraged this child to join in class discussions?

## Mena

I was the only black child in the school. It was a convent school in the North of Ireland. None of the other children would sit next to me and the nuns did nothing about it. I took all the money from my piggy bank one day so that I could buy sweets for the class and get some friends. The only time black children were mentioned was in geography and history and then it was as figures of pity. Whenever I did really good work, the nuns would be very suspicious and say, "Who did that? Who helped you?" It was as if they didn't think I was capable of doing it myself. Nobody could have helped me at home because neither of my parents spoke English.

*Questions to consider:*

- What could the nuns have done about the fact that no one would sit next to Mena?

- What effect would the curriculum content in relation to black children have had on Mena's self-esteem?

- Why were the nuns suspicious about Mena's academic achievements? To what extent does prejudice affect the way in which we assess children?

## Sarah

I was the oldest child in a well-off, white, middle-class family. My dad was a doctor and had a good reputation in the local community. He was very cruel, physically, emotionally and mentally, to me and my sister for years and I didn't dare tell anyone ... I never brought friends home to the house. I went to a small school with two classes. I had one teacher for four years. She thought that my dad was wonderful. I remember one day clearly. She got us to write about our last family holiday. I could only remember the horrible bits and I refused to write about it. She got very cross with me and told me that I was obviously a very lucky girl and didn't appreciate what my parents did for me. I wanted to scream at her but it was all locked up inside me.

*Questions to consider:*

- What assumptions was the teacher making about this child's home life?

- What signs might the child have been showing that all was not right in her life?

- What are the dangers inherent in asking children to write about their home experiences, and how can we ensure that this is done in a sensitive way?

Once we begin to listen to the voices of children and assess their needs as individuals, we begin to see how important it is that the curriculum content and delivery should reflect their varied experiences. For children who live in a high rise block of flats in an inner-city area, surrounded by a wide range of cultures and lifestyles, books which feature only white characters who live in houses provide them with little in the way of content that they can relate to. This would also be the case for traveller children and children who live in refuges. Other children may have families living in large cities in Africa. If the work in geography presents them solely with images of Africa as consisting of desert wastelands or rural villages, then their perceptions of their own realities can become confused.

Of course, it is important that all children, not just those for whom it is directly relevant, have a variety of images and experiences presented to them. For children in a rural village school, the teacher must ensure that the curriculum reflects their own experiences as well as incorporating a wider vision. However, we must be sure that the material we are presenting truly reflects the community and is not simply a stereotype of it. Many of the books which are set in the countryside present an idealized version of village life which is simply not the reality for some families who live in relative isolation and poverty in many rural areas.

Curriculum content needs to reflect the lifestyles and interests of the children in the class as well as introduce them to a wider range of experiences. We need also to be careful that the resources we use in the classroom include objects and artefacts that resonate with children and make the classroom environment feel less alien. For those children in all-white schools, it is important that they are familiarized with life in multicultural Britain. Teachers should ensure that they use a wide range of sources for display materials, artefacts that provide stimuli for a variety of curriculum areas and teaching resources that reflect our rich society. At the end of the chapter there are some suggestions for further reading and sources of relevant materials.

These resources should be used in a thoughtful and enriching manner rather than adopting a tokenistic, reductionist approach. For example, it is not very productive to focus solely on festivals as a means of introducing children to a range of cultures. If a child only ever has a chance to explore the culture and traditions of India through a Diwali project, he or she may get the impression that people in India spend a lot of time making Rangoli patterns and lighting diwas. This is clearly not the case. Rather, the cultures, traditions and practices of other cultures should be threaded throughout the curriculum in an integrated way in order to avoid further stereotyping and misrepresentation.

We should develop the ability to reflect on the provision we make in a detailed and sensitive manner in order to ensure that we are providing an inclusive rather than an exclusive environment for the children and parents we work with. In the following section, I will look at the issues related to working with parents in a diverse society and examine how we can ensure that we make the school environment welcoming for all parents, not just those who have had successful and inclusive experiences of school.

## WORKING WITH PARENTS

Partnership between schools and parents is a vital ingredient of a child's intellectual, emotional and social development. Much of the literature in this area stresses the need for open communication between home and school and the fostering of a degree of trust between parent and teacher. This section examines how teachers can ensure that they are considering the needs of all the parents they work with, not just those who are confident in their dealings with school.

British schools serve an ever-changing society. Single-parent families now outnumber people living in the more traditional situation of the 'nuclear' family. Of those children who are living with two parents, it cannot be assumed that they are a mother and father in the traditional sense. Children may live with a birth parent and a step-parent. They may be living with adoptive or foster parents. They may have gay or lesbian parents who are co-parenting with their partner. Children may live in an extended family group where their grandparents or aunts and uncles are their main carers. Children will have all sorts of relationships with the people they live with. Some will be intense and loving, others will be distant, perhaps even abusive. It is important to find out as much as you can about a child's family situation in order to inform your work with that child. There are many aspects of school life that are potentially difficult areas for relationships with parents and carers. We need to reflect carefully upon our work, in order to ensure that all families have equal access to the school and its staff. I outline below key areas and provide suggestions for improving communication with parents.

## Letters home

Letters home are a common feature of school life. If they concern general school issues, it is obviously easier to have these prepared centrally by the head or school secretary. These letters should be addressed to 'Parents and carers'. This is an inclusive opening and acknowledges the role that carers make. If parents speak English as an additional language, try to ensure that letters are translated into the appropriate languages. Parents may not be able to read in their first language. However, you are not likely to know whether or not they can and so you must make appropriate provision. Many LEAs have a translation service. If the letters sent home concern only your class they can be addressed more personally, as you will have relevant information that ensures they name the appropriate people.

## Open evenings

Provide a range of appointment times to suit a range of needs. Single parents may need to see you earlier in the evening, bringing the children with them. This is not ideal, but arrangements could be made for the children, for example by setting up a television and video in a separate area. Other parents may work late and need to see you later in the evening. Bilingual parents may need a translator. If you are going to provide a translator, let the parents and carers know in advance; otherwise they will assume that there is no provision for them and will be unlikely to attend.

## Celebrations

If you have detailed knowledge about a child's background, you can ensure that cards are sent to the right person or, indeed, allow the child to make a number of cards. If a child has parents who are separated and live in different houses then they might like to have a card each. Be careful about such events as 'Mother's day'. Here is one carer's experience of Mother's day:

> I foster a lively 10-year-old girl, Annie. She made a mother's day card at school and, well, she got into a complete state about it. She didn't know whether or not to give the card to her mum or me. She hid it in her bag … I only found it weeks later when I looked for her swimming goggles. She thought she would upset me if she gave it to her mum and not me. Of course I wouldn't have been, but she wasn't to know.

This situation could have been avoided if Annie had been allowed to make two mother's day cards at school. If children are living only with their father, it may be that they could be allowed to make a card for 'A special person' instead of a mother's day card; this would prevent them from feeling excluded from the occasion.

## Parent workshops

As stated above, parental involvement in children's education can enhance their academic performance. Many schools now hold workshops in which parents and carers can come into school and play language and maths games, read and work with their child. It is important not to put too much pressure on all parents to become involved in this way. Some people may not have the space or stamina to spend time in school. If a parent or carer is a single parent, living in financial poverty and poor housing, joining in with such workshops may be the last of their priorities. Schools should not add to their feelings of guilt about not being the 'perfect' parent.

It is important to assess each situation on an individual basis. It may be that a parent would be very keen to join in, but just needs a little more encouragement. Some parents may have had a very negative experience of schooling themselves and not feel confident about helping their child. Black parents who may have experienced racism within the education system could be reluctant to become involved with their child's school. By providing a warm, welcoming environment and treating parents with respect rather than patronizing them, you can begin to build up the trust necessary to foster more productive relationships.

## Home-school reading schemes

Research shows that the majority of parents want to help their children with reading (Hannon, 1995). Many schools encourage children to take books home to share with their parents and carers. Schools must not assume that parents know how to read with their child. It is advisable to provide specific guidance in the form of booklets that outline how to help children with reading. Some schools run workshops that take parents through the process of learning to read and provide strategies for supporting children. These sessions should be relaxed, supportive, and free of educational jargon which may alienate parents. Again, ensure that you provide adequate services for bilingual parents.

Some schools send home notebooks in which parents are encouraged to make comments about their child's reading. However, this can be difficult if parents do not read or write English, or if their literacy skills are limited. This needs careful handling. Indeed, it may be necessary to question whether such practices lead to such disparity between children's experiences that they need adapting in some way. For example, could older siblings be encouraged to write in such home-school books? Could children themselves be responsible for making comments in them about what reading experiences they have had at home? Is there a point at which such practices should be discontinued because of the inequality of experiences of children?

## Asking parents for money

Many schools ask parents for money for various things. This can be very problematic for poor families. As one single parent pointed out:

> In one week, my daughter's school asked for £2 for a balloon experiment in science, they wanted 50p a week for six weeks for cookery, they wanted you to buy books for the school's funds and then 50p a week for fencing lessons. This all added up to about £4 or £5 that week. I just haven't got that kind of money but I don't want her to miss out and not be like the other kids. I had to walk to college that week, I couldn't afford the bus fare.

Be careful that your school does not put pressure on parents in this way. Holding book fairs can create great difficulties for some parents and cause pain and embarrassment for some children when they see other children getting things that they cannot have. If you work in an area of poverty, then hold a second-hand book fair instead of a publisher's book fair. If you do ask parents to contribute towards special activities, try to ensure that these are spread over the school year. Most importantly, be prepared to understand that some parents simply cannot pay, and cover their child's costs through the school funds.

It is up to teachers to provide themselves with the means to find out about the many different cultures and communities they work with. Asking parents is an obvious starter but cannot be relied upon for a number of reasons. Parents may not speak English, they may not be aware themselves of the practices of their wider culture, they may not welcome such intrusive questioning. There are a number of other ways to seek out information. There are many books that outline key aspects of different religions and their practices. Most LEAs will have a central stock of such material. Some authorities may even have 'Multicultural' centres, which provide a range of resources and materials for use by teachers. Linking up with community schools can be a valuable way to exchange information about children and the curriculum.

However, simply listening to parents and children can be the most successful way of discovering their individual differences and needs. If we can open ourselves up to others' lives and learn not to judge them by standards which may be based on prejudice and misinformation we will be in a better position to provide an education system which is appropriate, challenging and meets both children's and parents' needs.

In this chapter I have looked at the ways in which the assumptions we make about children's backgrounds and cultures can affect the relationship we have with them and the curriculum we offer them. More critically, it can affect their academic development if the learning styles which the school values and promotes are different from the child's own. The chapter has briefly explored how the curriculum content and materials can reflect a range of lifestyles. It then moved on to examine the ways in which schools can develop open and honest relationships with parents and carers in order to facilitate their children's learning. The model that the chapter promotes is one of a reflective teacher, a teacher who examines carefully the messages she is giving in all areas of her professional life and works hard to ensure that she is aware of and sensitive to the multiple realities at work in any situation. It encourages an encompassing vision rather than one of exclusivity. We need our classrooms to be a meeting place for all our different experiences, beliefs, attitudes and knowledge. Only then can we ensure that we are providing rich and enabling contexts for learning.

I want to conclude by posing a few questions that we must ask ourselves if we are to begin to meet the needs of all children. These are followed by some suggestions for further reading and useful addresses for obtaining resources.

*Questions we need to ask:*

- What assumptions do I make about children and families from different communities? On what information are those assumptions based?

- What information do I have about the children and families I work with? What do I need to know? How will I find out?

- How can I vary my teaching strategies to meet the needs of a range of pupils?

- How can I ensure that the curriculum reflects the lives of the children as well as incorporating the content of the National Curriculum?

- What resources do I need to use in order to ensure that I am incorporating materials from a range of cultures and communities? How can I be sure that these resources are not presenting stereotypes or used in a tokenistic way?

- How can I ensure that I involve as many parents as possible in school events? Are there any parents whom I feel uncomfortable about approaching and why? What can I do about this?

- How can I ensure that I encourage the children I teach to question, explore and appreciate differences?

## REFERENCES

Gillborn, D. and Gipps, C. (1996) *Recent Research on the Achievements of Ethnic Minority Pupils*. London: Ofsted.

Hannon, P. (1995) *Literacy, Home and School: Research and Practice in Teaching Literacy with Parents*. London: Falmer Press.

Kendall, F.E. (1996) *Diversity in the Classroom: New Approaches to the Education of Young Children*. New York: Teachers College Press.
Vernon-Feagans, L. (1996) *Children's Talk in Communities and Classrooms*. Oxford: Blackwell.

## SOME RESOURCES AND SUGGESTIONS FOR FURTHER READING

Edwards, V. and Redfern, A. (1992) *The World in a Classroom*. Clevedon: Multilingual Matters.
Stones, R. (1994) *A Multicultural Guide to Children's Books 0–12*. London: Books for Keeps and The Reading and Language Centre.

ACER (African-Caribbean Resource Centre), Wyvil School, Wyvil Road, Vauxhall, London SW8 2TJ.
AIMER (Access to Information on Multicultural Education Resources), University of Reading, Bulmershe Court, Earley, Reading RG6 1HY.
Letterbox Library (Specializes in mail order of non-sexist and multicultural books for children), Unit 2d, Leroy House, 436 Essex Road, London N1 3QP.
The Multicultural Bookshop, Rashid House, Westgate, Bradford.

# CHAPTER 5

# Teaching, learning and standards

ASHER CASHDAN

## LEARNING TO LEARN

Even if you taught the same group of children for many years and you were a particularly creative and resourceful teacher, with access to the most powerful teaching equipment and techniques, you could not possibly teach them every single thing they need to know. This is not due merely to the limitations of teachers and learners. It is because the number of different facts we need to know at some time or other and the number of different actions we are able to perform is virtually infinite - and unpredictable.

Look again at the paragraph you have just read. It contains sentences that neither you nor I had ever seen before in exactly that form. Yet I was able to write them, and you (I hope!) could read and understand them. No teacher could have taught me all the sentences I would ever encounter or have to write.

What we are seeing is that teaching and learning are not about assimilating thousands of facts, but about learning and understanding a limited number of facts and skills, together with a fairly small number of organizing principles. Together they enable us to solve an infinite number of problems. *We learn how to learn.*

Nor are we talking merely about academic tasks. No coach could show a tennis player how to play every single stroke they would ever need. Each player has to learn how to apply his or her personal technique to a unique situation, including the opposing player's game, the type of court, the weather and so on - not to mention motivational factors such as whether the game is an important one and how much depends on the next point.

Teaching, then, is about helping pupils to be effective learners, running their own learning, constantly and cumulatively building up techniques for helping themselves to acquire knowledge, skills and understanding. This raises immediately the issue of how far the teacher's role should be an indirect one - facilitating learning by arranging the child's school experiences so that learning can occur, and how far direct instruction is desirable: that is, likely to succeed.

This has recently become quite a contentious issue, with a whole range of people outside the profession (parents, politicians, journalists, even HMI) complaining that standards would be higher if teachers did more teaching and there was less sand-and-water play, or less group/project work in which children are left to their own devices. Teachers, on the other hand, often feel that the best learning occurs when they are *not* standing talking in front of the class. I will return later to the question of standards – and to the issue of whole class teaching versus group work. For the moment, though, I would suggest that the question is not whether direct or indirect teaching is right, but rather *when* each is the appropriate method.

Moreover, we have to acknowledge that much of children's learning does not take place in the classroom and is not under the teacher's control. To take but one among many possible examples: the great majority of the children who start school at the age of 5 arrive as quite competent speakers of at least one language – and most, if not all, of this competence will have been acquired with no formal instruction at all, though they will have learned from adults and from other children around them.

In unsupervised play, too, children learn many things – about materials and construction, weighing and measuring and so on, as well as a whole host of social skills involving sharing, co-operating and settling arguments.

## THE TEACHER'S ROLE

Does this mean that teachers are not needed? Some educationists have in fact suggested this. John Holt, himself paradoxically a great teacher, insisted that teaching did not often lead to learning. He says:

> Organized education operates on the assumption that children learn only when and only what and only because we teach them. This is not true. It is very close to one hundred per cent false.
>
> (Holt, 1991, p. 160)

Psychologists and educationalists have studied the learning process for many years, systematic work in this field having started with studies of mental abilities towards the end of the nineteenth century. But we have not yet arrived at a comprehensive account of how learning takes place or how a teacher can ensure that it happens, though we do have a number of partial insights. It is possible that there never will be a full-scale, adequately tested theory of learning. For the time being at any rate we therefore have to accept that teaching is part science, part art. With experience and with critical examination of our practice (see Chapter 6) and taking research into account, we can constantly improve. Teachers are always learning; this is one of the fascinations (and the frustrations) of our profession.

The American psychologist Jerome Bruner used to tell of a small experiment he once carried out. He observed an excellent nursery teacher working with a succession of 3-year-olds helping them to solve a specially designed wooden jigsaw-type problem. With two-thirds of them she seemed to be wasting her time: one-third of the children could do it straightaway so her help was redundant; another one-third found it so difficult that her help was again irrelevant – they were just not ready for the task. The remaining one-third, however, could not at first solve the problem unaided, but with the teacher's help they did reach the solution.

It would in fact be rash to deduce from this that two-thirds of our teaching is wasted, but it is important to make sure that there is as good a match as possible between the learner and the task. This is why whole class teaching is often problematic what is right for one child may be too difficult for another, and so on.

Think of a school assembly, for instance. Try asking your children what was said there, just a few minutes later. For both social and cognitive reasons you will find that many of them will not have understood what the headteacher said to them, even if they remember her words.

Even more interestingly, to return to Bruner's little experiment, what did the teacher do that helped those children who *did* eventually manage to fit the puzzle together? Was it what she said to them by way of explanation, the leading questions she asked to help them think it out, or the demonstrations she offered? Or was it merely that she had caught those particular children at just the right point when they could teach themselves to reach the solution and her teaching was irrelevant even with this group? The disappointing answer is that it is often very hard to be sure what contributes to children's successes, even if at times we can make some intelligent guesses. We must always be ready to analyse our teaching, to try a variety of approaches, to study each child's strengths and weaknesses.

## AGES AND STAGES

Are there any ways of knowing how far a child has reached in his or her development, so that we can decide what to teach them and at what level of difficulty? There are two questions here: are there well-defined developmental stages and if so, how do I find out which is the one that a particular child has reached?

Let us start with stages. There have been a number of attempts to lay down a series of developmental stages through which each child should pass, but by far the best known and most researched is the framework developed by the Swiss theorist and experimenter, Jean Piaget. He started out as a botanist and never really thought of himself as an educational psychologist at all, though his numerous followers have always saddled him with their interpretations of what his work means for education!

Essentially, Piaget saw children as passing through a series of stages (four main ones) in their thinking in which they become successively more able to detach themselves from their immediate experience and develop more abstract thinking capacities. Thus, in the *sensori-motor* period, children are entirely restricted to their immediate sensations and surroundings and learn through physical actions. As they develop, they are still bound by what they see and know, but passing through a *pre-operational* period they become gradually more able to learn by thinking. In the *concrete operational* period, then, the operations they use become mental, carried out in their heads, rather than direct actions. Finally, adolescents and adults become capable of *formal operations*, using abstract concepts at a purely theoretical level. (Margaret Donaldson (1978) gives a very clear, critical account of Piagetian theory in the Appendix to her book.)

The Piagetian stages have been linked closely to particular ages and particular sequences of skill development. However, as Di Bentley points out (Chapter 11), this has proved far less reliable (or fruitful) than the general theory itself. For instance, Piaget's distinction between *assimilation*, where the child fits new knowledge into its existing mental structures, and *accommodation*, where the structures themselves have to change to accept the new understandings, has remained a powerful concept.

These two concepts of *assimilation* and *accommodation* help us to see how the child's development represents an interaction of internal mental structures, largely given, and external experiences which enable their growth and change. Without the structures, which are part of the endowment of all of us, there can be no learning; but without the necessary experiences there can be no learning either.

The implications of this way of thinking about children are particularly important when contrasted with the more traditional, earlier emphasis on intelligence as a largely inherited quality which each of us has in a fixed quantity, the level of which sets definable limits on our educational potential. One can certainly devise tests that have the power to predict academic achievement, but they do not always tell us what we might think they do.

To go back a little in time. After World War 2 especially, there was a strong egalitarian movement to provide high-quality education for all those with the potential to benefit from it. It was thus hoped that if tests could be devised which picked out the potential high-flyers, even if their home or educational circumstances had not given them full opportunity to develop, they would be the success stories of the grammar schools and later of university education.

So eleven-plus tests of intelligence were devised so as to measure potential, without depending on life experiences. However, it slowly became apparent that any test, however 'culture-free' (or, later, 'culture-fair') it was designed to be, could not eliminate the effects of experience and thus those from favoured backgrounds continued to do better than the rest, even in such tests. Interestingly – and counter to expectation – children from 'disadvantaged' backgrounds typically gained lower scores on non-verbal than on verbal tests, showing perhaps that an impoverished background can affect learning over a wider front than just the verbal sphere.

What are the implications of all this for the teacher? The most useful one is to be aware of sequences of learning in school subjects, and to see where individual pupils come in terms of these, but not to rely on them too heavily. A child may be more advanced in one area than in another, even if that is not what we normally expect. But most importantly, it is far more accurate to think in terms of *achievements* than of *abilities*. If I am trying to help a child who is behind most of the others in the class, I want to know what he or she can actually do now - where they are up to - so that I can try to help with what may come next. Besides, we all function at so much less than our maximum potential nearly all of the time that we do not usually need to be great geniuses to manage the next steps. What hampers achievement is far more likely to be discouragement through poor results in the past than some major inherent lack of ability.

So try to find out where the child is, ignore pessimistic forecasts and encourage him or her to take the next step - but make it a small one, so that success is guaranteed.

## AN EXAMPLE - LEARNING TO READ

Many of the above points are relevant to thinking about children learning to read. For instance, it used to be fashionable to spend considerable energy on tests, working out whether a child was ready to start work on reading. Reading readiness tests can involve matching pictures, spotting differences, putting cartoon pictures in order and so on. Then there are all those workbooks, which give children practice in the prerequisites of reading; then, when they are 'ready', they can begin the real thing. Some teachers still do this, but for most children they are an irrelevance.

If we want to know whether a child is ready to read, the best thing to do is to make a start, with letters, words, a book, with talk about these and with demonstrations. If the child is not ready, little of this will make much sense, but provided that inappropriate pressure has not been applied, no harm will be done. In fact, the child may have understood more than we give credit for and foundations may have been laid that will lead to progress at a suitable later time (Similarly, in the Bruner experiment we discussed above, the 'unsuccessful' children may have learned more than we realize.)

More important than readiness exercises is the provision of a context in which the meaning of a task is learned. Thus readiness for reading is best fostered by reading to children, showing them that you are a reader (sometimes a silent one!), discussing signs and labels, the child's name on a coat peg, writing on supermarket packets and so on. Recent research has shown that word play, particularly with rhymes and sounds, is a potent preparation for reading. Note, too, that these are worthwhile both in their own right and as fun.

If the child knows what reading is, and has seen its uses and benefits in his or her own environment, he or she will be ready - and keen - to start an activity he or she understands. If the child understands his or her own learning processes (sometimes known as *metacognitive* skill) that will help even more.

Such children notice similarities and differences: 'That's just like the one we looked at yesterday', 'My name begins with a 'k' too; is it kitten, then?', 'I knew it was $x$, because ...'. All these tell you that the children are aware of the nature of the task and of how it needs to be approached. That is your cue to make some suggestions, or to put in the right question.

Do not be afraid to formalize some of the children's learning. Regular practice in learning tables and whole class work on letter-sounds do have their place, but they will be vastly more successful if the children have a clear understanding of why they are learning these things (see Susan Cameron, Chapter 10 for the maths side) and what use they will make of them.

## FITTING THE LEARNER AND THE TASK

As we have already noted, everyone, whether child or adult, learns far more effectively if they understand the nature of the task and know what they are trying to achieve. Equally important is that the task should be an appropriate one for the learner. Let us examine both of these aspects.

First, if I have something new to learn, I ask a lot of questions. 'What are we going to do? What is it all about? How am I to start? What will we do with it?' If the teacher just says, 'Trust me, do as I say, just get on with it and things will eventually become clear', she will have an anxious, easily confused and possibly easily demoralized student to manage. Many of us were completely turned off algebra, or French or even learning to swim, because no explanation was forthcoming, or at best an incomprehensible one. To learn well, students need a context that is meaningful to them and linked as far as possible to what they already know, so that the new knowledge or skill builds from what they can cope with already. If that does not happen, there can be trouble.

To take a personal example, I could start to learn Spanish with very little preparation: I already know some French and Latin plus a little Modern Greek, and I am a native English speaker. Whether I know it or not, I have a range of techniques for learning languages. If, on the other hand, I attended a class on motor repairs I would not know where to begin and would soon become confused. I lack sufficient 'hooks' on which to hang this new learning. Other people might be in exactly the reverse position. 'Knowing where to begin' is a crucial phrase. If we want children to acquire new knowledge, we have to help them to understand the nature of the task as well as its specific content.

One of the reasons why project work has acquired such a bad reputation is because teachers have not always realized that it requires skills and insights which pupils do not automatically have. Instead of approaching the resource material with focused questions in mind and techniques to extract relevant answers, the pupils of these teachers end up simply copying large chunks out of reference books.

Second, little progress will be made if the starting point of the task is either too easy or too difficult. In the one case, the student may become bored and lazy; in the other, discouragement may follow. Many psychologists have written about these issues. The two terms I find most useful are *scaffolding* and *matching*. Scaffolding means helping the pupil by providing the right amount of context and support in the learning situation. Matching is getting the right gap between the learner and what is to be learned – not too big, not too small.

Unfortunately, doing both of these well demands at least some individual work with each learner, to assess where they are and exactly what help they need. This is why the recent demand for greatly increased amounts of whole class teaching in the primary school needs to be handled with some care. Explaining a new area for the first time, engaging in corporate activity, sharing information, all have their place in whole class work. But time must also be spent, usually when the class is engaged in small group work, for the teacher to give tailored help to her students in twos or threes or, best of all, individually.

Moreover, there are a number of significant differences in pupils' preferred learning styles, possibly constitutionally determined. To take one example: some prefer to take a broad look at a new area of study before they begin to see any light. Others would rather work steadily through a narrow sequence and come to the broad picture much later. The former have been dubbed *holists* and the latter *serialists*. Again, the teacher can take such differences into account to a greater extent in group or individual work than in the whole-class situation.

To conclude this section, a word about learning motivation. Most children come to school eager to learn, curious about the world and everything in it. They study keenly and work hard to please both themselves and their teachers. Yet within a few years we know that many will have become bored, resentful of school and reluctant learners. Of course these changes are to a large extent due to factors outside the school, being concerned with much wider aspects of the society in which we live. But part of the change, I would suggest, is a result of being asked to do things that pupils could not understand, with inadequate explanation and no clear relevance to the rest of their lives. We can do a great deal to help here through the planning and organization of our curricula and by careful thought about fitting the task to the individual pupil. This inevitably brings in the question of standards in education, and in the final section of this chapter I hope to shed some light on what has in recent years become such a thorny issue.

## STANDARDS IN EDUCATION

It has become virtually impossible in the last ten years to open a newspaper, listen to the radio or switch on the television without hearing that standards in education are falling, that lack of sufficiently trained personnel is damaging our competitiveness in international markets and that some government project, agency or working group is being set up to tackle the problem. While some of the claims about lower standards are ill informed, there are some real issues here which we need to consider.

## Some background

Testing of 11- and 15-year-olds in reading and numeracy has been conducted regularly since before World War 2. The results of these surveys show steady improvements over the years until the 1980s, since when there has been a slight drop. How far these changes are really significant is debatable. Foxman *et al.* reviewed this whole area in 1993 for the National Commission on Education. Their summary includes the following points:

- Reading standards among 11 and 15 year olds have changed little since 1945, apart from slight rises around 1950 and in the 1980s. Among 7–8 year olds, however, standards fell slightly in the late 1980s. In writing performance, there was no overall change during the 1980s.

- British school students are above average in geometry and statistics, but below average in number skills, compared with other industrialized countries. Britain also has a wider spread of mathematics attainment, mainly due to the weaker performance of lower attaining pupils.

- Nationally, there was a fall in attainment among 11 and 15 year olds in number skills between 1982 and 1987, and a rise in geometry, statistics and measures.

(Foxman *et al.*, 1993)

They point out that we no longer have systematic information on changes in pupil attainments. Despite government claims, National Curriculum (NC) assessment does not provide information on educational standards throughout the country. This is partly due to the type of testing used; but in any case NC assessment is carried out against pre-set criteria. If pupils under- or over-achieve against these criteria it may be that the tests have set too high (or too low) a standard, rather than that the pupils are doing badly.

Moreover, there is no agreement among the experts on the relative significance of school factors as opposed to external social and economic variables in causing changes in standards. If poverty levels have risen (and educational achievement is certainly linked to health, housing and other social indicators) or there are more children in an area who do not hear English spoken at home, this can certainly affect standards in school. On the other hand, there can be wide variations in average achievement between pupils in schools with very similar catchment characteristics in the same inner-city area, pointing to school factors such as the competence of the headteacher, the quality of the school's organization and its whole educational approach as significant influences on pupil attainment.

## The current situation

So does all this mean that there is nothing to worry about and that all the talk of falling standards is simply yet another example of the 'teacher-bashing' that the profession has suffered from ignorant politicians and journalists over the last few years? Not quite.

First, we do live in a climate of international competition whether we like this or not. Comparative studies of attainments in different countries are notoriously unreliable. But we in the United Kingdom certainly have no grounds for thinking that we are doing particularly well on the international scene; when we take our past achievements and our aspirations into account, it is probably fair to say that the educational attainments of our population are somewhat disappointing.

More important, though, is the fact that small falls or rises in school attainment are beside the point when we see the vastly increased demands on literacy, numeracy and other core skills made on us in the modern world. There can be no doubt that major improvements in these, together with technological and other skills, are needed if we are to maintain our standard of living, let alone enhance it.

So schooling needs to be more efficient and to strive for progressively higher standards of achievement in all our pupils. The foundations for this are laid in the primary school, so this is a particularly relevant issue for the readers of this book. Many of the points highlighted in this and other chapters offer helpful ideas, but there are dangers, too, if we define standards too narrowly. For instance, Guy Merchant hints in Chapter 9 that the new 'literacy hour' currently being established in our schools will not prove the hoped-for success if it pushes up achievements in the short run, but fails to maintain pupil motivation. As we saw above, narrow teaching, where pupils do not see the point of what they are doing, can be counterproductive. So make sure that your literacy hour is meaningful (and enjoyable) as well as technically well organized and structured. That way your children will not only become better readers; they will also continue to read!

## REFERENCES

Donaldson, M. (1978) *Children's Minds*. Glasgow: William Collins.

Foxman, D., Gorman, T. and Brooks, G. (1993) Standards in literacy and numeracy. In *Briefings for the Paul Hamlyn Foundation National Commission on Education*. London: Heinemann.

Holt, J. (1991) *Learning all the Time*. Ticknall, Derbyshire: Education Now Publishing Co-operative/Lighthouse Books.

## SOME SUGGESTIONS FOR FURTHER READING

Desforges, C. (ed.) (1995) *An Introduction to Teaching: Psychological Perspectives*. Oxford: Blackwell.

Donaldson, M., *Children's Minds*, as above.
Holt, J. (1969) *How Children Fail*. Harmondsworth: Pelican Books.

Donaldson and Holt are classics, written from their authors' individual perspectives. They are both well written, easy to read and stimulating. Desforges' book provides a wider range of material.

CHAPTER 6

# Thoughtful teaching

ROBIN SMITH AND JOHN COLDRON

## INTRODUCTION

In this chapter we will examine some ways in which teachers can extend their expertise by thinking about their teaching. Whether you are a student teacher, recently qualified or more experienced, you can gain useful insights by reflecting upon your classroom practice and on the situation in which you are working. Some of these insights will be of immediate use – for instance, reviewing the difficulties experienced by a child in understanding your explanation of place value may help you to realize how you misinterpreted his or her questions and enable you to present the topic in a more accessible way in the next lesson. Other insights may not be directly applicable in subsequent lessons, but they can accumulate to alter your views of teaching or learning. For example, when you set pupils problem-solving tasks, do they see them as opportunities to develop the skills you have in mind or are they more concerned to get 'the right answer', or simply to earn your approval? Sometimes reflecting upon teaching raises awkward dilemmas – after lots of hard work you may have found strategies that ensure your class stays on task and completes the prescribed curriculum, but as a consequence they may have become dependent on you and seem to lack initiative.

As former primary teachers who have worked with hundreds of students and experienced teachers, we are well aware that teaching is a demanding job. Each day can be felt as an achievement or a struggle. It might seem like imposing an extra burden to ask teachers to reflect upon their work as well. However, we believe that the practice of teaching and thinking about it are intimately linked. Teaching provokes thinking and it requires thinking in order to do it better.

When you start as a teacher, most of the activities you carry out in order to achieve a successful lesson have to be thought through. But in time many become routines, so you are able to concentrate on other aspects of your teaching and, crucially, upon your pupils' learning. Even then, there are so many demands on your time, so much to do in and out of lessons, that time for thinking is limited, so you need to have a focus for your thinking. If you can share this with others who have similar concerns, you are more likely to benefit and to feel encouraged to examine your teaching. Courses for teachers in training or in-service can provide the focus and the community for this dialogue. The climate in schools does not always make it easy because of the isolation of class teaching, preoccupation with everyday pressures or sometimes a reluctance to question taken-for-granted practices. Collaborative planning in teaching teams and with subject co-ordinators, or supervision by mentors, may offer the opportunity.

## THINKING ABOUT THE SUBJECTS AND CHILDREN YOU TEACH

In recent years there has been growing emphasis on teachers' understanding of the subjects they teach. Although there has been a move towards more subject specialism, most class teachers in primary schools teach a wide curriculum and need to have knowledge of many subjects. Whether or not you are a specialist in the subject, in order to prepare yourself for teaching a new topic you have to research or refresh your background knowledge. However, it is not always obvious what you need to know until you think about how you will use the knowledge.

A depth of knowledge about a topic, for instance the environment you are going to map with a class, or the history of local housing, or the rocks from which the building materials came, will help you to plan how to present it for your class. You will feel more confident in explaining ideas and answering pupils' questions if you have thought about what they might ask, the difficulties they might face and mistakes they might make. Thinking ahead and imagining the lesson may lead you to see the need to find out more yourself, or to consider alternative ways of explaining difficult ideas.

Three student teachers nearing the end of their course were teaching electricity to pupils using familiar practical tasks – getting the children to make simple circuits, to predict which would work and check if they did. They felt that the learning would be more effective if, before doing those activities, children were given explanations of some key ideas about electricity that would usually be left until secondary school. Before they could test out their ideas, they discussed what sorts of explanations to offer and found they needed to check their own ideas about electric current and resistance. They experimented with several circuits, seeing what happened when they put more bulbs in series or in parallel. They discussed how the idea of resistance explained what they saw. When they had done this they felt more confident about their own understanding of current and clearer about how to present their lessons.

But they then thought of some awkward questions which children might ask, such as 'Why isn't the first bulb brighter? Doesn't it use up some of the electricity before it gets to the second?' So they had to decide how they might answer such questions. This led them to consider different analogies they could use to help primary pupils make sense of the abstract ideas. They read about how the flow of current could be likened to water flowing in pipes, or to lorries delivering goods, or dramatized by children passing objects round a circle or moving round themselves. Each of these had limitations, but they now knew several approaches which they might use when appropriate.

Thinking about lessons afterwards will help you to build up a repertoire of teaching ideas and of insights gained from pupils' responses. What worked well with the class last time I did it? How should I change the content? What really were the key ideas I wanted them to grasp and do I need to check my own understanding of those? Talking with other teachers or reading vivid accounts of their experiences can add to this repertoire. (There are good examples in the books by Woods (1990) and by Woods and Jeffrey (1996))

The picture we are painting here of a teacher's subject knowledge is one that grows and changes with experience and especially with thinking about that experience. It has been analysed by researchers as subject content knowledge and pedagogic content knowledge, meaning not only knowing the subject at your own level but also knowing ways of representing it so that pupils can make sense of it. This links with a more general understanding of teaching strategies and of children's learning; for example, in knowing the sorts of ideas which pupils themselves are likely to hold in a subject. There is now a large body of evidence of the conceptions children already have which can affect what they learn from your lessons.

For example, teachers often set pupils work sorting items into groups such as living/non-living or animal/plant. However, children often have their own concepts of living or animal that may be reinforced by everyday language. Some will insist that cars or fires are living. They will often resist the classification of insects or worms as animals, reserving the term for those which biologists classify as mammals. People may not be included as animals. You can probably think of signs and situations that seem to confirm this classification, rather than that of the biologist!

It is useful for teachers to be aware of the ideas which their pupils might bring to lessons. However, in any class, children will have a particular set of ideas and their teacher needs to find these out. There are a number of ways of eliciting these in class and working with them. One technique that has proved popular with many primary teachers is concept mapping, in which the associations children make with the topic are mapped out. This can be done individually or as a group, or even as a class, to gain insights into ideas which pupils have about the topic. With younger children it can be done by scribing for individuals or for a group. (See the example in Figure 6.1.)

Other techniques for bringing out children's ideas include listening to a group talk about a situation shown in a picture, getting individuals to do their own drawings or to complete or add captions to a drawing, or beginning a demonstration, then asking the class to predict what they think will happen and to offer their explanation. Thinking about the variety of ideas thrown up should alert you to the different interpretations the children might make of the experiences you have planned for them. It can be daunting if there are lots of unexpected ideas and you want to ensure they all achieve some common

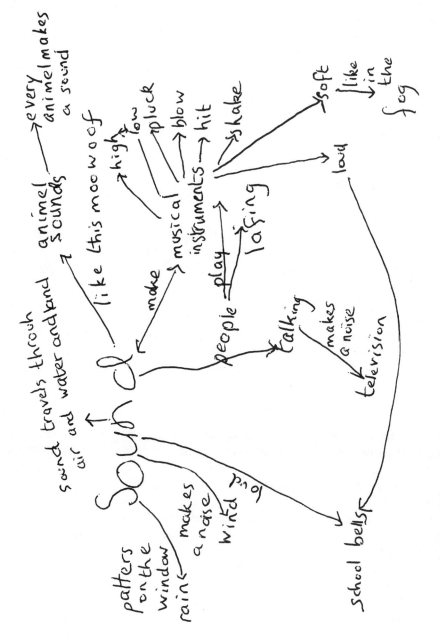

**Figure 6.1** Concept map drawn by Rebecca, aged 7

understanding. You will need to reconcile that goal with the wish to value children's own ideas.

One view of learning, the constructivist approach, suggests that you should help children to test out their own ideas, discuss them and see if the standard ones which you are offering make better sense (see Chapter 11 for more on constructivism). Many primary teachers are sympathetic to this approach but find it is not always easy to achieve in practice. First, the teacher needs to create situations where all the children can explain their own ideas. Second, the teacher may be overwhelmed if pupils do produce many non-standard ideas. Third, to work with those ideas requires more time than direct instruction. Finally, the pressure to teach standard ideas specified by the National Curriculum can make a teacher reluctant to air alternatives. However, this sort of dilemma is a feature of teaching, and is one reason why thinking about classroom practice raises bigger questions about how we teach and why.

One dilemma you have to live with as a teacher is the tension between controlling pupils and fostering their independence. Closely related to this is the concern to build a classroom atmosphere in which children respect one another and value their different viewpoints. But this ideal of a community may be hard to reconcile with the pressure to avoid disputes and run a quiet class. The balancing of different purposes is a characteristic feature of teaching. To the subject and pedagogical questions above, we should add reflection on the moral and social environment of our classroom, such as 'What approach to learning did I encourage, did I make them feel responsible for their own learning or did I make them "guess what teacher wants"?'

## THINKING ABOUT THE SORT OF TEACHER YOU WANT TO BE

During initial training you come into contact with many experienced teachers. As you watch them teach, listen to the way they talk to individuals, deal with disputes and talk about teaching, you use them as models. Sometimes you are lucky enough to meet a person who is inspiring in every aspect of the profession, more often it will be someone who is good in many respects but not in others – and of course you also meet those who exemplify for you everything you think is bad about teachers! These models are crucial in helping you to reflect on your own identity as a teacher – ' I want to teach like her'; 'I like the way he does that, but not this'; 'I will never become that sort of teacher'. When you use models like this, you can identify aspects of teaching which are sometimes very difficult to make clear in any other way. Thus seeing and using examples furthers your thinking about teaching. Teachers who are striving to improve constantly check themselves against such models and try to be more and more discriminating about what they like and don't like about what they see – 'I want to teach like her, because …'; 'If I could do what he does in those circumstances, then I would achieve …'; '*That* way of relating to children is wrong.'

Unfortunately, once training is finished and you are in a post, this way of thinking about your teaching can, for a number of reasons, be more difficult to do well. One reason is that, although based in school, you have far fewer opportunities to observe how other teachers really work in the intimacy of their own classrooms. A second reason is that in order to make as good a job as you can of the first year, you focus on your immediate practice and do not notice so much what others are doing, or you may only look for what will help with narrow, but urgent, practical concerns. Another danger is that as you become more confident from year to year in your way of doing things, it is tempting to relax and enjoy the relative ease compared with your first year and not to seek alternative models of practice.

Having constructed your identity, what need have you for further building blocks? Well, looking at the way others are doing it should be not only an initial stimulus but also a source of continuing challenge. As a thinking teacher you should therefore take every opportunity to observe others and to talk with them about their aims and style. Team teaching is an excellent means of doing this. School management can also help by using in-service days to allow teachers to go to other schools or to observe each other in a planned way. Reading descriptions of other teachers' practice is a good substitute for actual observation, since the best accounts give a real flavour of the teaching and classroom atmosphere.

Here is an extract from Woods (1990), in which some Year 6 children described their teacher's way of establishing a classroom atmosphere where their views were relevant:

> She talks to the whole group together and then we just tell her our ideas, and other people comment on them and suggest this and that and then we put it all together. She lets us talk about it more than other teachers. She lets us have our own conversations and arguments and then gets us back to the point. She lets us speak, she lets us vote although we're not 18. ... She lets us breathe more. Most of all she listens, unlike other teachers who jump to conclusions.
>
> (Woods, 1990, p. 76)

You will inevitably think about day-to-day details of classroom practice such as 'What is the most effective way to give children access to the art materials?' What is harder is to reflect on issues of style and relationships; for example, 'Does my humour suit all the children in my class?' and 'Do I allow my children to be independent in the classroom?' It is almost impossible to find time, or the company, in which to ask the more fundamental questions: 'What do I mean by education?', or 'Why are schools the best places to educate children?' When you are immersed in the urgency of daily practice, questions like this can seem at best a luxury and at worst an irrelevant indulgence.

But in fact, consideration of these questions has the potential to develop your practice more radically than do those that seem more directly relevant.

Think of a house: the type and quality of the rooms and facilities are dependent on the foundations. To change these will inevitably change the living space and what is possible in that space. The pressures to be unthinking are very powerful. The urgency of day-to-day concerns, the culture of the school and the social position of teachers conspire to make you accept the status quo. It is therefore necessary to force yourself to think about the more fundamental questions in order to keep a critical perspective on your own current practice and to develop and improve.

Much of what you do as a teacher is determined by the need to survive in a reasonably dignified way from day to day. Survival is always set in a specific context. It means particular children and their parents, a particular head teacher, perhaps with her own view of how you should be teaching, a particular community of school colleagues and support staff who over the years have built up a school identity in a specific building and community, with a way of doing things, an approach best described as an ethos, with all its overtones of territorial identity. These things exert powerful social forces on you which makes questioning them very difficult, but they do need to be questioned. Schools can develop ways of working that help the school but are not good for children. For example, control and discipline are central concerns of headteachers, teachers and parents because without a calm, harmonious atmosphere schools cannot work. But in striving for control, teachers can forget that it is a means to an end, not an end in itself.

Ways of dealing with children that have emerged over time in a school can become unquestioned habits, but they may be disrespectful, violent or simply thoughtless in relation to children. For example, in one primary school, where the staff were extremely caring and responsive to the children, they tried to mark events that were special for individuals. Over time it became the custom that when it was a child's birthday that child was invited to the front during school assembly and everyone sang 'Happy birthday to You'. At some point a child must have said, 'Can I show my cards and presents?' and before long it had evolved into a regular display of child wealth and the success of television advertising. Some children of course had no, or very few, cards or presents. They must have looked forward with dread to when it was their turn to have their birthday. But the staff just stuck to the way things were, unable to see the dubious values the practice was purveying or the suffering it was causing. The school's 'common sense' and habitual practices may need to be questioned by you as a developing teacher and that may sometimes take courage and strength of mind.

Similarly, the National Curriculum and the increasing prescriptions as to teaching method, because they come from central government, have immense power to affect what you do; but this does not mean that you should not, in the interests of the children, consider the rights and wrongs of what you are being asked to do. We do not mean a knee-jerk rejection, but a coming to a professional judgement.

A powerful way of enabling yourself to question the way things are is to work at more than one school. Our advice to young teachers is to spend from two to three years in one school, then to move on and do the same in another. By working for that length of time in three schools you will have gained a critical perspective on ways of doing things and not be confined by the horizons of a single school community.

## WHAT DOES IT MEAN, THEN, TO BE A THOUGHTFUL TEACHER?

What do all these points add up to? You need to be able to think beyond the confines of your own classroom needs, the school's habits, the community setting and the apparently all-powerful dictates of government. This means being committed to continually learning about teaching, education, children, and yourself as a teacher. Student teachers often express envy at what seems to be the unassailable confidence of the experienced teacher. For reflective teachers it is not like that. Yes, you are comfortable with your craft in that you know how to survive and at the same time to deliver what is asked of you. As a successful, experienced teacher you will have immense skill and ability. But as the problems of survival fade, so experience gives you new insight into your failings. Because your aim is no longer set merely on getting through, you become only too aware of how far your practice falls short of your more considered ideals.

Uncomfortable questions crowd in on you: 'Do I do enough in my class of 30 for the low attainers *and* the high attainers?'; 'Do I teach more to deliver knowledge rather than for understanding to be achieved?'; 'How can I teach better to lead someone to real understanding?' ; 'Do I handle the children with humour and affection?'; 'Despite all of my and my colleagues' efforts, have we only played the school's part in allocating most children to their pre-ordained place in society rather than giving them opportunities for self-fulfilment or betterment?'

A teacher who is continuing to develop is someone who enjoys the challenge of being creative in practice and thoughtful about theory. She enjoys the tension between what actually happens, what she thinks ought to happen to children in her classroom, and the constraints imposed by the education system of which her classroom is a part. By theory, we mean what you gain from all the ways of being thoughtful about teaching described in this chapter – deepening subject knowledge, using models offered by others as a means of discriminating your own preferred style, discussing educational questions with colleagues, gaining a critical perspective on the school's ethos and 'common sense', being determined to ask and to answer impartially how far what is imposed by others (from the head teacher to the Secretary of State for Education and Employment) are in the best interests of children.

One way of engaging with theory has so far not been stressed in this chapter; that is, by teachers acting as researchers. Traditionally, there has been an apparently unbridgeable gulf between classroom practitioners and educational researchers. For all of the hours spent on finding good answers to significant educational questions, such research seems to provide little of benefit to teachers in schools. At the time of writing there is a determined effort by the Teacher Training Agency to encourage teachers to identify research questions about classroom practice, to read and analyse educational research that addresses those questions and to engage in small-scale research projects themselves in pursuit of the answers. It is an initiative that has great potential and is aimed at enabling teachers to be more reflective.

We have been writing this for teachers who are at the beginning of their careers. However, it is worth noting that the approach we advocate can make teaching more creative and fulfilling throughout a career. Here are two examples.

- A primary class teacher who had been carrying out action research for many years told us how the systematic reflection he had carried out had improved his teaching and made it more satisfying. When he first embarked on an in-service course he had looked closely at particular aspects of his classroom practice. Then he had worked with colleagues as a subject leader to change the science curriculum throughout the school. Looking back on that, he reported enthusiastically about how much progress had been made over the years. This had placed the school in a stronger position when it was inspected as well as giving him a personal sense of achievement. His current work was on bullying. Following his involvement in a local project about bullying, he had researched the issues thoroughly in his school, getting evidence from children and parents. This had led him to reconsider some assumptions about what children saw as bullying and how it might best be tackled. He developed ways of dealing with name-calling, which he found was a crucial first step in bullying, and taught victims 'fogging' strategies for deflecting and diffusing the aggression. His work had very obvious, immediate benefits for children in the school. Although he had found it hard to involve other teachers, who were often preoccupied with curriculum matters, he emphasized how thinking deeply about the issue had enhanced his personal professional development.

- A greatly respected deputy headteacher in an infant school explained how writing the reports for her class had stimulated her to look afresh at their achievements. This had given her new insights into children whom she already knew well. She was in the final term of a long career but she was still learning and being enriched by thinking about her pupils. Teachers, parents and children who had been fortunate enough to know her all recalled how much they had learnt from her. Thoughtful, creative teachers have much to offer their pupils, but also much to gain in their professional lives.

## REFERENCE

Woods, P. (1990) *Teacher Skills and Strategies*. London: Falmer Press.

## SOME SUGGESTIONS FOR FURTHER READING

Louden, W. (1991) *Understanding Teaching: Continuity and Change in Teachers' Knowledge*. London: Cassell.
A detailed case study of one teacher by a researcher who worked alongside her.

Pollard, A. (3rd edn, 1997) *Reflective Teaching in the Primary School*. London: Cassell.
Ideas and activities to structure thinking about teaching.

Woods, P., *Teacher Skills and Strategies*, as above
Woods, P. and Jeffrey, B. (1996) *Teachable Moments*. Milton Keynes: Open University Press.
The last two books contain many vignettes of thoughtful, creative teaching.

# PART 3

# Teaching in the classroom

# CHAPTER 7

# A golden age? New technologies and learning

MOIRA MONTEITH

> How can we manage with the curriculum nailed down and technology bursting through the roof?
>
> (Steve Heppell, at an ITTE conference in 1997)

Information and communications technology (ICT) may be compared metaphorically with Janus, the two-faced guardian god of doors and beginnings. This new revolution stimulates us to look forward, to take advantage of a new opening. At the same time we look backwards, wondering how to accommodate traditional learning needs. Are teachers and pupils to look back to basics, using a computer or even an integrated learning system (ILS) for drill practice in spelling, number exercises, constructing sentences and cloze comprehension? Would this hinder us from encouraging children to be intuitive and creative, qualities more openly in demand in job advertisements since what might be called the computer age? How do we ensure standards in literacy and numeracy? Do we add computer literacy and then visual literacy to the list of essentials which pupils must achieve?

If we consider recent history from a technological viewpoint, the timing of the debate about 'back to basics' (which is still continuing) was no accident. The slogan and the debate first occurred in the US and subsequently in the UK at a time when computers were becoming familiar in classroom learning and, even more significantly, computerized data could be collected and transferred comparatively easily. Schools now need to produce a considerable amount of information about every individual pupil, in terms of assessment, partly for the Department for Education and Employment (DfEE) and partly for parents.

Software designers have seen the opportunities of this new market, and have created programs so that schools can organize the data and also 'write' reports. League tables, where schools are ranked according to examination results, came into being when the software to create them became available (as well as when it was seen as politically desirable). The computer age offers every one of us immense opportunities for both individual and collaborative learning; it also provides the power for a highly centralized curricular system.

If we are able to achieve the balance between individual learning needs and national requirements, ICT can open the door to a golden age for education. One thing is sure: the door cannot be shut – whether or not the future is golden.

## PROVISIONALITY: JUST-IN-TIME EQUIPMENT AND LEARNING

Provisionality may seem an unpleasant new word. However, it does define very effectively the situation as regards current knowledge about ICT and the equipment we use. First, it is extremely difficult for us to foretell the future as regards ICT, and when people do it seriously they tend to get it wrong. The National Council for Educational Technology (NCET) tried exactly this with a group of eminent educationalists and technologists in 1993 and published a document proudly entitled *The Future Curriculum with IT* (1994). There was no mention of the Internet anywhere, CD-ROMs were deemed to be rather too difficult for teachers to use, and electronic mail was mentioned only twice. This is not in any way to criticize the contributors to that publication, merely to give a clear example of how difficult it is to be sure of the technological future. We can have only a provisional view based on our current knowledge.

A sensible approach in the face of this difficulty is not to worry that you have a mixture of probably outdated computers in any given school, but to build an ICT policy on what resources the school has now and plans to have in the next three years or so, and then to fully exploit the expertise and equipment you have now.

The second consideration is the nature of learning ICT skills. What you learned a few years ago is now superseded. No one can remain an expert for long. While this is frightening in one way – how can we continue to teach when our knowledge slips away inexorably in front of us? – it is also comforting. Provisionality is a great leveller. We all have to make new starts again and again, so we should have less and less trouble accommodating. If we are on our third start, we may be with people on their first or their ninth. A new motto for ICT policies might be live for *today*, plan for *tomorrow* and *not more than three years ahead*.

Of course, this provisionality of expertise has particular applications for teachers, students and pupils. The teacher, or any single individual, cannot sustain the role of expert as regards either factual information (there is far more to be gained from a selection of CD-ROMs and the Internet) or thorough awareness of the media for learning. There were always more books than anyone could read; now there are films, videos, music, computers, recorders, software, hook-ups from phones and computers and fax messages. From the time I am writing this to the time you are reading it, there will have been new developments, new integrations of what were previously separate entities. Some industries now use what they call 'just-in-time' training about every eighteen months to keep the expertise of their workforce currently viable.

Part of a teacher's sense of security in their role used to come from the belief that they knew more than their pupils. There is a story of one of the early Labour leaders, who was basically self-taught and later became an MP. He began to teach Greek in order to earn money. He always tried to keep fourteen lessons ahead of his students. This strategy presupposes a sequential line of learning and some clear, if narrow, water between student and teacher. No doubt, as an intelligent man, he thought up tactful ways of getting out of the difficulties when his students asked questions that required an answer further ahead or way off to the side of his current knowledge. Or perhaps he did not allow questions. This situation may never have been desirable or even tenable for a long time. It just is not possible now.

Teachers have to adapt their centres of expertise. They should be better than their students at the management of learning and at assessing the value of different learning approaches in different contexts. They need to take the lead in

- organizing and promoting opportunities for learning

- providing contexts in which all pupils and they themselves as teachers can continue to develop

- advising on the revision and construction of new learning programmes for individuals

- ensuring by assessment and evaluation that their pupils are progressing as well and as quickly as they can.

## CAN WE HAVE A STABLE NATIONAL CURRICULUM?

What can we say about the National Curriculum (NC) for ICT in the light of the previous statements made in this chapter? In some senses such a curriculum must be out of date in places by the time we read it. Yet it is still difficult for schools to achieve the totality of its requirements owing to the lack of hardware and software and, currently, expertise. There are a plethora of education papers at the moment to consider: the Stevenson Report (ICT Commission, 1997), prepared for Tony Blair while he was still leader of the Opposition and now about to be implemented; a working party set up by the Teacher Training Agency (TTA) to look at the NC in ICT for teacher education; the White Paper, *Excellence in Schools* (DfEE, 1997a) and, just published at the time of going to print, the government's consultation paper, *The National Grid for Learning: Connecting the Learning Society* (DfEE, 1997b). I suspect that this state of affairs will not alter very much, in that we shall frequently be in the position of having research just published, reports just about to be made, committees or working groups just about to be established.

It is a parallel situation to that of buying new ICT equipment. There is always the definite knowledge that computers of a given performance will become cheaper soon after you buy them. But there is little sense in waiting to buy, because you will be in exactly the same position in a year or eighteen months' time. Ron Dearing proposed a moratorium on changes to the NC on the basis that teachers were becoming annoyed and frustrated by the almost yearly changes. It is clear that you cannot have a moratorium on ICT progress, because it just goes on progressing. Discussions, working parties, government pronouncements and a variety of publications (including cyber-hype) will continue alongside technological development.

This situation actually provides an extremely helpful and healthy educational debate. At the same time, current technology, let alone future advances, allows all teachers and students to feed in their research findings.

## THE NATIONAL CURRICULUM FOR SCHOOLS

Originally, IT (as it was still called in the last NC documentation) was included as part of the technology subject area, which is an indication that educationalists did not know quite where to put it. The revision of the statutory orders in 1995 included IT as a separate entity, although legally still within technology. Every subject order, with the exception of PE, included the statement 'pupils should be given opportunities, where appropriate, to develop and apply their information technology capability in their study of ...'. This meant that teachers had to indicate within each subject area where pupils would be using IT. *The Framework for the Inspection of Schools* as published by Ofsted (1995) recommended that 'in information technology, the report should draw on evidence from all the other subjects inspected'. However, many inspectors were not qualified in terms of inspecting IT and their school reports were considered rather bland when it came to IT. Indeed, the Stevenson Report calls for better training for inspectors in this area.

Nevertheless, the Ofsted review of inspection findings 1993/4, published in 1995, found that

- More rigour is needed in meeting the requirements of the NC at all Key Stages, to ensure that pupils gain their entitlement to all aspects of IT capability.

- Teachers' competence with IT and ability to use it fruitfully in teaching need strengthening.

- There is a lack of differentiation in teaching IT capability.

- Teachers at all Key Stages need to feel more confident in judging at what levels of IT pupils are working.

- In primary schools, specific discussion and teaching should be offered so as to extend pupils' understanding of, and competence with, major IT applications.

- The great variation in teaching IT capability in different classrooms in a primary school needs to be reduced.

Emphasis on subject use of IT revealed an ambiguity in terms of focus, which did not help teachers in general. This may be one explanation of why many schools and teachers have not been active in promoting the use of IT. Some schools, mainly secondary where more computers were available, literally moved computers out of IT labs and into classrooms, for specific use by subject teachers. In some cases this actually decreased pupil/student use and the computers were moved back again.

The primary programme of study has been based on communicating and handling information, controlling, monitoring and modelling. Primary schools have worked heroically, often with antiquated equipment (the Stevenson Report recommends that no computer over five years old be 'counted' as part of the ICT resource within a school) to meet these requirements.

*Approaches to IT Capability: Key Stages 1 and 2* (NCET, 1995) states very clearly the relationship of IT to the rest of the curriculum and includes 'A suggested framework for an IT policy'. NCET proposes that in the introduction to the policy a school 'should state what IT is, in the school's view, and the importance of IT to a broad and balanced curriculum'. There seems, then, to be room for a variety of interpretations of IT.

Subsequently, *Approaches to IT Capability*, when considering 'an IT development plan', states:

> Where teachers have appropriate access to IT, in the staff room for example, or through the loan of portable computers, this emphasises the value of IT as a professional resource and helps to raise its profile.

There is here an acknowledgement of the current situation, in that some teachers do not have appropriate access to IT and others do not yet consider IT to be a valuable resource. The language is hesitant and accommodating.

## GENERIC SKILLS

It was, until quite recently, generally accepted that there were a number of ICT skills associated with specific kinds of software – 'the major IT applications' referred to in the Ofsted Report. These included: word processing, use of spreadsheets, involving also the creation of graphs and charts, use of databases (and again, allied graphs and charts), use of graphic /arts/design packages, and use of computer mediated communication (CMC), which includes e-mail, computer and video conferencing. If primary school children could attain a basic functionality in most, if not all of these applications they would have an excellent foundation for subsequent use. You may ask: Why not include use of CD-ROM and desktop publishing? Where do we put use of video images, scanners, digital recording and editing of music, creation of animation and so on?

Software developments increasingly fuse functions, so that many word processors, for instance, now contain many desktop publishing features. The use of software has become more integrated, so that the results from database and spread sheet work can be easily transposed into a word processed document, images can be scanned and transferred into databases, word processing attached to e-mail or published on the Internet. It is increasingly less easy therefore to plan a primary school ICT checklist based merely on what might be called generic skills. Some teachers claim that it is difficult even now to fulfil NC requirements relating to database skills, since their new software has 'got rid of' some search strategies and simplified their use. Pupils now do not need to go through the previous search procedures. Technological developments will increasingly change skill-related competences.

## *THE STEVENSON REPORT* AND THE GOVERNMENT WHITE PAPER: *EXCELLENCE IN SCHOOLS*

> A realistic Government strategy for ICT will consist of mainly small and low key initiatives which, if consistently sustained, will over a 5–10 year period lead to comprehensive progress all over the UK.
>
> (*The Stevenson Report*: ICT, 1997)

This statement relates in part to government expenditure. However, since the government is now prepared to raid lottery investment and is quite likely to broker deals with telecommunication industries, comparatively low-level funding may produce results far beyond current expectations. Electronic communication can upgrade a school's entire level as regards ICT usage. Low-key initiatives also encourage schools to keep moving and to review their progress continuously. The report recommends support for teachers and student teachers in developing their own expertise, the development of educational software as opposed to industry standard software and proposes that it is a 'priority for Government to find a way of making the cost of usage of external networks by schools easily affordable and predictable'. Fifty per cent of pupils over age 9 will be given their own e-mail address, and should be able to send electronic messages from libraries and community centres as well as schools. This in itself will revolutionize the learning context.

The action plan recommends a *National Grid for Learning* (DfEE, 1997b), with access to the Internet for all teachers and pupils. Local grids are already coming into existence, such as that being developed by Sheffield Hallam University and Sheffield LEA, whereby all schools and the University School of Education will be linked via First Class computer conferencing. In this way, schools will be able to contact each other, the LEA and university tutors (particularly important with regard to students training in partnership schools). They will be able to discuss new initiatives from government or industry and, perhaps even more significantly, share resources such as policy documents, lesson plans, tips on where to buy ICT equipment, and solutions to problems.

This form of discussion may well be one of the achievements of the communications revolution. Just as research has shown that children's talk can have a profound effect on their learning, perhaps this discourse will have a considerable effect on educational development: and indeed mainly 'small and low key initiatives ... consistently sustained, will over a 5–10 year period lead to comprehensive progress'. Schools are to be encouraged to report back on the implementation of their ICT policies and 'every organization and individual involved in the profession [inspired] to participate in a coherent and productive way' (DfEE, 1997b).

The action plan also picks up on two other important issues. It asks the government to 'ensure that the external networking is devised in such a way that the growing number of computers in the home complement those in schools'. In addition, it is concerned at the growing disparity between children and some schools who have little equipment and no access as yet to the Internet, and those more fortunate, who have expensive technology available both at school and in the home. It suggests a number of pilot strategies to see how best to bring electronic access to the less privileged members of our society. Public libraries were established at a similar time of technological growth, and they may well fit into a similar niche once more.

The government White Paper published in July 1997 includes specific reference to ICT in the section 'Modernising the comprehensive principle'. Comprehensive schools were established to build up a secondary school system that would support the majority of pupils and get rid of the eleven-plus examination divide. ICT is now seen as underpinning that general level of support and improving the quality of educational resources and opportunities for learning. New legislation will ensure 'access to new technologies for all', with a 'clear national strategy' for ICT. 'Schools will be linked to a National Grid for Learning providing modern teaching and resource material, supported by initiatives such as Net Days' and there will be continuing research to maintain informed school development. The White Paper states in language certainly not hesitant:

> We are determined to create a society where, within ten years, information and communications technology (ICT) has permeated every aspect of education. Better teaching and understanding of ICT can both improve the process of teaching and learning itself and develop pupils' awareness of the potential uses of ICT in work and society.
>
> (DfEE, 1997b, p. 41)

The Secretary of State, David Blunkett, has called for readers to 'join us in a crusade' and offers opportunities for comment on the White Paper by post or e-mail. In the future, government documents will be published on the Internet as soon as they are written and consultation can be widespread. Just as the new technologies have delivered the actuality of a centralized curriculum and national league tables, they can conversely be used for individual pupils' curricular benefit as well as for mass consultation.

## THE NATIONAL CURRICULUM FOR TEACHER EDUCATION

There is to be a National Curriculum (NC) for all intending teachers, as outlined in Chapter 1. Currently, the DfEE has proposed that all students, at the point they leave their training, should 'have a working knowledge of IT to a standard equivalent to Level 8 in the National Curriculum for pupils and understand the contribution that IT makes to their specialist subject(s)' (DfEE, 1997c, p. 8). However, 'trainees may omit the *control* elements of the IT National Curriculum Order if this is not relevant to their specialist subject' (*ibid.*, p. 8n.)

In some ways a standard related to another accredited level is appropriate, in the sense that as the NC changes so do the requirements for teacher trainees. This is only a short-term strategy and a far better planned curriculum, particularly suitable for teachers, will be forthcoming from the TTA after wide consultation.

It thus follows, that whatever level student teachers should have reached at the exit point from their course should be attainable by all other teachers currently in schools. This will entail considerable in-service training in terms of the current workforce. If we then include the concept of 'just-in-time learning', all teachers will need an update every two years or so. Such an approach would not be linked to a skills-only approach but would include knowledge of recent research on the application of ICT in education.

## A NOTE FOR THE FAINT-HEARTED

There are many reasons why anyone might consider themselves as faint-hearted when thinking about new technologies, but do not despair. First, find out where you might get help. Tell yourself that you will spend at least ten minutes a day on ICT. Everyone can nearly always find ten minutes. (I always use this strategy when I am writing, as otherwise I put off the dreaded task for as long as possible. However, after ten minutes I can either leave the task or continue, and often I am able to continue, as I have 'killed' the apprehension.)

As soon as you have a basic working knowledge of a Windows environment on a computer (which will be most computers these days), do go where you can get on the Internet or send e-mail. You will be surprised at how easy it is. Some cyber cafes appear to have times when not many people are on the computers, so that could be one way to find a helpful guide. Public libraries are also becoming increasingly helpful in this direction. If you can find a few people to e-mail – cousins in South America or somewhere, possibly other teachers or schools – and e-mail them regularly, you will soon see an increase in your own ICT confidence. Once you have done this, encourage someone else you know – there is no better method of learning than teaching, as we all know.

## PREPARING FOR ICT

What might teachers do now to help prepare themselves in ICT for the next few years? A short answer: learn how to use e-mail, computer conferencing, some of the resources of the Internet, and seriously look at what is happening to home computers. Keep up to date with reading about what might be included in the National Learning Grid. Access the World Wide Web and look at some of the relevant materials there with a view to classroom use and research. It is easier to use e-mail and search the Web now than it was to use some of the earlier databases, so it could be that we are about to see some steady progress – a comforting number of 'small initiatives'.

The NCET has a number of web pages with resources designed often in collaboration with schools. For example, in July 1997 the Internet page at http://www.ncet.org.uk/ncet-info/links/primary.html contained sections on the following:

*Exploring English* – This site contains support for learning alphabet sounds, parts of speech, sentence construction and much more. (KS 2–4)

*Children's Literature Web Guide* – Story-books for children, with online conferences and pointers to resources for parents and teachers.

*Treasure Island* – Pages all about the book *Treasure Island* and other related stories. Also includes a 'design a pirate' section where children can e-mail descriptions of their pirates to be included in the gallery. (KS 2–3)

*MathsNet* – More for older children, but some activities are suitable for Key Stage 2 – check out the logo section, for instance. (KS 2–4)

*Using IT in Primary Science* – A series of five articles on using IT in Primary Science, first published in *Questions Magazine*.

*Schools online* – Science pages with activities to try, teacher support and 'ask an expert' pages. (KS 2–3)

*History* – All Souls School / British Museum Ancient Greeks. Virtual tour of the Ancient Greeks – artefacts from the British Museum prepared by a teacher for KS 2 teachers and children. There are downloadable worksheets and images as well as pointers to other sites. (KS 2–3)

From the last section we click to:

> *Room 68: Everyday Greek Life*
> Click on the pictures to see a larger version of the picture and questions. This room is probably the most valuable of all to teachers wishing to teach the Ancient Greeks at KS 2 (7–8-year-olds).

Such Web pages give an indication of what we can hope for in the future Learning Grid. They are available to anyone (with access to the Internet, of course), so parents and governors can access them just as well as schools. Information and suggestions are available to anyone who reads these pages and readers can also contribute; they can send in reviews, pupils can join in science experiments and also ask questions of science experts. In other words, the pages are interactive.

If you have pupils who are clearly more advanced than their peers, you can gain help and ideas for their development by looking at other key stages, as the maths item suggests. In addition, of course, there are museums and art galleries which pupils and teachers may visit. In the NCET example, a teacher has already put in some work on the Ancient Greeks as part of the history syllabus. Since the British Museum apparently does not like visitors to stay too long in this room, there are illustrations of what is in the room, superb examples of pottery and sculpture, and you can look at these by clicking on the appropriate link.

## COMPUTERS IN THE HOME

Many homes now possess one or more computers and as the prices come down this trend will increase. Some home computer systems are far more sophisticated than those in schools, so it is to be expected that some children will have had opportunities to become far more expert than many teachers. Such a situation does give added impetus to schools to encourage the sharing of all expertise within the classroom and to encourage collaboration with work at home.

Children with access to superior systems can bring information and extra skills to aid collaborative work with their peers. At the moment, though, a few children find the change from their home computer to the one at school an uninviting prospect, since their one at home is more powerful or has different software. It is good to find the Stevenson Committee seeking to address this problem. In the future, many pupils may learn much from individualized tuition online, whether at school or at home, so some close liaison needs to be assured.

PIN, or Parents' Information Network, describes itself as

> an independent organization set up to help parents and carers cope with the fast-moving world of computers, specifically how they are used in schools and how they can support learning at home – for children and the whole family.

This is an example of a new kind of consumer group, which has aims that go beyond simply scrutinizing merchandise or services. PIN's growth has been rapid and has obviously fulfilled a need, and perhaps other similar organizations or associations will follow.

# CONCLUSION

ICT does give help and hope for the future of education. A teacher with 25 years' teaching experience stated on the Apple Education Research Series WWW pages: 'It totally rejuvenated me. ... Now, I can't retire.' The more teachers can research their own use of ICT and can access others' research, the more they can have an impact on the future development of the NC. 'Interactive' could be applied not only to software, but to a lifelong educational debate, which informs the nature of the National Curriculum.

# REFERENCES

DfEE (1997a) *Excellence in Schools*. London: DfEE.
DfEE (1997b) *The National Grid for Learning: Connecting the Learning Society*. London: DfEE.
DfEE (1997c) *Teaching: High Status, High Standards (10/97)*. London: DfEE.
ICT in School Commission, 1996/7 (1997) *The Stevenson Report*. Published on the Ultralab Website at Anglia Polytechnic.
NCET (1994) *The Future Curriculum with IT*. Coventry: NCET.
NCET (1995) *Approaches to IT Capability, Key Stages 1 and 2*. Coventry: NCET.
Ofsted (1995) *Framework for the Inspection of Schools*. London: Ofsted.
Ofsted (1995) *Information Technology: A Review of Inspection Findings 1993/4*. London: Ofsted.

# SOME SUGGESTIONS FOR FURTHER READING

Elliott, D. and Pettigrew, M. (1998) *Student IT-Skills: A New Approach*. London: Gower.
Monteith, M. (ed.) (1998) *IT for Learning Enhancement*. Oxford: Intellect.
Underwood, J. (ed.) (1994) *Computer-Based Learning: Potential and Practice*. London: David Fulton.

MAPE (Micros and Primary Education) is an association which links primary schools together to share experience and information on ICT. You can obtain either individual or school membership. It publishes a very helpful magazine, *Microscope*. Further information is available from: Y Peers, MAPE, Technology Centre, Newman College, Genners Lane, Bartley Green, Birmingham B32 3NT.

NCET publishes booklets on many aspects of learning and managing ICT. Its name is now British Educational Communications and Technology Agency and its address is: Milburn Hill Road, Science Park, Coventry CV4 7JJ.

PIN (Parents' Information Network) is at PO Box 1577, London W7 3ZT, UK, Fax +44 (0)181 566 3336.

CHAPTER 8

# The National Curriculum: background, approach, content

DAVID OWEN

## INTRODUCTION

> Be gentle with me ... I'm having a National Curriculum crisis.
> (Poster on Year 1 classroom door, Sheffield school, June 1997)

It is difficult to play down the impact of the National Curriculum in terms of the transformation of primary schools and primary teachers. The schools in which you will work or work in now have experienced massive change in the last ten years. Teachers who have been in a post for some time will tell you of how they worked long and frustrating hours implementing an untested curriculum. They can explain how they grappled with new subjects such as technology and piloted a new assessment and testing system. If you are studying for a teaching degree as you read this, the National Curriculum will have changed again by the time you start your first teaching post. The challenge is for you to interpret those changes for the benefit of the children you will teach – without a crisis!

This chapter has four main aims. The first is to explore what the National Curriculum (NC) is, why it was formed, and how it has changed. The second is to discuss what types of curriculum have been present in the primary school and what approaches teachers have taken to implement the NC. The third aim is to look at the content of the NC as interpreted by the teachers of two Sheffield schools. Finally, I will explore the future of the National Curriculum, as we race towards curriculum review in the year 2000. A key part of this exploration centres on the extent to which you will be told *how* to teach as well as *what* to teach.

## BACKGROUND

### What is the National Curriculum?

Kenneth Baker, then Secretary of State for Education, introduced the National

Curriculum as part of the 1988 Education Reform Act. It is a statement of the minimum education a child is entitled to during his or her compulsory education. It is not meant to be the whole curriculum and schools are expected to implement the NC while still reflecting the particular needs of their children and the individual circumstances of the school.

The structure of the NC at KS 1 and 2 is as follows:

- The core subjects are English, maths and science. The foundation or non-core subjects are art, geography, history, information technology, music, physical education and technology. Schools have been required to teach religious education since the 1944 Education Act. The NC does not prescribe the content for this, although SCAA published model syllabuses for RE in 1995.

- All the subjects with the exception of RE have their content, method and approaches specified in the *Programmes of Study (PoS)*. Each subject has one or more *attainment targets*, which set out to define the expected standards of pupil performance. These standards were designed for the majority of pupils, rather than the whole school population. The standards of performance were what was thought to be reasonable by subject and assessment groups during the planning process. They were therefore not based on what children could achieve, but rather on what they *should* achieve.

- Performance is assessed against *level descriptions*. Each attainment target is now divided into eight levels, which is a reduction from the ten levels in the first version of the NC. For KS 1 and 2 the expected range of achievement is Level 1 to Level 5. Not all the NC subjects have level descriptions. Art, music and physical education have *end of KS descriptions*. These give a picture of what children should know, understand and be able to do by the end of KS 1 and 2.

- Assessment should be carried out on a day-to-day basis by teachers to inform their planning, but assessment against level descriptions at the end of KS 1 and 2 is also required in some subjects. Statutory tasks and/or tests take place in English and maths at the end of KS 1 and in English, maths and science at the end of KS 2.

- Teachers must report annually to parents on their children's progress in each NC subject. This report does not have to make reference to levels. At the end of KS 1 and 2 teachers must also report on performance in the core subjects and make brief comments on the assessment results.

- Special provision for children with special educational needs should be made by teachers. Within the *common requirements* for each subject is a statement on access to the particular PoS. This details how work can be selected from earlier or later key stages to meet children's needs. Provision should be made for children who need to use a range of communication methods and learning aids.

You can find further details of the subject orders and the special requirements for schools in Wales in the official publications listed at the end of this chapter (DfEE, 1995; SCAA, 1995).

The above brief description details the legal requirements on schools and teachers to deliver the National Curriculum. But why is there a National Curriculum? Why does an Education Act state what should be taught? The following section will briefly describe the creation of the NC in order to begin to answer these two questions.

## WHY WAS THE NATIONAL CURRICULUM CREATED?

For most of this century primary teachers have had considerable freedom to decide what should be taught in schools. Teachers had fought hard to be seen as professionals who had the expertise to make all curriculum planning decisions. The inclusion of the National Curriculum in the Education Reform Act in 1998 imposed a 'top-down' model of planning which has fundamentally altered how primary schools function, how teachers see their roles, and how children are taught.

So why was the National Curriculum introduced? Since the 1920s government has seen the school curriculum as the responsibility of teachers. However, government, media and public interest in the school curriculum grew during the late 1960s and early 1970s. The economic problems facing the UK in the early 1970s prompted several questions. Was money spent on the education service used efficiently? Did the school curriculum produce citizens with the skills to improve the nation's economy?

The nature of the teaching approaches used began to be questioned. Was the child-centred approach effective or did it contribute to a decline in standards? The well-publicized inquiry into William Tyndale Junior School, London in 1975 did much to damage the reputation of child-centred education and the perceived ability of teachers to plan their own curriculum. The report states how the headteacher described the school's teachers as being the only people who could make judgements about what was best for the children.

In the light of these economic and curricular concerns, James Callaghan, the Labour Prime Minister, made a speech at Ruskin College in 1976 which is widely seen as the start of a process that culminated in the introduction of the National Curriculum. This speech covered many of the issues that are still hotly debated today: the content of the school curriculum, preparing young people for the world of work, standards in literacy and numeracy and concern over 'informal methods' of teaching. It initiated the shift from a curriculum controlled by teachers to one controlled by the state.

This process was formalized in the Education Reform Act some twelve years later. The National Curriculum was introduced to promote many features of the government's thinking on education and the provision of services in general. There was an emphasis on learning the 'basics' and knowing about British achievements, history and literature. Science and technology became important subjects in both the primary and secondary curriculum. The idea of applying market forces to the provision of education was important. This weakened the role of the local education authorities in allocating school places and influencing the organization of schools. As the results of core subject tests at KS 1 and 2 are published in 'league tables' the argument was that schools would be more accountable. This gave parents more evidence on which to base their choice of school for their children. Control over the structure and delivery of the school curriculum therefore became much more centralized.

## How was it introduced and how has it changed?

The National Curriculum was introduced very swiftly and with little consultation. The original NC was quickly seen to be too complex and too prescriptive. Teachers needed to work towards hundreds of statements of attainment at KS 2. Covering nine subjects and RE in such detail was impossible for junior school teachers. At KS 1 teachers were under great pressure during the first full run of the English and maths standard assessment tasks in 1991. Many commented that the time spent on reading, writing and maths had actually been reduced by the new curriculum due to the demands of teaching the other subjects as well. Research commissioned at the time by the teaching unions showed that teachers' workloads had greatly increased and that there were also increased levels of stress and 'burnout'.

By 1992 the need to review the NC was clear. Sir Ron Dearing was appointed to review the NC and the present day 'slimmed down' curriculum was introduced in 1995. The following changes occurred as a result of the slimming down process.

- The volume of content to be taught by law was reduced and 20 per cent of teaching time was freed up for use at the discretion of the school.

- The number of attainment targets was reduced.

- The complex ten level system of statements of attainment was replaced by the more general system of level descriptions and the number of levels reduced to eight.

- The national tests in the core subjects were slimmed down and the importance of teacher assessment was reasserted.

Schools were advised to exercise their professional judgement, especially outside the core subjects, as to which elements of the curriculum to pursue in depth and which to cover 'with a lighter touch' (SCAA, 1995, p. 3). The importance of the basics was again highlighted. The following section discusses the approaches teachers are taking in implementing this curriculum. As you will be aware from your school experience, the actual curriculum children experience is a combination of what is prescribed and what teachers in individual schools feel is important in meeting the needs of their children. Complete government control of the curriculum has perhaps been replaced by a partnership between government and teachers, although further prescription in the areas of literacy and numeracy is likely. Recently, too, schools have been informed that to give any necessary extra time to the teaching of literacy and numeracy, full coverage of all parts of the foundation subjects need not be undertaken.

## APPROACHES TO THE NATIONAL CURRICULUM

Reflect on the different schools you have gained experience in or work in now. You will have talked to teachers, observed how children learn, taught groups and whole classes and shared what you have learned with fellow students or staff. What did you find out about how the NC was taught in each school? Does each school have the same approach? Or is the curriculum tailored to the needs of the children, the strengths of the teachers and the locality of the school? Are the NC subjects taught through topics, or as single subjects, or a mixture of both? Are children coached for the tests at the end of each Key Stage? Is the presence of the National Literacy Project a common element in the delivery of the English curriculum? It is likely that in discussion with your colleagues you have had many different experiences. These experiences are also likely to include some common threads. How each school implements the NC will depend on what sort of curriculum they see as appropriate for the age and ability of their children. The following section briefly describes some of the types of curriculum to be found in schools.

## DIFFERENT PRIMARY CURRICULUM STYLES

What 'styles' of curriculum are present in the primary school as we approach the millennium? The child-centred or 'progressive' approach has been and still is important in primary schools, even after ten years of the NC. The key features of this approach, highlighted in the Plowden Report of 1967, are that the child learns best from his or her direct experiences, that learning should be an active process of discovery, teachers should know their children and be able to respond to their individual needs and that there is a holistic approach to learning, best facilitated through integrated topic work.

Individual teachers had a great deal of independence in planning topics, with such titles as 'Houses and Homes', or 'Growth and Change'. The child-centred approach has been criticized by the media, politicians, and some educationalists who are in favour of a more 'knowledge-based' curriculum. But as you will have found out in your school-based work or recent teaching experience, a great many primary teachers still see the child-centred approach as the most suitable for primary age children.

The original 1989 NC ushered in a subject-based curriculum, where knowledge, understanding and skills were divided up into discrete subject units. The key features of this approach are to introduce children to the characteristics of traditional subject disciplines. The children can then develop their abilities in these subjects and continue this study in secondary school and beyond. This approach has been roundly criticized by primary teachers as not reflecting how primary children actually experience and learn about the world. Another widely held criticism is that the NC resembles the curriculum of a 1950s grammar school and therefore does not prepare children for 'real life' in the next century. Many KS 2 teachers see this curriculum as not being suited to the needs of the less able, as well as finding it impossible to cover all subjects effectively.

Will the revised NC and any changes in the year 2000 create a new style of curriculum in the primary school? The Dearing Review in 1995 highlighted the importance of using any time freed up by the 'slimming down process' on teaching the basics. Most teachers interpreted this as more time for literacy and numeracy. Within a month of being elected, the Labour government advised schools to concentrate on English and mathematics and that inspectors would take this into account when looking at 'breadth and balance' during primary inspections. Information and communications technology (ICT) is also now highlighted as an area in which teachers must both improve their own skills and use more effectively in their teaching.

Are we witnessing the evolution of a curriculum that focuses on the core skills of literacy, numeracy, oracy and the process of enquiry? This curriculum would seek to equip children with the skills to 'learn how to learn' and the ability to make sense of the huge amount of information and experience available to them from all over the globe. Or are we again seeing the professionalism of teachers questioned and a 'top-down' planning approach being imposed again? The National Curriculum for Initial Teacher Training, outlined in Chapter 1, certainly seeks to specify what teachers must know in the core subjects and how they should teach them.

Whatever laws are passed, guidance given and training undertaken, individual teachers may still interpret the NC differently. They may favour a child-centred approach, or a knowledge-based approach, or a literacy, numeracy and enquiry approach. They may favour a combination of all these, or be in the process of changing approaches. They may vary in the amount of time they use for whole-class teaching, individual work or group work. This is extremely frustrating for those who would wish a standardized experience for all children from Year 1 to Year 6! Ensuring a common entitlement to the NC is still a challenge for everyone, from a subject co-ordinator to Her Majesty's Chief Inspector.

## SCAA GUIDANCE ON DELIVERING THE NC

This section looks at how teachers in schools can deliver the NC using SCAA guidance. SCAA is the Schools Curriculum and Assessment Authority (now renamed the Qualifications and Curriculum Authority, QCA). Its role is to monitor and review the curriculum, school examinations and assessment. As part of this role it publishes many useful publications which will be available in your school or college library.

When the revised NC was introduced in August 1995, SCAA published guidance on how it could be implemented. *Planning the Curriculum at KSs 1 and 2* was written with the help of practising primary teachers and was piloted across the country before being published. It is an example of a partnership approach to curriculum development, rather than the top-down approach of the earlier 1989 curriculum.

Implementing the NC is the responsibility of all teachers and of the governors of the school. The whole process, however, is co-ordinated by a senior member of the teaching staff, either the headteacher or deputy. The stages of planning that schools will have gone through are shown below:

- *Identifying the whole school curriculum*
  Reviewing the school's aims, objectives, policies and priorities so that the taught curriculum will be an integral part of the whole curriculum.

- *Highlighting school priorities*
  Identifying areas where the school chooses to have extra curriculum provision.

- *Long-term planning*
  What will the children be learning in each year?

- *Medium-term planning*
  What will the children be learning each half-term?

- *Short-term planning*
  How and what will the children learn each day?

Another source of guidance that schools may have used comes from the local education authority advisory staff. They may have drawn up sample plans for each year and be keen for them to be implemented, to standardize educational provision across their authority.

## MORE DETAIL IN LONG-TERM PLANNING

So how is the long-term planning process carried out? How do teachers decide when subjects are taught in Year 1 and Year 6? How do they ensure progression in mathematics or continuity in the English curriculum from KS 1 to KS 2?

Many schools have answered these questions by following a similar planning process to the one recommended by SCAA/QCA. The process organizes the curriculum into teaching units. SCAA/QCA uses the term 'units of work' but many schools have stayed with 'topics'.

Units of work or topics can be divided into three types: *blocked*, *linked* and *continuing*. This approach creates a compromise between single subject delivery (based on the secondary school model) and an integrated topic approach (based on the child-centred primary model). Instead of looking for opportunities in a topic entitled 'Wheels' for children to learn maths, science, technology, art, music (perhaps singing 'The wheels on the bus go round and round …'), a more focused approach can be used which seeks to exploit opportunities for meaningful integration but also to deliver single subject learning when necessary.

- *Blocked* units are drawn from a single subject or aspect of the curriculum that forms a coherent body of knowledge, understanding or skills. An example is a mathematics unit investigating fractions (AT 2 Number and Algebra) in Year 4.

- *Continuing* units are also drawn from a single subject of the curriculum. These are areas that require regular teaching to ensure progression and need frequent practice so that children can develop their knowledge, skills and understanding. The daily National Literacy Project exploits this continuing unit approach.

- *Linked* units are similar to integrated topics from pre-NC days except that they should not have more than three subjects as a focus. A Year 5 unit of work linking the weather theme in geography and the water cycle in science clearly links areas of the NC which have shared content.

## CONTENT

This section contains two examples of the content of the NC as interpreted by two Sheffield schools. The first shows how one infant school in Sheffield includes the National Curriculum as part of its whole school provision, using the SCAA planning model. The second discusses how teachers at a junior school are thinking of planning their KS 2 curriculum in the future.

## Case study 1: How Pye Bank Nursery and Infant School implemented the revised NC

Pye Bank Nursery and Infant School is a friendly and organized school with a well-planned curriculum. The headteacher and her staff used the SCAA planning process to revise their curriculum after the Dearing Review.

The school serves the Pitsmoor and Burngreave communities in Sheffield.

Sheffield City Council has designated these areas as 'areas of acute poverty'. Unemployment is high, as is dependency on social services. Recently renovated local authority housing surrounds the school, which has a hilltop location overlooking central Sheffield. Over one-third of the children have special educational needs and a similar proportion are from homes where English is a second language. There were 132 children on roll at the time of writing, and 102 received free school meals.

The planning process that the teaching staff went through is shown below. A key part of successful NC planning is that the planning process is a whole school one. All the Pye Bank staff were actively involved during planning.

## Stage one – identifying available teaching time

First, the planning team (at this stage the headteacher and deputy) established the amount of time available for teaching and assessing the curriculum. This is the statutory provision laid down by the NC, religious education and any other curriculum priorities the school identifies.

## Stage two – highlighting school priorities

Second, they identified aspects of the curriculum such as the NC subjects, themes and dimensions, RE and school priorities which needed specific timed provision. Priorities were then established for each year group. At Pye Bank these aspects included additional time for whole school discipline, using the assertive discipline approach; and time for personal and social education, developing the use of 'circle time'.

## Stage three – ensuring breadth and balance across the curriculum

Third, set amounts of time were allocated to each aspect of the curriculum for each year group. Each year group was allocated similar time in this case (see Table 8.1).

How similar is the provision at Pye Bank to what you may have seen during your school experience or in your present teaching post? What do you think about the time allowances for the core subjects? What is your reaction to the teaching time for art?

The headteacher stated that art is seen as a common medium for communication and leads to further work in the core subjects. This is important so that children whose first language is not English can develop speaking and listening skills in an informal situation. Will the school still have the freedom to use art in this way in a few years' time? Or will prescription of English teaching methods lead to a reliance on teacher-directed whole class teaching? The tensions exposed here between school autonomy and DfEE directives are explored further in the section on the future of the National Curriculum.

**Table 8.1** Teaching time allocated to each area of the curriculum

|  | English | Drama | Maths | Science | Design/technology |
|---|---|---|---|---|---|
| **Per week** | 5 hrs | 32 mins | 3 hrs 20 mins | 1 hr 40 mins | 1 hr |
| **%** | 23 | 3 | 15.5 | 7.5 | 4.5 |
|  | **Information technology** | **History** | **Geography** | **Art** | **Music** |
| **Per week** | 1 hr | 1 hr | 1 hr | 2 hrs 33 mins | 50 mins |
| **%** | 4.5 | 4.5 | 4.5 | 11.5 | 4 |
|  | **Physical education** | **Religious education** | **Cross-curricular themes** | **Whole school discipline** | **Personal and social education** |
| **Per week** | 1 hr 40 mins | 20 mins | 25 mins | 30 mins | 50 mins |
| **%** | 8 | 1.5 | 2 | 2 | 4 |

## Stage four – long-term planning

Fourth, the school divided up the curriculum into units of work as described above. The planning team and subject co-ordinators then decided which aspects of the curriculum could be taught as *continuing*, *blocked* and *linked* units of work and allocated them to year groups. The whole staff were involved in this process and many extra staff meetings were used to contrast the previous topic-based planning with the new approach.

The science planning in Table 8.2 shows the result of this process. Looking through it you can see how the staff have taken the KS 1 science PoS and identified that the investigative approach, as explained in experimental and investigative science (Sc1), can be developed through continuing work. They have studied the other attainment targets for science: life processes and living things, materials and their properties, physical processes, and picked out the key areas of knowledge and understanding and named these areas as blocked units of work. A progression has been developed, with some areas, such as plants, being visited in Reception and Year 2.

Finally, linked units replace the multi-focus topics of old where similar content occurs, such as weather which links geography with Sc2/2b changing materials.

**Table 8.2** Science units of work

| | Continuing | Blocked | Linked (linked subject shown in brackets) English has a substantial element in all topics |
|---|---|---|---|
| **Reception** | Investigations Interactive displays | People Animals Plants Sand, water, wood and paper, plastic and metal Cooking (*NB: choose 1 per half-term*) | All about me (RE) Living things Growing Materials (technology/art) |
| **Year 1** | Investigations Interactive displays | Floating and sinking Fish Hot/cold (absorbency and insulation) Food Keeping healthy Sound magnetism (*NB: all blocks must be covered*) | Water (maths) The weather (geography/maths) Food (technology) Change (PE) Communication (maths/art) |
| **Year 2** | Investigations Interactive displays | Electricity Light Decay/recycling Natural/manmade Air resistance/gravity Minibeasts Plants (*NB: all blocks must be covered*) | Power The earth and beyond (geography) Growing Living things Light |

## Stage five – medium-term planning

SCAA recommends allocating each unit to a specific half-term or term. At Pye Bank the staff have some flexibility in when they cover each unit, although detailed records are kept showing the place of each unit for each year. Out-of-school visits and fieldwork are also formally linked to units of work and planned to fit with each half-term's work.

## *Stage six – short-term planning*

Staff record exactly what they teach in weekly planning books. These books allow for continuity and progression as classes move from Reception to Year 2.

Staff in the school and also students who have gained school experience at Pye Bank feel that the curriculum that has been developed is very successful in both meeting the needs of the children and delivering the NC statutory provision.

## Case study 2: How Nook Lane Junior School, Sheffield is planning to develop its KS 2 curriculum

Nook Lane Junior School is located on the fringe of northern Sheffield and serves part of the Stannington community. The school is surrounded by a recently built private housing development and has impressive views of the fields and moorland that border this part of Sheffield. Both students and teachers have stated that it is an enjoyable place in which to work or gain school experience. The school has recently received a positive Ofsted report.

The staff here have also used the SCAA model, but have recently begun to re-evaluate their curriculum in the light of potential changes in the future. The headteacher is concerned about the KS 2 curriculum being interpreted as just a set of 'facts' and 'content' that must be transmitted to all children. The staff have reflected that this can encourage didactic teaching methods. These are manifested in such practices as teachers 'doing' science investigations for the children (see Chapter 11), and 'leading' children through technology tasks rather than letting them experiment and be creative.

The headteacher and her staff wanted a curriculum that gave prominence to the skills inherent in each NC subject. They envisaged a curriculum that developed skills through the content specified in the NC but which also equipped the children with both the ability to learn more independently and to value and enjoy the process of learning.

## *The planning process*

First, they took two subjects traditionally associated with afternoon topic work – history and geography – and studied the NC orders in depth. The head, and staff with appropriate curriculum strengths, isolated the key skills in both subjects and created a skills progression that the children could develop from Year 3 to Year 6. In history, for example, skills leading to an understanding of *chronology* and *cause and consequence* are developed through study units concerning the Tudors and the Egyptians. Learning 'the facts' about each study unit is seen as secondary to developing an ability to use historical skills. Experiential staff meetings were held where staff took part in learning activities which developed historical skills, so that they might interpret the history units of work from the perspective of skills development.

Significantly, the curriculum is planned so that teachers have some autonomy in terms of how they teach each study unit; they must develop the appropriate skills, depending on which year they are teaching, but can approach the unit from a different angle each year if they wish, so that they stay fresh and interested themselves.

A similar approach was taken in technology, stressing skills progression and the development of independent learning. Science in the school is based on an investigative science project, which again stresses skill acquisition over learning the 'content', in science attainment targets 2, 3 and 4. The whole staff are involved in planning and implementing this project which allows individual teachers to make the planning their own and to share individual strengths and successful past practice.

The headteacher sees the development of ICT skills as crucially important for the children. The school has an integrated resource unit for children with special needs. Staff in the unit have been very successful in their use of ICT; however, the school is under-resourced in terms of computer hardware at the present time. Nevertheless, the same skills progression is evident in information technology, with a focus on ICT in Year 5 to make the most of teacher expertise and available hardware. Future planned developments include developing Internet searching and communication skills.

Skills in English and maths are similarly identified. Skills, teaching strategies and targets for each year have been identified, written up and used as a basis for informing teaching and building a partnership with parents. This is evident in English where the targets for reading, spelling and writing are given to parents alongside advice on strategies for helping learning at home.

The headteacher sees this curriculum as one that meets the demands of the NC and also develops forward-looking pupils who are learning how to learn. This certainly fits in with the view of many commentators, who see this ability to learn how to learn and make sense of the 'global information society' as a key set of skills for life in the twenty-first century.

## THE FUTURE OF THE NC: PRESCRIPTION OF TEACHING METHODS AND CONTENT

As mentioned earlier, the NC will be formally reviewed in the year 2000. The process of consultation has already begun and subject associations and other interested parties are at the moment lobbying SCAA/QCA and the DfEE. The publication in June 1997 of the Education White Paper *Excellence in Schools* gave some clear ideas about what the NC may look like in the early years of the next century.

The first change has been occurring since 1997. It is the focus on literacy and numeracy and ICT, as mentioned earlier in this chapter. SCAA/QCA have been instructed to find ways of enabling schools to give a sharper focus to literacy and numeracy in the way they interpret the NC. The daily literacy hour specified by the Literacy Task Force is seen as fundamental to this process. A Numeracy Task Force was established in May 1997 and has the brief to examine practice here and abroad. A numeracy hour is just around the corner. Children and teachers are also expected to be confident in the use of ICT and the White Paper unveils plans to set up a National Grid for Learning in which all school are connected electronically to share best practice.

## RECOMMENDATIONS OF THE WHITE PAPER WHICH AFFECT NC PROVISION

- Continuity between nursery provision and KS1 provision
- Baseline assessment at the start of KS1
- Targets for achievement in KS1 and 2 tasks and tests to be achieved by 2002 in maths and English
- Prescription of teaching methods in school:
  - A focus on whole class teaching and phonics in English
  - Interactive whole class teaching, mental arithmetic and distrust of calculators in maths
- A national curriculum for teacher training which may lead to the prescription of particular teaching methods to students in training.

The prescription of teaching methods at school and in training is a further attempt to 'get into' the individual teacher's classroom, something that has been desired by many, including the chief HMI Chris Woodhead, over the last five years. But within this development lies a conundrum. Can similar teaching methods be replicated across the country, when schools are full of very different individuals serving differing communities? (See Chapter 4.) We have seen that teachers at present construct the curriculum in different ways as they interpret the needs of their pupils in the light of their own teaching experience. Would you value more direction in how and when you should teach reading, grammar and mental arithmetic, or do you see such guidance as questioning your professionalism?

Will the statutory NC in the twenty-first century reflect a broad and balanced curriculum that equips children with 'the basics', enables them to learn how to learn, and also to live as global citizens of the twenty-first century? Or will we be able to explain the primary curriculum simply as English and maths in the morning and 'topic' in the afternoon, all based on national approved schemes and teaching methods? Whatever the outcome of planning, consultation and legislation at national level, you will still have the challenge of interpreting the NC with its associated approved teaching methods to ensure the best for the children whom you teach.

## REFERENCES

DfEE (1995) *Key Stages 1 and 2 of the National Curriculum*. London: HMSO.
SCAA (1995) *A Guide to the National Curriculum*. London: HMSO.

## SOME SUGGESTIONS FOR FURTHER READING

Moon, B. (3rd edn, 1996) *A Guide to the National Curriculum*. Oxford: OUP.
DfEE (1995) and SCAA (1995), as listed above, would both also be useful as
  follow-up reading.

CHAPTER 9

# Teaching primary English

GUY MERCHANT

## INTRODUCTION

In this chapter we address some important issues in the primary English curriculum. The language we use is an essential part of the learning and teaching process, and so the first section examines the relationship between children's acquisition of language and literacy and the English curriculum in our schools. We then look at the National Curriculum Orders for English, using examples of classroom work to illustrate the three programmes of study. The development of literacy and oracy are then discussed before we turn our attention to the area of language study. After this, we move on to the wider English curriculum, placing a particular focus on the expressive dimension of the subject. In conclusion, the section 'English teachers and English teaching' outlines the role of all primary schoolteachers in providing an enriching language curriculum.

## LANGUAGE, LITERACY AND THE ENGLISH CURRICULUM

Language plays a vital part in children's learning. In the classroom, all aspects of the curriculum depend to a greater or lesser extent on language skills. For children, such skills as the ability to answer questions, offer opinions and follow instructions are as important for the social life of the classroom as they are for formal learning – and they apply in all subjects. For the teacher, the task of providing a context for pupils to learn to *use* language, to learn *through* language and to learn *about* language must occupy a central position in planning.

By the beginning of their compulsory schooling, most children are skilful communicators in the oral form of their first language or mother tongue. They will have an implicit knowledge of how that language works. For instance, they will know some of the conventions of turn-taking, appropriateness and politeness in conversation. They will also know most of the grammatical constructions for language in everyday life (such as those necessary to offer and request information), they will have access to a substantial vocabulary and will be familiar with all the constituent sounds of their language.

For some children you will teach, there will be few differences between the language of the home and the language of the school. Others may have been brought up in a minority language community and will have developed as skilful communicators in languages other than English. There will also be children who are more familiar or more comfortable with a particular variety or dialect of English. In any group of children you meet, there will be some sort of diversity in language experience. A good teacher will recognize and give value to children's home language, as well as aiming to develop all children's understanding of the more formal English that is the medium of instruction in our schools.

In a similar way, in any classroom there will be a diversity in pupils' experience of the printed word. Some may be literate in a language other than English and come from a home background in which the ability to read and write is held in high esteem (Merchant, 1992), while others may come from homes which value different skills or where parents themselves have experienced difficulties in literacy. Again, the successful teacher will be sensitive to these differences, but will understand the central importance of reading and writing in English in all aspects of the curriculum.

These important abilities in oracy and literacy are often referred to as 'cross-curricular skills'. This serves to highlight the significance of spoken and written language in thinking and learning, whether the subject matter you are teaching is mathematics, science, technology or indeed any other area of the curriculum. These language skills are not only *used* across the curriculum, they are also *developed* in different subject areas. For example, children will learn the language of problem-solving as well as the specific vocabulary of key concepts in mathematics, just as they will learn how to ask relevant questions, record observations in chart form and write up an experiment in science.

The skills of oracy and literacy are, of course, a fundamental part of English as a subject at both KS 1 and KS 2. Although much of your time will be spent on developing these skills, you will also be introducing children to the study of language and literature and the enjoyment of poetry, creative writing and drama.

## ENGLISH IN THE NATIONAL CURRICULUM

The National Curriculum subdivides the subject of English into three programmes of study: *Speaking and Listening*; *Reading*; and *Writing*. Within each programme of study, consideration is given to the range, key skills and aspects of language study that you are to address at each Key Stage. Although it is not suggested that these elements of the English curriculum will be taught in isolation, it is helpful to look at each in turn to understand the conceptual framework.

In reading, children will be introduced to a variety of texts from an early age. They will learn about reading for information as well as enjoying and responding to literature and poetry. They will also be reading from other printed sources such as posters, signs and labels, and from computer screens. This breadth of reading experience is referred to as *range*. In a similar way, in the programme of study for writing, consideration of range includes a variety of reasons or purposes for writing for a variety of different readers. The range of writing that children will produce, even in the early stages, will include things like lists, instructions and stories.

*Key skills* are an important aspect of each programme of study, too. In writing, for example, we are required by the National Curriculum to teach about planning and composition as well as the presentational skills of spelling, handwriting and punctuation. Clarity of expression and the conventions of turn-taking are referred to in speaking and listening. Key skills in reading include the development of word recognition and strategies for the decoding of unfamiliar words. These strategies include the use of phonic, graphic, grammatical and contextual understanding – we will be looking at the meaning of these terms in the following section.

Finally, each programme of study features an element of *Standard English and language study*. This element includes statements about spoken and written standard English as well as grammatical features of the language. Grammatical concepts such as clause, phrase, noun, verb and so on are referred to at various points, receiving more specific attention in Writing at KS 2. The use of standard English is seen as an important aspect of the curriculum. So, at KS 2, in speaking and listening not only are children to be shown the *differences* between dialect forms and standard English, they are also to develop the *use* of 'spoken standard English'. This is a particularly problematic area, which we will return to in the section on language study.

These three elements – range, key skills, and standard English and language study – constitute the conceptual framework of the three programmes of study. However, these elements are clearly interrelated, and although we are required to teach them, interpretation in terms of actual classroom practice may well vary from school to school. Similarly, you may choose to teach aspects of the programmes of study for speaking and listening, reading and writing within a single lesson.

Classroom work that integrates the three programmes can be particularly fruitful. For instance, by reading *The Angel of Nitshill Road* by Anne Fine (1992), either as a group or a whole class, children are introduced to the work of a significant children's author. Looking at how Anne Fine develops character and plot will address aspects of the reading curriculum. The story raises the sensitive issue of bullying, and through discussion children can explore how it feels to be bullied and even how it may feel to be a bully. Written outcomes could include producing an advice leaflet for other children in the school; and the report of a fictitious bullying incident could be performed as a 'news item' as a way of looking at more formal spoken language. In this way, many teachers are able to plan integrated work in speaking and listening, reading and writing that share a meaningful context.

## LITERACY SKILLS

Concerns about the level of children's literacy skills have tended to dominate recent discussion about education. Although evidence of a decline in standards is not entirely convincing, all of us would agree that any improvement in pupils' performance at school will be largely dependent upon successful literacy teaching. The study of how young children learn to read and write is a rich and fascinating topic, which draws on disciplines as diverse as psychology, sociology and linguistics. Here we will have to be content with a brief overview of the processes involved. For a more detailed study you should consult some of the titles at the end of this chapter.

As we saw above, the National Curriculum draws our attention to the key skills that are used in learning to read. The skilled reader is able to recognize the majority of words he or she will encounter both quickly and automatically. This ability is referred to as 'rapid automatic whole word recognition' (see Harrison, 1992) and it implies that a skilled reader will spend very little time on actually decoding words, concentrating instead on building up meaning. In contrast, the beginning reader will only have a very small stock of 'sight vocabulary' words. Thus in the early stages of learning to read, children will be dependent on other strategies in tackling unfamiliar words. The National Curriculum Orders for English refer to these other strategies as phonic, graphic, grammatical and contextual understanding.

*Phonic* knowledge is concerned with the relationship between print symbols and sound patterns. Children learn that certain letters or combinations of letters represent particular speech sounds (for instance, 'f', 'ch', 'oo', 'str'). Although there is considerable variation in the sound–symbol correspondences of the English language, alphabetic knowledge and a growing familiarity with common letter-strings are very important to the beginning reader.

*Graphic* knowledge is derived from learning about word meanings and common parts of words. This includes becoming familiar with root words, plurals and verb endings, as well as prefixes and suffixes. *Grammatical* understanding is the use of our knowledge of the word order or grammar of English. Even very young children know that 'the barking dog the door is at' is wrong but that 'the dog is barking at the door' is right. Beginning readers bring their understanding of the patterns of spoken language to the task of reading. Finally, *contextual* understanding is meaning derived from the text as a whole. It includes the skills of prediction and the use of pictures as cues for meaning. Most young readers expect to find meaning in what they read and will relate this to what they already know.

Carefully chosen reading material for young readers supports them in making use of these different strategies. For instance, the repetitive patterning and illustration of *Brown Bear, Brown Bear, What do You See?* (Eric Carle and Bill Martin, 1995) help children to use their contextual understanding. Similarly, the question and answer format of the written text draws on implicit grammatical understanding. As you hear children read, you will be encouraging the use of these key skills through the questions you use (e.g. What sound does this word begin with? Does that sentence sound right?). You will also be making assessments of which skills are used or over-used.

Although word recognition and the other key skills are of fundamental importance to the development of reading, your classroom practice will need to include a broader conception of text and the uses of the printed word. Important learning about the place of literacy in our society is derived from the child's everyday experience. We live in a world that is rich in print. Before they start school, many children will have learned how familiar logos and slogans appear on the packaging of their favourite food or drink, or how the curves and lines of particular letters represent their own name. They will have seen text on page and screen and may have some knowledge of how their parents or other adults make use of print at work or in leisure time.

As a teacher, you will be building on this knowledge by using and discussing the print environment both inside and outside the classroom. Taking your class on a 'print walk' around the school and its catchment area provides an opportunity to draw attention to different kinds of signs and notices, the messages they convey and their use of features such as capital letters and punctuation. You will also be able to draw children's attention to a variety of scripts, some of which may represent different languages.

Follow-up work may involve your class in recording and classifying the print they have seen, or devising signs, notices or advertising slogans of their own. In a similar way, the 'M' of McDonald's or the 'K' of Kellogg's are an interesting way of introducing the letters of the alphabet – a way that can involve colourful interactive display. Older children can learn about alliteration from advertisements (such as 'a better bit of butter') and the play on spelling conventions in the commercial world ('kost-kutting at Kwik Save').

In the early years, teachers capitalize on children's fascination with role-play by providing contexts for structured play that incorporate the use of both reading and writing. For instance, by creating an area in the classroom that is 'an opticians', children involved in shop-play will also use print in creating a window display with sale signs, and using an appointments book or a computer for recording details about their clients. By conducting 'eye tests' they will rehearse their learning of the letters of the alphabet.

The primary classroom will also be equipped with a wide range of books, often including reading schemes and their support materials, fiction and poetry by well-known children's authors and texts for information and reference (Moon, 1997). In addition to this you will commonly see books made by children, stories recorded on audiotape and IT texts of various kinds. These and other materials should be stored so that they are accessible to children. Notices may be used to draw children's attention to new or featured reading.

Many classrooms will be arranged so that there is a quiet, comfortable area which provides an attractive reading environment. Book provision should cater for the wide range of children's interests and needs. In the early years, favourite books will include those with patterned and predictable language so that the child's knowledge of how they should sound will support their skills in tackling unfamiliar words. At all stages, familiar material should be available for re-reading.

In most primary schools literacy work is an integral part of classroom life, so one would expect to see a variety of print-based activities taking place. Teachers throughout the primary years will be reading to children from a range of different texts, modelling the sorts of reading behaviour and discussion that they are expecting from children. They may also use enlarged texts, large format books (big books) or sets of books for guided or group reading. In these sessions they will be developing the key skills and drawing children's attention to certain features of the text. They may focus on specific features, such as individual letters or combinations of letters, unfamiliar words or a particular use of punctuation. Alternatively, they may be encouraging discussion about plot, setting or character and leading children to an understanding of literal and inferential meanings.

In most of the schools you visit, children will, at times, be involved in individual reading. This may take the form of reading aloud to the teacher or another adult, or it may be in a period of silent reading. In addition to this, there will be the direct teaching of key skills. For instance, children may be involved in oral or written word games designed to teach or practise letter sounds or more complex letter patterns.

It is quite common for reading and writing activities to be closely related. Thus, for instance, children may have specific questions in mind when reading information books on woodland animals. They may wish to know the feeding habits of animals, where they sleep, whether they are nocturnal, how they raise their young and so on. Follow-up work may involve recording the information that they have found out in chart or poster format. As well as this sort of work, children will be engaged in activities where writing is a starting point. Planning, drafting, redrafting and proofreading a story for younger children prior to presenting it is an example of this sort of writing process. Inevitably, on some occasions, writing will be an end in itself; on other occasions it will be part of the learning process in another curriculum area.

In some schools you may see structured literacy programmes in operation. Reading Recovery is one such programme that has been particularly influential in recent years. Originally designed in New Zealand, Reading Recovery is an intervention programme of one-to-one teaching which aims to help children who are having difficulties in the initial stages of literacy before they fall too far behind their peer group. Family literacy describes a variety of schemes that aim to provide literacy support for both parents and children. These schemes aim to break the cycle of inter-generational illiteracy and also to provide educational success for both parents and their children. More recently, the National Literacy Project, which began in September 1997, has been introducing an approach to literacy teaching in the primary years that is far more structured than that described above. Although the project includes some of the features of existing good practice, these have been drawn together to form a daily literacy hour and a detailed term-by-term syllabus. Teaching objectives are set out in three strands: word level (phonics, spelling and vocabulary); sentence level (grammar and punctuation), and text level (comprehension and composition). The English standards in the National Curriculum for Initial Teacher Training will ensure that you have the relevant subject knowledge to teach to these objectives.

Many teachers have now adopted the daily literacy hour. During the hour, roughly 60 per cent of the time is spent in 'direct' class teaching and 40 per cent on independent work in groups. Class teaching includes work on a shared text (usually a big book), skills teaching (at word, sentence or text level) and a plenary period in which children will reflect and review the work they have done. Independent work includes both reading and writing activities organized so that the teacher will have sustained contact with each group at least once a week.

At the time of writing, there is little hard evidence with which to evaluate the effectiveness of the literacy hour. However, all schools are now being encouraged to adopt this way of working. The project may well succeed in promoting more systematic and confident teaching of literacy skills. However, the time and organizational constraints of a daily literacy hour could well result in a narrowing of the English curriculum. In the following sections, as we deal with different aspects of English, you will be able to see how it may be possible to incorporate some of these within a literacy hour. Other aspects of the subject will need more time and greater flexibility in teaching approach.

## ORACY SKILLS

Oral communication in the classroom is as important as written communication. In fact, without oral communication it would be very difficult for most of us to get anything done at all! Many studies have shown how teachers dominate classroom talk. Often the giving of instructions, the management of behaviour and the use of closed or convergent questioning have characterized the teacher talk sampled in such studies. The programme of study for speaking and listening shifts the focus on to a consideration of the importance of pupil talk.

As we have already seen, most children have achieved an impressive level of competence in oral language when they begin their school life. However, in some senses they are still learning to talk. Anyone who has tried to conduct a discussion with a group of thirty 6-year-olds will tell you that managing turn-taking and keeping the discussion focus are by no means easy for the adult. So, at this age, children are still learning about the conventions of large and small group talk. But there is also a sense in which they are learning about new kinds of talk – how to describe what they found out about the load-bearing capacity of different materials, or why they liked a particular character in a story they have just heard. They will be using language for new purposes, exploring new grammatical structures and incorporating new vocabulary. Oracy, from this point of view, is as much about 'talking to learn' as it is about 'learning to talk'.

The work of the Centre for Language in Primary Education (CLPE) has been influential in the way that many teachers plan and assess speaking and listening. The *Primary Language Record* (Barrs *et al.*, 1989) draws our attention to two important dimensions of oracy. These are the social and learning contexts of classroom talk. The social context refers to the situation in which the child is working. For instance, the child could be the member of a small group working without direct contact with you or the teacher. Alternatively, the child could be part of a whole class discussion led by the teacher. Clearly, a range of other social contexts is likely.

The learning context refers to the specific content of the activity or discussion. This might involve any of the curriculum areas, a theme such as 'friendship', or a simple recounting of events. Over a period of time, children should have experience of speaking and listening in a variety of different contexts and your planning needs to take this into account. This is quite a challenge for students and newly qualified teachers who may lack confidence in their skills of classroom control. For many of us, the idea that a quiet class is a well-behaved class is deeply rooted in our experience of schools. Furthermore, we often assume that a quiet class is an indication of a good teacher, but classroom control is, of course, more complex than this. The successful teacher will be able to create situations in which there is plenty of purposeful talk; she will also be able to gain everyone's attention when appropriate.

Language diversity in the classroom raises some exciting opportunities for oracy work. We have already drawn attention to the importance of valuing other languages and dialects of English and there will be some situations in which it will be quite appropriate for the teacher to encourage discussion in children's own language or dialect. Bilingual teachers, adult helpers and parents are useful sources of support for this kind of work.

For example, in undertaking work on food at KS 1, children may be encouraged to use their own language or dialect in a role-play area based on a shop or market stall. In small group discussion, they may to talk to each other or to an adult about their favourite fruit. Class discussion on vegetables, culminating in a wall display, might look at different words for vegetables (such as the English 'potato'; 'aloo' in Urdu; 'pomme de terre' in French; 'spud' or 'tattie' in the informal regional variety of English), and different recipes for cooking these vegetables. This sort of work is encouraged in the National Curriculum:

> The richness of dialects and other languages can make an important contribution to pupils' knowledge and understanding of standard English. Where appropriate, pupils should be encouraged to make use

of their understanding and skills in other languages when learning English.

(DfEE, 1995)

## LANGUAGE STUDY

One of the most contentious aspects of the programmes of study is those statements that refer to standard English and language study. Most primary schoolteachers feel at ease with helping children to understand ideas like the differences between formal and informal, or written and spoken language. However, the more traditional grammatical features of language study are more problematic.

First, teachers may lack confidence in teaching grammar and may be confused by the variety of grammatical terms that are used. Second, they may themselves have unpleasant memories of being taught grammar, particularly if this teaching was based on repetitive exercises without the support of a meaningful context or purpose. Finally, grammar teaching, where it refers to a 'norm' or standard English, can contribute to the devaluing of other varieties of English and may not take into account the stages of development of children who are learning English as an additional language.

Standard English is notoriously difficult to define. There is a long history of educational and linguistic debate on the subject. Even if we were to agree on a definition of spoken standard English, and to accept that it is desirable to teach it to primary school children, there is a lack of practical guidance on how to go about it. What is more, it is by no means certain that all primary schoolteachers would have a comprehensive knowledge of the standard form, whatever that may be. Certainly the idea that standard English can be learned by the teaching of formal grammar has little support.

Written standard English raises different issues, but clearly a knowledge of the standard written form of English is an essential part of becoming literate. Learning to read and write is rather like learning another language, and that language is, in most cases, the standard written form.

The study of language does, however, have an important role to play in the curriculum. An awareness of the patterns of language use in different contexts is important in learning *about* English. Furthermore, an awareness of how particular uses of language involve making choices from the language system is part of understanding how different texts work. In looking at range (in reading or writing) these language choices can be highlighted. So, for example, the use of prepositions and questioning constructions in *Where's Spot?* (Eric Hill, 1988) are useful talking points for the developing reader. The terminology of a descriptive grammar is a useful part of developing a language for talking about language. But its application in understanding how real texts work is surely more important than learning terminology in isolation.

## THE WIDER ENGLISH CURRICULUM

Although literacy and oracy occupy a central place in the primary classroom, there is a fear that, if the curriculum is reduced to a set of basic skills, the wider and more expressive aspects of English will become marginalized. Drama, poetry and expressive writing have an important role to play in the education of young children. Not only do they involve quite distinctive processes and skills, they also constitute different ways of seeing and making sense of the world.

The imaginative play of young children is one way in which ideas about feelings, relationships and the dynamics of everyday events are explored. In the early years of schooling, good teachers capitalize on this sort of behaviour by helping children to work together in more structured socio-dramatic play. The role-play area of an infant classroom is a significant aspect of educational provision, which owes its origin to the dressing up and domestic play of what was once referred to as the 'Wendy corner'. Role-play areas such as booking offices, cafés and information centres allow children to interact with each other by taking on different roles and to engage in the sorts of spoken and written communication found in such settings.

More formal drama work will enable children to develop their thinking and understanding of issues that are important to them. Even though the starting point for such work may be a theme from another curriculum area or a story read in class, the children you teach will be moving beyond this and exploring their own reactions through the language of drama. This will involve speaking and listening as well as other skills – but we must not forget that the experience of drama, in its own right, as an expressive medium, has an important contribution to make to a child's education.

As with drama, poetry builds on the everyday experience of many children. Playing with words, memorizing simple rhymes and clapping chants are part of most children's early experience of language. Research has shown how this sort of play develops the kinds of awareness of language patterns that are of key importance in early reading (Goswami and Bryant, 1990). Work on the skills of rhyming and alliteration are currently given high priority in KS 1 classrooms for this very reason. However, poetry as an expressive form involves far more than word play. Reading poetry to children introduces them to texts in which quite specific choices about language are used to express meaning. In helping children to craft their own poetry, you will be turning their attention to the possibilities of language in expressing feelings and experiences in new forms.

As we saw above, the National Curriculum encourages a range of different forms of writing. At KS 1 these include lists, captions, observations, notices, instructions and so on. Although there are references to the development of imaginative work (stories, poems, dialogues, drama scripts and diaries), the potential for exploring personal perspectives and imaginary worlds through writing cannot be overlooked. While most of the different forms of writing are likely to be practised in other subject areas, personal and expressive writing will be developed in the English curriculum.

## ENGLISH TEACHERS AND ENGLISH TEACHING

Largely as a result of the pioneering work of advocates of language across the curriculum, such as Douglas Barnes and his colleagues (1971), teachers are now far more aware of the role that English language skills play in the learning of different curriculum subjects. It has often been said that 'all teachers are teachers of English', and of course this is particularly true in our primary schools. Even though you may have other subject strengths, as a primary schoolteacher you will need to be confident in your ability to teach this important core subject.

All primary teachers need to understand the importance of children's language as a way of developing, organizing and communicating new ideas and understandings. The adult's use of skilful questioning to encourage children to clarify their thinking is central to the process of teaching and learning. Good teachers will welcome and value the contribution of all children, without over-emphasizing the correctness or completeness of what is expressed. They will also promote a sense of enjoyment in playing and experimenting with language.

The direct teaching of literacy skills will also be the responsibility of all teachers. Your classroom will provide opportunities for children to develop these skills through a variety of activities in different curriculum areas. Reading skills will need to be given a high priority and children will be given the motivation to explore different forms of writing. In setting writing tasks you will need to recognize the influence of processes such as planning and assembling on the quality of the finished product.

In order to foster the development of literacy skills, all teachers need an ongoing interest in the development of reading and writing in children. Part of the task of primary teaching is to create a love of books and an enthusiasm for reading from a variety of texts. An understanding of the different ways in which we read will be important. In your training you will learn about the different ways in which we read for information and the particular demands that non-narrative texts place on the reader. But you will also need to understand the power of story and to develop good story-telling and story-reading skills. In this way, you will be able to bring a story to life by reading with expression, stimulating children's imagination and promoting enthusiasm and discussion about the texts you choose. As with all primary teachers, it will be important for you to be up to date with children's literature and poetry for your age group and to be familiar with key children's authors (see Moon, 1997; Powling and Styles, 1996).

Thus all teachers need a good working knowledge of appropriate written resources for children, whether this is print or IT-based material. Choices need to take into account age suitability and appeal in terms of quality of presentation and illustration. A sensitivity to issues of equal opportunities will help us to choose material that offers a variety of adult role models for both girls and boys. Written material and illustrations will provide positive images of ethnic minority communities. Dual text or bilingual books which show English alongside other scripts are also useful in any classroom, for the way in which they provide recognition and raise awareness of language diversity.

To conclude, we have seen how all teachers have a responsibility for English teaching. We have also recognized how language skills are used in teaching and learning across the curriculum. At the same time, however, we have suggested that English as a subject is much more than a set of basic skills. It is a subject in its own right, part of the core curriculum, and all teachers need to be confident in teaching it. Each primary school you visit will have a member of staff who is a curriculum co-ordinator for English and it will be his or her task to provide a coherent view of English teaching through each Key Stage. The co-ordinator will also be a source of advice and guidance and will provide support for other teaching staff in the school. As a student or a newly qualified teacher, you should seek to benefit from the co-ordinator's expertise.

English is a vitally important core curriculum subject, and one in which you can make the most of your enthusiasm and creativity to inspire the children whom you teach.

## REFERENCES

Barnes, D., Britton, J. and Rosen, H. (1971) *Language, the Learner, and the School.* Harmondsworth: Penguin Books.

Barrs, M., Ellis S., Hester, H. and Thomas, A. (1989) *The Primary Language Record.* London: CLPE.

Carle, E. and Martin, B. (1995) *Brown Bear, Brown Bear, What do You See?* Harmondsworth: Penguin Books.

DfEE (1995) *English in the National Curriculum.* London: HMSO.

Fine, A. (1992) *The Angel of Nitshill Road.* London: Heinemann.

Goswami, U. and Bryant, P. E. (1990) *Phonological Skills and Learning to Read.* Hillsdale, NJ: Lawrence Erlbaum.

Harrison, C. (1992) The reading process and learning to read. In M. Coles and C. Harrison (eds) *The Reading for Real Handbook.* London: Routledge.

Hill, E. (dual-language edition) (1988) *Where's Spot?* New York: Crocodile Books.

Merchant, G. (1992) Supporting children for whom English is a second language. In M. Coles and C. Harrison (eds) *The Reading for Real Handbook.* London: Routledge.

Moon, C. (1997, published yearly) *Individualised Reading.* Reading: Reading and Language Information Centre.

Powling, C. and Styles, M. (eds) (1996) *A Guide to Poetry 0–16.* London: Books for Keeps.

## SOME SUGGESTIONS FOR FURTHER READING

Barrs, M. and Thomas, A. (eds) (1991) *The Reading Book*. London: CLPE.
Browne, A. (1993) *Helping Children to Write*. London: Paul Chapman.
Lockwood, M. (1996) *Opportunities for English in the Primary School*. Clevedon: Trentham.

# CHAPTER 10

# Teaching primary mathematics

SUSAN CAMERON

## INTRODUCTION

This is a significant time for mathematics education. We have increasing evidence that standards of pupils' achievement are low in mathematics and may even be declining. Too many pupils, students, adults – and teachers – have a negative view of mathematics as a difficult or just boring subject. In Britain, we have a major job to do to reverse these trends.

In this chapter, the nature of mathematics and the current concerns in mathematics education, both nationally and internationally, are considered. Strategies for the effective teaching and learning of mathematics are explored along with the need to use the outcomes of research and anecdotes of good practice. The areas of mathematics in the National Curriculum are discussed and the teaching of number is highlighted, as it is in this area that we appear to be least successful as a country.

## WHAT IS THIS THING CALLED MATHS?

Each of us has our own view of mathematics which is based on our experiences, particularly at school. For many, that view is of a subject which is based on given rules that we must learn and try to remember, that there is only one correct way to do any given task and that the answer is always right or wrong. It may be these views which contribute to our lack of success at mathematics.

Certainly $2 + 3 = \square$ has only one answer (well, in the decimal system anyway!), but what about $\square + \triangle = 5$? Or $2 + \square > 5$?

How many 3-digit numbers can you make using the digits 1, 2, 3? Six? 123, 132, 213, 231, 312, 321. But what if you can use each digit more than once? 111, 112, 113 …. How many then? How do you know if you've got them all? Pentominoes are shapes made from five equal squares joined together.

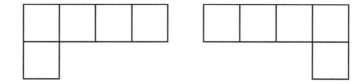

What about this?

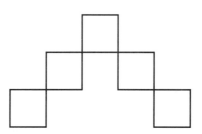

How many different pentominoes are there? Look it up and a book or scheme might tell you there are twelve. How many can you find? Are these the same or different?

How many pentominoes are there joined corner to corner? How many pentominoes there are depends on how you define them! More mathematical learning can be gained from discussing which are the same and which are different, what is the relationship between shapes: reflections, rotations – deciding which rules to adopt – how you know if you've got them all, than in searching for the twelve the teacher has told you that there are!

Some questions in mathematics have just one answer, some have several different answers and some have no answers at all, at least for primary school pupils. What number squared is $-2$? Young pupils believe that $3 - 5$ has no answer, but as they develop they realize that there can be an answer. Not so much of mathematics is as cut and dried as we may think. Pupils need to explore mathematical questions that lead to different sorts of answers. They need to ask, 'How do I know?' and develop the skills to check and justify their answers.

Mathematics is a source of awe and wonder. The discovery that numbers go on forever is exciting ... and daunting until you discover their pattern. You do not need to learn each number separately; after the first few you can generalize: 20, 21, 22, ... 520, 521, 522, ... 7820, 7821, 7822 ... . Numbers continue infinitely, not only as they get larger, and smaller: 0, $-1$, $-2$, $-3$, but between any two numbers there is also an infinity of numbers.

Identifying patterns and making generalizations are at the heart of mathematics. They enable us to use a simple starting point to generate countless other facts.

If we are going to improve achievement in mathematics, we must change the way in which people view the subject and the ways in which teachers teach and pupils learn about mathematics.

## INTERNATIONAL COMPARISONS

International studies suggest that standards of mathematical achievement in Britain are significantly lower than in many other countries. Although our pupils compare favourably in questions on shape and space and data handling, they are well behind in number skills and number problems. The recently published Third International Mathematics and Science Study Report (1997) provides some worrying examples (see Table 10.1):

**Table 10.1** Some international comparisons

| Here is a number sentence:<br>2000 + □ + 30 + 9 = 2739<br>What number goes in the □ to make this sentence true? | | |
| --- | --- | --- |
| | **% correct for Year 4** | **% correct for Year 5** |
| **England** | 27.9 | 49.1 |
| **International mean** | 44.3 | 62.6 |
| **Highest scoring country** | 86.2 | 92.0 |
| Approximately one-quarter of English pupils in each year gave the answer 7. 10% at Year 4 and 5% at Year 5 did not attempt the question! | | |

| Addition fact<br>4 + 4 + 4 + 4 + 4 = 20<br>Write this as a multiplication fact: __ × __ = __ | | |
| --- | --- | --- |
| | **% correct for Year 4** | **% correct for Year 5** |
| **England** | 39.0 | 52.9 |
| **International mean** | 63.2 | 76.6 |
| **Highest scoring country** | 90.7 | 94.8 |

Pacific rim countries consistently achieve the highest scores in international studies, and while we might argue that this reflects specific cultural differences, our pupils also perform significantly below those from the Netherlands, Hungary and the United States.

In exploring factors which might contribute to our lack of success, the organization of mathematics lessons presents clear differences between British methods and those used in other countries. Although each country has its own characteristic styles of teaching mathematics, it is possible to draw out some important generalizations. Other countries give greater emphasis and more time to basic skills, including mathematics. British primary schools are unusual in not consistently timetabling mathematics as a whole class lesson. Our pupils also spend significantly more time on individual work, with teachers providing support. In other countries the teacher is much more central to the lesson, using questions and answers to explore problems and involving pupils in explaining, comparing different methods and often scribing on the board to show their working. The majority of the lesson is spent with the whole class working together interactively, with only a small proportion of time given to individual practice.

While countries like Singapore gain consistently high scores in these studies, they have also identified problems with their teaching styles, as reported in the *Times Educational Supplement* in June 1997, where the Singapore Prime Minister launched a challenge to traditional methods:

> Your whole life is memorise, memorise, memorise, but afterwards you remember nothing. ... What is critical is that we fire in our students a passion for learning. ... Their knowledge will be fragile, no matter how many A grades they get, unless they have the desire and the aptitude to continue discovering new knowledge well after they leave school. It is the capacity to learn that will define excellence in the future, not simply what young people achieve in school.

## THE NATIONAL CONTEXT

Concerns about the low levels of basic skills in school pupils, entrants to further and higher education and employment, as well as in the adult population, have led the drive to get education in general, and literacy and numeracy in particular, to the top of the political agenda.

The National Curriculum was introduced in 1989 defining, for the first time, the content of the mathematics curriculum to be taught to all pupils of school age. The mathematics curriculum started out with fourteen different areas or attainment targets. With ten National Curriculum subjects and religious education to address, the primary school curriculum was set to change dramatically. Basic subjects like mathematics were squeezed as teachers had to work hard to develop and implement new areas.

The National Curriculum Non-Statutory Guidance for mathematics (1989) provided advice on using the new curriculum:

> Although mathematics does contain a hierarchical element, learning in mathematics does not necessarily take place in completely pre-

determined sequences. Mathematics is a structure composed of a whole network of concepts and relationships, and ... creative activity. The structure of mathematics within the National Curriculum recognizes the need for a common framework within which all schools can plan, but which also enables a flexibility of response to the needs of individual pupils. The programmes of study and attainment targets ... provide the basis upon which teachers must plan their teaching, and the broad objectives against which pupils' progress can be assessed.

(p. A3)

The Dearing Review of the National Curriculum in 1995 made some reductions and mathematics at KS 1 and 2 was reorganized, but little changed, into four sections: using and applying mathematics; number; shape, space and measures and handling data. A moratorium on further curriculum changes before the year 2000 was guaranteed. But concerns about content overload, particularly at KS 2, and insufficient attention to basic skills, make an early review likely. As a core subject, it is likely that mathematics will be given greater prominence. Indeed many primary schools are already beginning to shift the emphasis of their curriculum to increase the amount of time given to mathematics.

The introduction of national standard assessment tasks and tests (SATs) for 7-, 11- and 14-year-olds, as well as the increasingly regular use of standardized tests, provide us with some basic measures of achievement which we can use to identify areas of weakness and chart improvements.

We now have national targets for improved achievement in primary mathematics:

---

By the year 2002
75% of 11-year-olds will achieve level 4 or above

---

In the 1997 SATs: 62% of 11-year-olds achieved level 4 or above (54% in 1996);
84% of 7-year-olds achieved level 2 or above (82% in 1996).
In May 1997, the government set up a Numeracy Task Force with the remit to:

- review existing international and national evidence about achievement, teacher effectiveness and school effectiveness in mathematics;

- investigate the educational and social factors which are determinants of that performance;

- propose appropriate policies for all parts of the educational service to tackle underachievement, including classroom teaching, whole school practice, teacher training and development and action by local and national government and its partners.

Their interim report is due at the time of writing, with the final recommendations expected later in 1998.

## THE NATIONAL NUMERACY PROJECT

The National Numeracy Project was set up by the DfEE in April 1996 to raise standards of numeracy by improving teaching skills and the management of numeracy in schools. The Project's definition of numeracy is:

> more than knowing about numbers and number operations. It includes an ability and inclination to solve numerical problems, including those involving money or measures. It also demands familiarity with the ways in which numerical information is gathered by counting and measuring, and is presented in graphs, charts and tables.

In April 1996, numeracy centres were set up as the first phase of the project in fifteen local education authorities, supported by specific grant for five years. Numeracy consultants work with targeted schools, training teachers and providing advice on implementation.

While the National Curriculum sets out the mathematical content that all pupils should be taught, it does not explicitly define the teaching methods to be used. In contrast, the National Numeracy Project provides a highly defined approach to the teaching of numeracy based on three key principles:

- regular lessons each week
- a clear focus on instructional methods
- a clear focus on oral work and mental calculation.

The Project provides clear guidelines on what to teach each year group to secure good progression through defined learning objectives and suggested activities. Each Project school is expected to timetable each class for four lessons of forty-five to fifty minutes each week for the teaching of numeracy. Further lessons are needed to cover those aspects of mathematics not included in the Numeracy Project, particularly shape and space.

The Government's White Paper, *Excellence in Schools*, published in July 1997, proposes that, subject to the recommendations of the Numeracy Task Force, a national numeracy implementation programme will be introduced, probably from September 1999. This will involve national advisers training local numeracy consultants, who will work with primary schools in their area on the introduction of a structured hour a day for numeracy for all pupils.

## TEACHING STYLES

How can we help our pupils to succeed mathematically? The most important resource we can provide is an enthusiastic, knowledgeable and skilful teacher. Teachers need to have a good understanding of mathematics content and processes. They need to understand the different ways in which children learn and be able to structure lessons for effective learning. Critically, they need to provide a positive image of mathematics as an exciting, creative and useful subject.

The youngest pupils in nurseries and reception classes benefit from a mixture of well-structured situations in which they can explore mathematics: construction materials, sorting activities and role-play situations; small group teacher-led activities in which new ideas and skills can be introduced and developed; whole class activities where they can develop and practise their mathematical language, skills and confidence through rhymes, games, counting and predicting.

At KS 1 and 2, mathematics is more effectively taught through a daily whole class lesson, where the focus is on one particular aspect of mathematics. These lessons are likely to form part of an ongoing mathematics topic or unit of work, perhaps over a number of weeks. Over a half-term, the class will have worked on topics within or across each of the aspects of mathematics: number; shape, space and measures, and handling data.

Few teachers can teach mathematics effectively when the pupils in their class are engaged in a range of work on different subjects or on different aspects of mathematics. Typically, much time is wasted explaining different tasks to different groups, with each group having to wait for their explanation. A stimulating teaching input is often dissipated when pupils learn that it will be their turn to try it out tomorrow. In these situations, teachers often spend much of their time organising groups and ensuring all pupils are on task. Interactions are often reduced to helping pupils when they are stuck – a very negative role. Teachers often find they are explaining the same point to individual pupils over and over again. This cannot be efficient use of a teacher's time.

Another organizational style, based on the use of published or teacher-produced schemes, involves pupils working through the material 'at their own pace'. Again, it is a talented teacher who can use this system to provide an effective structure for learning. With individual pupils each working on different sections, there is little opportunity for whole class explanations, discussion or questioning. Pupils' 'own pace' of learning is generally very slow without the stimulus and challenge provided by the teacher.

Ofsted reports have identified teaching pace, challenge and motivation as key factors relating to pupil achievement. The simpler whole class mathematics lesson generally provides more efficient opportunities to achieve these goals through: defining and discussing clear learning objectives (maybe written on the board or on a poster and copied into books by older pupils);

using questions and answers to check out what pupils already know about the topic; addressing key teaching points in a way that stimulates and challenges pupils' thinking; picking up common problems and misconceptions, and providing pace and variety through the lesson.

Whole class lessons do not mean that all pupils will do exactly the same work. In any class there will be a range of ability and successful differentiation will involve targeting questions at appropriate levels, setting tasks at different levels for individuals, ability pairs or groups and working with pupils to set individual targets.

Whole class lessons do not, however, mean a return to past teaching methods. Reports over the past 150 years have identified concern about attainment in mathematics, as in the HMI comments described by Alistair McIntosh (1977) in his well-known article 'When will they ever learn?':

> ... the oral test shows that the children are working in the dark ... far too much time is given to the mechanical part of the subject. The result of this unintelligent teaching shows itself in the inability of the upper standards to solve very simple problems.

We need to explore and evaluate different teaching approaches, building on accounts of successful teaching, in order to find ways to raise achievement.

## THE USE OF PUBLISHED SCHEMES

There are many published schemes available for primary mathematics. Each scheme is a fund of valuable explanations, activities and resources. Most schemes have particularly useful teachers' handbooks. These handbooks often identify the need for teachers to use the scheme materials as a resource alongside other resources to plan their own teaching programmes.

In practice, there are too many examples of the poor use of mathematics schemes. At the most extreme, some teachers do not do any planning for their mathematics because 'we use the scheme'; some ignore the advice on introductory work and pupils spend their mathematics lessons working through cards or books.

Because the schemes have been written by 'experts', some teachers believe that the scheme must be a better teacher than they are. This clearly suggests that we need to increase teachers' confidence and expertise – and enjoyment – in the teaching of mathematics.

Publishers have also supplemented their schemes with consumable work-books, cards, games, posters and other extension materials. Schools using published scheme materials need to plan their teaching of mathematics and their use of these materials effectively. No school should be wholly reliant on one set of published materials. Pupils need to see mathematics presented in different formats rather than get used to one house style. Schools need to spend their annual mathematics budgets carefully to ensure a range of different practical and printed materials. One local school spends the whole of its annual mathematics budget of £1350 on consumable workbooks! Most importantly, teachers need to take responsibility for the planning and teaching of mathematics and pupils need to be very clear that what they are learning is mathematics, and not 'Cambridge' or 'Steps'.

## MATHEMATICAL LANGUAGE

In learning, we use words and symbols to help us construct the meaning of mathematical ideas. Mathematical language includes: mathematical words such as circle, addition, tessellation; the use of everyday words with their usual meanings; and, confusingly, the use of everyday words with different, mathematical meanings, such as odd, unit, volume. Pupils of all ages need regular, planned opportunities to develop mathematical language. This includes: oral work; discussions associated with practical work; reading aloud and silently, and writing in a variety of ways.

Key words need to be clearly identified in planning and can be usefully displayed on a classroom poster for a particular lesson or topic. The words and their meanings need to be discussed. Pupils need to hear teachers using correct mathematical vocabulary and to have opportunities for plenty of repetition of important terms. Activities can be structured to emphasize vocabulary. When checking multiples of 9 with the whole class, the teacher might say, 'I'll say a number, you repeat the number and say is/is not a multiple of 9'; so: 72 → 72 is a multiple of 9; 100 → 100 is not a multiple of 9. This simple device enables repeated use of the key word, which yes/no answers would not achieve.

Practical work is most often carried out by individuals and small groups, at times independently of the teacher. It is critical, however, that the teacher targets time to spend with each group, establishing the vocabulary needed to discuss and develop these ideas. The links between practical and formal work, for example, three cubes and another two cubes and 3 + 2, are not easily achieved and need to be supported through repeated discussions. Mathematical symbols might appear simple, but each expression represents a range of abstract ideas. Pupils need to make connections between these concepts, their practical representation, the appropriate symbols and their application in everyday life.

Pupils need a wide range of opportunities to see and read written mathematics. This should include a range of texts, board work, displays of pupils' mathematical work and real life data. Each class should have access to mathematical dictionaries. Many good examples for pupils of different ages have recently been published.

We should expect pupils' mathematical recording to develop over time. Too many teachers move too quickly to the use of mathematical symbols and formal layouts. We can support the development of understanding much more effectively by encouraging pupils to record their practical work in a mixture of pictures, words and symbols and to produce written descriptions of their oral explanations and methods. As a whole class, we might explore patterns in a 100 square and identify key words: multiple, diagonal, column, increases and so on. Individual pupils can then be asked to write descriptions of two or three patterns. These can then be read out for others to find.

## MENTAL AND ORAL NUMBER SKILLS ...

All pupils need to have a wide range of number facts at their fingertips, facts that they have learned by heart and can recall quickly. They also need to be able to use known facts to work out more complex calculations in their heads. They need to develop a range of mental methods and choose the most appropriate for a given task. We should encourage pupils to use mental methods wherever possible and only resort to written calculations or the use of a calculator for problems that are too difficult to work out mentally.

It is worrying to see older pupils, including those in secondary schools, still using very inefficient methods: counting on their fingers or adding by drawing marks on a page. For many pupils their only methods are the standard written algorithms that predominate in current teaching. These are used without too much thought, say, to subtract 992 from 1000 by decomposition! Mistakes are often made by trying to remember procedures, rather than thinking about the numbers involved. Too few pupils even recognize when their answer is clearly incorrect: 47+28 = 615! An emphasis on mental rather than written methods can help pupils to develop a feel for number, to treat each number as a whole rather than as individual digits and, with discussion, to reach a better understanding of what they are doing.

A daily ten- to fifteen-minute mental and oral session provides a regular opportunity to teach new skills and strategies and continue to improve confidence and expertise. The sessions can stand alone and do not need to be directly connected to other current work in mathematics. They might be at the start or end of the daily mathematics lesson, but could be at a different time in the school day.

Each session needs to focus on one aspect, with a clear, shared learning objective: count in fives to 100, add 10 to given numbers, recall multiplication facts to 5 × 5, estimate prices to the nearest £1. Sessions need to have a brisk pace and involve every pupil: counting together, testing each other on number facts, answering quick questions. There is no need for pupil recording, they should be free to think and respond. At times, the teacher might use the board to scribe numbers and methods. What is this number? Is this a multiple of 5? What numbers can you make from these digits? Let's look at the different methods you have used to work that out. The board may be used to show and compare different methods of working out. How did you add 45 and 23?

At other times the questions should be wholly oral to encourage pupils to hold more information in their heads.

Although all pupils are working on the same objective, the teacher should

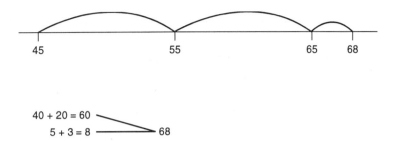

target the questions at appropriate levels for different pupils: Which of these are multiples of 3 ... 18, 30, 360, 51, 252? Individual pupils should be encouraged to set themselves targets, perhaps recording them on their target card. These could be checked by parents and friends as well as by teachers.

## ... AND PRACTICAL AND WRITTEN NUMBER SKILLS

Pupils of all ages need regular opportunities to work with mathematical ideas in practical, mental, oral and written ways. Most importantly, teachers need to help pupils to build meaningful connections between these different models.

Practical work provides concrete images, which support the development of mathematical ideas. Askew and Williams (1995) report that:

> while practical work and 'real' contexts can be useful ... they need to be accompanied by careful dialogue with pupils to establish the extent of their understanding. Pupils' success on a concrete task should not be taken as an indication of understanding the abstract .... How links are perceived between the two needs to be the subject of considerable discussion between pupils and teachers.
>
> (p. 10)

The mathematics National Curriculum states quite clearly that pupils should be given opportunities to develop flexible and effective methods of computation and recording, and to record in a variety of ways, including ways which relate to their mental work. We need to encourage pupils to develop a variety of methods for calculations and not impose a single style and format for recording.

## SHAPE, SPACE AND MEASURES, HANDLING DATA, USING AND APPLYING MATHEMATICS

Shape and space activities provide particularly valuable ways in which to help pupils to develop mathematical thinking. In recent years the quality of available shape resources has improved dramatically, providing opportunities for pupils to manipulate, sort and fit together two- and three-dimensional shapes. Solid shapes can be passed around a circle of pupils with each describing one property of the shape: 'It has rectangular faces; there are triangles; it has six vertices; it's like a Toblerone.' If you can't think of anything you can pass it on or swap it for another shape.

Measuring and handling data provide excellent opportunities to relate mathematics to everyday life, and are often best taught in realistic contexts. A topic on supermarkets is a stimulus for exploring questions: 'How many packs will fit on the shelf? Which holds the most? Can you make a replica package?' and so on.

Using and applying mathematics is defined in a separate section of the National Curriculum, but it is not intended to be taught separately. Instead, the opportunities to use and apply mathematics in practical tasks, in real life problems and within mathematics itself and to explain thinking to support the development of reasoning, should permeate all of our teaching and learning of mathematics. Many closed tasks can be restructured to provide more interesting activities. A page of sums can be replaced by the question: 'The answer is 100, what is the question?' Asking which quadrilaterals will tessellate encourages the exploration of many different four-sided shapes instead of sticking to squares and rectangles. Not only are these problems more interesting for pupils, they also save on worksheets!

## CONTINUING PROFESSIONAL DEVELOPMENT

If we hope to raise significantly standards of achievement for all our pupils, we need to ensure that every school is an improving school and every teacher an improving teacher. The completion of a course of initial teacher training is the start of a professional journey, not the end of the learning process. All teachers need to continue to work at improving their teaching through activities in the classroom and working with their colleagues in school. Local education authorities, higher education institutions and a range of other groups provide further opportunities for continuing professional development.

Mathematics education has two major subject associations: the Association of Teachers of Mathematics (ATM) and the Mathematical Association (MA) which produce regular journals: *Mathematics Teaching and Micromath* (ATM) and *Mathematics in School* (MA). Both run annual national conferences, usually at Easter time, as well as local groups and working parties. ATM, in particular, develops and markets a wide range of innovative resources.

Every teacher should be a researcher in their own classroom, continually trying to find ways of making their teaching and their pupils' learning more successful. There are many networks locally and nationally which can support this challenging task.

## REFERENCES

Askew, M. and Williams, D. (1995) *Recent Research in Mathematics Education 5–16*. London: Ofsted.

Dickson, L., Brown, M. and Gibson, O. (1984) *Children Learning Mathematics*. Holt Education for the Schools Council.

Floyd, A. (ed.) (1981) *Developing Mathematical Thinking*. London: Addison-Wesley/Open University Press.

Hughes, M. (1986) *Children and Number*. Oxford: Blackwell.

McIntosh, A. (1977) When will they ever learn? *Forum*, **19** (3), 6–11.

National Curriculum Council (1989) *Mathematics: Non-Statutory Guidance*. York: NCC.

Third International Mathematics and Science Study (1997) *Second National Report Part 1*. Slough: National Foundation for Educational Research.

## SOME SUGGESTIONS FOR FURTHER READING

Useful further reading on topics covered in this chapter would be the books by Dickson, Brown and Gibson (1984), Floyd (1981) and Hughes (1986), as listed above.

CHAPTER 11

# Science for the twenty-first century

DI BENTLEY

## INTRODUCTION

This chapter looks at some of the key issues in science education which have been active for a number of years, as well as others which have become important in primary schools since the 1988 Education Reform Act. It raises a number of issues that are crucial features of science for young children and of particular importance for primary teachers to take into account. What it will not do is show you how to teach the National Curriculum. What I will hope to do is to focus your attention on some key principles of learning and teaching in science, and by helping you to consider them, to assist you in your teaching of the National Curriculum.

The chapter begins with some key features of science that you as a teacher need to consider when embarking on that exciting venture of helping children construct their ideas of the natural world. These key features are followed up in the rest of the chapter, but in some cases are particularly intertwined, so there will not be a subheading for each key feature. Nor is the same emphasis given to each one.

## SOME KEY FEATURES OF SCIENCE

First, science is a practical subject in British primary schools. This is an important point. In many countries, children learn their science by reading and by watching the teacher conduct demonstrations. Here in Britain we believe that practical work is an essential feature, because it opens up to children the whole of the methodology of science. They learn about key ideas such as predicting, fair tests, hypothesizing, measuring and observation by actually practising. While in reading this you are perhaps surprised that it should be mentioned, because you had taken for granted that this was the case, it will nevertheless create some challenges for you.

Because science is practical, it needs to be well managed. It needs very careful planning to ensure the key ideas mentioned above are planned for so that children can practise them. Grouping the children needs careful thought. Research shows us that boys and girls bring different skills to science as a result of their socialization (Reay, 1991). Both sets of skills are important in learning science. Planning the best ways of helping children to explore investigative work can be quite taxing, and often children feel it can be repetitive. Later in the chapter, I suggest that problem-solving, as opposed to just investigative work, is what is needed in a modern primary science curriculum. This encourages wider skills than investigative work – skills that are crucial features of lifelong learning. And it's never too soon to start!

Second, and again something we take for granted, science has a body of knowledge, the content of the National Curriculum; or is it? Well, actually no. There is of course far more to science than the content of the National Curriculum, but as a teacher you will need to ask yourself two questions. What content do you want to teach – are some of the ethical issues of, for example, pollution, BSE, global warming, all part of science? Should you be teaching about them? Or is it your role to ensure that children understand the facts which, because of what science is, have often developed with little consideration for ethics? And what of your own knowledge? Research (Bennett *et al.*, 1992) has shown that for many primary teachers this is really the nub of the matter. No matter how confident they feel as a teacher, no matter how expert they are at asking questions to help children move on, if they themselves don't know where it is the children should move on to, they lack confidence, and not infrequently either don't help them to move at all, or direct them into a cul-de-sac.

Third, exactly what is science? Is it simply a body of knowledge, supported by a set of fairly precisely defined methods? Or is it much more problematic than that? Are the facts of science actually representations of the reality of the physical world, which have been discovered because scientists controlled variables in order to find out about nature? After all, most of us would argue, there are some facts – for example, the boiling points of liquids are dependent on a combination of heat energy being transformed to kinetic energy at particular conditions of pressure. Children need that knowledge, and that at the pressures we normally experience in our homes, it means that water boils at 100°C.

But is all scientific 'fact' quite that straightforward? I prefer to think of science as a set of explanations which human beings have put forward to make sense out of the natural phenomena that they observe. Because they are explanations, they are made within a particular historical and social time, within the limits of the available technology, and by individuals who bring their own understandings, biases and prejudices to the interpretation of what they observe.

Of course, thinking of science in this way implies that explanations can change over time. It also implies that some of the important features of science that we try to teach children might not be quite so important. We teach them to control variables, or factors that influence how phenomena behave. We call this being objective, ensuring that all biases are designed out of our finding out about the physical world. However, some scientists, philosophers of science and sociologists consider that this is simply not possible. Because we are human, they argue, and we interpret from within our own social and psychological world, we don't always recognize our biases. Thus no matter how well you design the experiment, it cannot be objective in the way which traditional scientific methodology implies.

Finally, what about children's learning? After all, as teachers that is what we are planning for, assessing, developing and working at all the time we are in the classroom. Schooling is about learning, not about teaching. In science, there has been a huge effort put into research in understanding how children learn. That area of literature is well worth reading. It will help you to make all your lessons fit better to the needs of the youngsters for whom you are responsible. Of course, like many areas of education, and I would argue of science too, there are competing ideas about how children learn. At the end of the day, like all of us, you will develop your own ideas in this area. You may not articulate them or make them explicit - even to yourself, but you will have your own theories of learning. They will guide how you plan lessons, how you treat children, how you interact with them, how you manage and control your classroom and how you assess what takes place there. What is important as a teacher is that you feed the development of your own theories by reading the work and books and thinking which researchers are producing. In that way your teaching stays fresh and children's learning remains at the centre of your concerns.

## CHILDREN'S LEARNING IN SCIENCE

There are a variety of theoretical bases to understanding children's learning. In particular, in primary education and science there are probably two major and related areas that have influenced the work in the field. The earliest work was the cognitive developmental psychology developed from the work of Piaget. As the term suggests, his theories centred on the developmental nature of children's learning, and he proposed a set of stages through which children pass, when given suitable stimulation in the development of their thinking. In the past, much time was wasted in discussion of the stages themselves. They were often, erroneously, linked very closely to particular ages and a multitude of tests developed to determine what stage children had reached. It was declared that some children never reached the final stage - what Piaget called *formal operations*. This involves the capacity to manipulate two or more factors in one's head at the same time, being able to cope with 'what would happen if this changed or that changed'. Since this is a crucial part of scientific thinking, it is easy to see how Piaget's ideas became important in science. In fact, the stages he identified seem to underpin many areas of scientific thinking, such as classification, hypothesizing, predicting and deduction. What is probably more true than the stages being linked precisely to ages is that children do develop their thinking, that the development is progressive, and different children may be at different stages of understanding, not just in different subjects of the curriculum but in different concepts too.

For example, a child may have a very well-developed understanding of time, but find volume particular difficult to conceptualize. Piaget suggested that the age at which children reach the different stages is influenced by both experience and natural development and his followers advocated different learning strategies for each stage, from a hands-on type of learning when the child is very young, to more abstract and second-order forms of support as they progress.

Another important feature of the Piagetian theory of learning is that it sees children as active learners, continuously constructing and reconstructing their internal understandings or conceptual framework as they gain experience. It is the role of the teacher to plan that experience, recognizing the rate at which the child can progress due to the rate at which his or her brain, thinking and nervous systems are developing. As Piaget (1970, pp. 153–4) pointed out:

> Intellectual adaptation is thus a process of achieving a state of balance between the assimilation of experience into the deductive structures and the accommodation of those structures to the data of experience … adaptation presupposes an interaction between the subject and object, such that the first can incorporate the second into itself while also taking account of its particularities

In Britain, since the Plowden Report was published in the 1960s, there has been a large measure of support in primary schools for a so-called Piagetian approach to learning. This has meant that teachers see children as being active in their learning, needing hands-on experience in which they practise and develop their deductive structures themselves as a result of the experimental learning which the teacher instigates. When it is done well, it is a joy to watch. However, as Ofsted (1993, p. 15) point out, it is not always done well:

> In both Key Stages (one and two) a significant minority of lessons significantly lacked purpose. The pupils were often busily occupied in activities but were unclear about what they should be doing and why they were doing it.

Thus applying any learning theory needs careful thought. It is important not to lose sight of the goal. Learning has a purpose, it is not sufficient in itself. In the worst case scenarios of experiential learning, the structures which help children to relate the learning back into their conceptual framework and then to move on towards a clear goal were not provided in the activity. The 'scaffolding' for the learning was never planned, because experience was all. Scaffolding is an idea that comes from another interesting theorist, Vygotsky (1962), whose work on thought and language, although somewhat outside the remit of a chapter on science, is well worth while. He supported social constructivism, one of the group of theories which the next section considers. Like Piaget, he believed that children develop in their thinking and that to assist this development teachers need to provide a series of small and planned steps – a scaffold – towards the goal.

## CONSTRUCTIVISM

Major aspects of the research in science education in the last two decades have focused around constructivist theories of learning. In brief, constructivism is a philosophy and a psychology about the way people make sense of the world. Constructivist learning theory as described by, for example, Driver *et al.* (1994) suggests that all learners construct new meaning by using their existing conceptual frameworks to interpret new information and make sense. The central feature of all types of constructivism – twenty-one at the last count (!) – is that people are intellectually active; they do not learn passively, but go out of their way to try to make some meaning from what is taking place in their environment. Our constructions of life are conditioned and constrained by our experiences and this means that, since we all have different experiences, we are all likely to have different understandings. Given the description above, one could in many respects describe Piaget as a constructivist.

Constructivism's influence on science education has spawned a burgeoning library of research papers on children's conceptual understandings at different ages and in different aspects of science. For many teachers it is using this huge mass of understanding about children's conceptual understanding of science that is a major appeal of constructivism. Knowing what ideas children have about science – for example, what do they think an animal is? What do they understand about temperature or heat when they reach the classroom, having seen animals, experienced cold days, watched weather reports on television? Many teachers have found that having some guidance in these areas is very helpful in planning the activities to help in refining or changing the conceptual understandings which life experiences helped children to develop before they reached the classroom.

For others, constructivism suggests a methodological approach to science education and provides the opportunity to use this method in their teaching. The generalizability of constructivism to most learning situations is the appeal which is most common for many teachers. Despite the twenty-one varieties, the majority of constructivist research and writing falls into two main camps, that of social or radical constructivism. Rosalind Driver describes social constructivism like this: 'novices are introduced to a community of knowledge through discourse in the context of relevant tasks' (Driver *et al.*, 1994, p. 7).

As a teacher, one can take a strong or a weak approach to social constructivism. Watts and Bentley (1991) have pointed out that schools have difficulty with the strong position of social constructivism. To help young people understand the processes of science and develop an understanding of its content, schools must help children understand what science *is*. They must discuss the nature of science itself. Most schools do not, or cannot, do this. In schools, the nature of science and the working practices of scientists are rarely discussed and in primary science almost never.

For teachers wanting to be strong social constructivists, there are some dilemmas in the interpretation of the nature of science. One needs to be clear what one thinks science is. Would you, for example, go as far as Rosalind Driver? She says:

> Scientific knowledge is symbolic in nature and socially negotiated. The objects of science are not the phenomena of nature, but constructs that are advanced by the scientific community to interpret nature.
>
> (Driver, 1994, p. 5)

Jonathan Osborne (1996) suggests that social constructivists treat science, as was being explored earlier, as something that is less a set of facts, which represent the truth about the physical world, and more a set of explanations which are subject to change over time:

> the social constructivists would portray the world as being full of peculiar symbolic entities such as atoms, electrons, ions, fields, genes and chromosomes. These are organised by ideas such as evolution or the nuclear model of the atom, but essentially there is nothing special about the truth of science.
>
> (Osborne, 1996, p. 61)

Osborne suggests that being a social constructivist when teaching science dictates the role of the teacher to be 'a guide mediating and negotiating between children's everyday world and that of science'. He is critical of such a role because, he says:

> Never once in the dialogues does the teacher address the important epistemological issues and ask of the student 'How do you know?', 'How would you justify that?'. ... that is, the issue of evidence and the act of reference are omitted and instead the function of the teacher is to negotiate with and persuade the student towards a scientific way of seeing through discussion.
>
> (*ibid.*, p. 62)

The other main version of constructivism to be found in science education is that of radical constructivism. If social constructivism, even in its weak version, is challenging the links between science as representing the truth about the real world, radical constructivism makes a deliberate attempt, as von Glaserfield (1989) states, to 'cut loose from the philosophical tradition that knowledge has to be a representation of reality. Instead truth is replaced by the notion of viability' (p. 123). Osborne is no more comfortable with radical constructivism than he was with social constructivism. His critique lies in the issue that radical constructivism has failed to put forward any criteria by which one may make judgements as to the viability claims of competing theories.

Radical constructivists do not believe in scientific knowledge having any different or more important status than any another kind of knowledge. This causes some of its critics some difficulty. Osborne, for example, has this to say:

> Science education should attempt to communicate not only the practice of science but also the beliefs that are widely held in the scientific community and one of the basic tenets is that scientific knowledge is different.
>
> (Osborne, 1996, p. 68)

I know very few teachers who would admit to practising radical constructivism in their classroom when they teach. It is particularly difficult to do this in primary education. To discuss what science is, before children have really gained any theoretical understanding of science, is very difficult. Most primary teachers who like this approach to learning use it only in KS 2. They generally come at it by using the competing theories approach, so children can see that data can be explained in different ways and that science might need to be viewed as being viable because it fits the available evidence, rather than valid because it represents the truth of the reality of nature and how it works,

One of the most important features of constructivism for science education has been its contribution to how teaching takes place. This has involved a wide variety of suggested and tried methods, from developing notions of autonomy in experiential learning, through group discussion and a wide range of other techniques such as DARTS (Directed Activities Related to Texts) activities, word association, predict–observe–explain sequences, and concept mapping. Associated with these are ways of approaching learning that rely on experiential, co-operative, discussion-based approaches.

Some good examples of the types of approaches associated with constructivist ways of teaching are to be found in Baird and Northfield (1992), or Bentley and Watts (1994). Some critics, for example Osborne, feel that methods such as demonstrating, showing and telling are missing from the approaches which constructivists use. His main criticism seems to be that despite the large variety – by his own admission over eighty in one book alone – of learning styles which constructivists advocate, these will not fit for all children. This is certainly something to take into account when planning.

Whatever brand of constructivist you are – or become – one of the important tenets is that you will see learning as being an interpretive process involving individuals' constructions of meaning, which are related to specific occurrences and phenomena. New constructions are built through their relation to previous experience and prior knowledge. The challenge for the teacher is to focus on students' learning-with-understanding rather than the more common and straightforward emphasis on 'covering content'. To learn science from a constructivist philosophy implies using concepts and experiences we already possess, and which we then change and elaborate on the basis of fresh meanings. These fresh ideas are commonly negotiated through everyday interactions with peers and teachers.

## CLASSROOM CONSTRUCTIVISM

It is possible, as with several of the writers quoted above, to be very purist about constructivism, but whatever else it is, it is a theory that adapts to everyday practice. Previously I have written about the five main tenets of 'classroom constructivism' (Bentley and Watts, 1994) which are:

1. Start where the learner is. This is a very common dictat of constructivism and most primary teachers are aware of working this way. They enable individual learning through focused experience and then use children's range of experiences to further understanding.

2. Help progression through a process of 'orientation', 'elicitation', 'restructuring' and 'application' (Driver *et al.*, 1994). This is about structuring the learning environment to encourage the explication of ideas and to provide challenging experiences. So, for example, teachers are used to developing children's language skills in all contexts in order to help children explain and develop their ideas.

3. Design 'bridges' to take the learner to the desired point. The task of the teacher is to know the pupils well enough so that instructional steps are strong and help transport ideas for particular individuals. Primary teachers know their children very well and are commonly able to do this through the careful and targeted questioning of children.

4. Use different forms of active learning. Learning is not just listening and writing. Group work and collaborative learning are all examples of techniques that play upon ideas of active learning.

5. See yourself as a facilitator. Classroom management is important: teachers must design and organize situations in which ideas can be discussed without fear and ridicule. Many primary teachers are expert at this way of teaching. They use sophisticated questioning techniques to lead children along different paths of thinking. They encourage children to explore ideas themselves rather than being directive.

## SCIENCE: THE PROCESS AND THE CONTENT

In designing the National Curriculum, the government of the day gave a rule of thumb about the amount of time to be spent on investigative or process-based work in science. Their guidance was about 50 per cent of the time in KS 1 and 2. What is crucial, however, is that teachers plan the needs of children in investigative science. Simply carrying out the investigations and assuming that children absorb the skills and processes by some kind of osmosis is not enough. Nor is it sufficient to assume, when developing a scheme of work, that as long as the content is being planned, and activities are taking place, there is no need to map out the steps of investigative science. Many schemes of work plan very carefully for the content areas of science – forces, light, materials, structures, astronomy, earth, space, etc. and forget that crucial skills and processes need to be planned for just as carefully.

Children need to practise such aspects. Simply planning an investigation into the work periodically, or just as bad, fixating, as many primary teachers did early on in their unfamiliarity with the science curriculum, on 'fair testing' as an investigative process, will not help children to develop the skills. As the Ofsted report of 1993 (p. 5) pointed out: 'Investigative skills developed at key stage 1 were not always adequately built on, with pupils in KS 2 less often required to plan investigations.'

The National Curriculum Council (1993, p. 12) was reporting similar findings:

> Research has shown that few children make use of the results from their investigations when interpreting their meaning and coming to a conclusion. In many instances, children's conclusions are based upon observation made during the investigation or are simply a repeat of the beliefs held at the beginning. Others draw conclusions that are a description of how they did their investigation.

Not much evidence of classroom constructivism here, then! However, what the quotation does point up is the extraordinary difficulty of planning successfully for investigative work. In this final part of the chapter, I want to suggest problem solving as a holistic way of looking at investigative work, but at the same time ask you to keep in mind that although the investigative work is exciting and motivating when it is holistic, you still need to enable practice of different skills and processes.

In keeping with my position as a strong social constructivist (well, actually a radical constructivist, but that's not what this section is about, so I'll temper my beliefs to fit with the moment), I want to go beyond mere investigation and suggest that what teachers need to develop is children's ability to solve problems. So what, you might ask, is the difference? Problem solving, I would argue, encompasses investigations, but contains and develops many more skills and components such as the following:

## Inquisitiveness

Problem solving encourages inventiveness because it provides opportunities to explore playfully. For some this is easier than others, since some people are naturally inquisitive and seem to leap at the chance to play and experiment with things. This is easily apparent when children want to 'see how it works' or 'find out what it does'.

## Prior experience

Problem solving is a way of developing children's 'prior experience', those experiences they can call on to provide context and significance. The context helps to make sense of the problem and leads (hopefully) towards a solution. So, for example, if children are making something that needs to be supported off the ground, they need some appreciation of the strength of materials and so of what might be appropriate in the circumstances. Some of this appreciation comes from direct experience of using, say, a range of domestic materials, building blocks or construction toys, while some comes from tests and trials in the problem-solving situation. Prior experience also involves other kinds of knowledge, such as an understanding of situations (what is likely to happen in certain circumstances) and relationships between materials (like card and glue).

## Transferring contexts

If children can see the solution of a problem in one situation they are more able to transfer this understanding to a slightly different problem in another context. This is a vital feature of problem solving: using knowledge in maths, for instance, in the context of a science problem; using construction skills from one project to another.

## Investigative skills

Problem solving helps to develop the skills of conducting tests and trials, studies and explorations of how and why things work. Children need to understand the factors (and/or variables) associated with problems, selecting the appropriate or manageable ones, exploring how they relate to each other and to the central purpose involved, and how they can be quantified and measured.

## Motivation

One could argue that with young children this is hardly a problem for teachers! In the classroom there is no doubt that the activity of problem solving itself is highly motivating. Children enjoy the relative freedom and autonomy of making their own decisions, correcting their own mistakes and reaching their own solutions.

## Self-directed learning

More importantly, problem solving develops self-reliance and good group work. Being both scientific and technological involves moving between acting as a self-directed individual and as a good member of a team.

So what does problem solving entail? Watts (1994, p. 103) argues thus:

> Problem solving is quintessential constructivism. The task is open, learning starts with the learner's own experiences, the learner is responsible for how he or she works, it is rooted in relevant activities and contexts, it is motivating and encouraging of language develop- ment and conceptual shift, it is skill based and the teacher is facilitator all through the activity.

However, planning it is not straightforward. It does develop skills and understanding of processes for children, but it tests your skills as a teacher.

Juniper (1989) suggests that in planning problem solving, teachers need to be:

1. *decisional*: taking account of what you are aiming at before you begin

2. *procedural*: establishing priorities among all the organizational details to be considered

3. *solutional*: organizing the work so that children seek some precision in solutions – choosing clear objectives to be achieved

4. *generative*: developing materials or outcomes which will carry over to other problem-solving sessions.

### 1. Making prior decisions (decisional)

There are a large variety of decisions that face teachers in planning for problem solving. Some crucial ones are:

- How open will the problems be – carefully structured and constrained or wide open to a range of solutions?

- Are all the children tackling the same problem or different ones? If they are tackling the same problem, can it be divided into related sub-problems or will all pupils undertake exactly the same task?

- If the problems are different, or are sub-problems of a main theme, will these all be at the same level of difficulty?

- Who chooses the problems – are they teacher provided, or can the children choose and generate their own problems?

- How long do they have for the problem – is the timing appropriate?
- How can the materials and equipment be constrained – are they free to find specialist items from sources outside the classroom? From outside the school?

## 2. *Thinking through procedures and priorities (procedural)*

Any form of classroom work, including problem solving, must entail the provision of learning opportunities which:

- set clear aims and objectives for the activities and their outcomes
- ensure progression in both knowledge and understanding
- enhance skill learning
- allow for individual needs
- meet the requirements of cross-curricular themes and dimensions
- enable the provision of equal opportunities in the school.

## 3. *Aiding children to reach solutions (solutional)*

To facilitate children reaching solutions rather than just reverting to experiential learning, you need to ensure that they know what the requirements are for the project – the time, the possible resources, the possible strategies to be used, the broad range of acceptable outcomes, the nature and level of negotiation possible for the task, the form of recording and communication of results, the mode of assessment and the overall pattern of work. These are all decisions which teachers need to make before they begin, so that, conceptually, the members of the class reach their goals while, managerially, the teacher reaches hers.

## 4. *Providing ideas and materials (generative)*

Some of the above is simply a collection of ideas, hints and suggestions. However, successful problem solving also involves the collection of a bank of equipment and resources. Many of the physical materials for problem solving revolve around household packaging and waste. Such materials are cheap (free), easily available, versatile, safe to work with, quickly bonded, recyclable and familiar. They should not be a substitute for high tech materials such as commercial construction kits, computer-driven models, electrical circuit components and the like, but they are a highly useful format for introducing children to simple construction.

In all this planning, however, to develop skills, to enable team work, to encourage motivation and inventiveness, one must not lose sight of the

# Science for the twenty-first century    139

content. However one thinks about the nature of science, whether or not one is a radical constructivist, there is a body of knowledge to science, even if that body of knowledge shifts and changes according to the researcher and the social and political conditions of the time.

There is, nevertheless, a kind of received orthodoxy - what we traditionally call 'the facts', so problem solving has to be about something. It means solving a problem in a real context. Children will learn scientific concepts and be able to apply their understanding of existing concepts to new areas of work through problem solving. As science teachers, once the excitement of the problem-solving work is over, the hard work begins. We need to explore what concepts children have developed, as well as what skills they have practised, and help them to consolidate it all. That, however, is the subject of another book.

## REFERENCES

Baird, J.R. and Northfield, J.R. (eds) (1992) *Learning from the Peel Experience.* Melbourne: Monash University.

Bennett, S.N., Wragg, E.C., Carre, C.G. and Carter, D.S.G. (1992) A longitudinal study of primary teachers' perceived competence in, and concerns about, National Curriculum implementation. *Research Papers in Education,* **7**(1), 53-78.

Bentley, D. and Watts, D.M. (1992) *Communicating in School Science: Groups, Tasks and Problem Solving 5-16.* London: Falmer Press.

Bentley, D. and Watts, D.M. (1994) *Teaching and Learning in Primary Science and Technology.* Milton Keynes: Open University Press.

Driver, R., Asoko, H., Leach, J., Mortimer, E. and Scott, P. (1994) Constructing scientific knowledge in the classroom. *Educational Researcher,* **23**, 5-12.

Glaserfield, E. von (1989) Cognition, construction of knowledge and teaching. *Synthese,* **80**, 121-40.

Juniper, D.F. (1989) *Successful Problem Solving.* Slough: W. Foulsham.

National Curriculum Council (1993) *Teaching Science at Key Stages 1 and 2.* NCC: York.

Ofsted (1993) *Science at Key Stages 1 and 2: Results of Inspection Findings.* London: HMSO.

Osborne, J. (1996) Beyond constructivism. *Science Education,* **80**(1), 53-82.

Piaget, J. (1970) *The Science of Education and the Psychology of the Child.* London: Longman.

Reay, D. (1991) Intersections of gender, race and class in the primary school. *British Journal of the Sociology of Education,* **12**(2), 163-82.

Vygotsky, L.S. (1962) *Thought and Language.* Cambridge, MA: MIT Press.

Watts, D.M. (1994) Building on experience. In D. Bentley and D.M. Watts *Teaching and Learning in Primary Science and Technology.* Milton Keynes: Open University Press.

Watts, D.M. and Bentley, D. (1991) Constructivism in the curriculum. Can we close the gap between the strong theoretical version and the weak version of theory-in-practice? *The Curriculum Journal*, **2**(2), 171–82.

## SOME SUGGESTIONS FOR FURTHER READING

Bentley, D. and Watts, D.M., *Teaching and Learning in Primary Science and Technology*, as above. This book focuses on managing primary science and technology in the classroom. It contains helpful case studies written by teachers, to give ideas of how they approached tasks with children in KS 1 and 2. It addresses ideas of constructivism, conceptual development and language, curriculum planning, classroom organization and management, effective questioning and equality of opportunity.

Sherrington, R. (1993) *The ASE Primary Teachers' Handbook*. Hemel Hempstead: Simon & Schuster Education. This is a very helpful book, with chapters that cover a range of advice for teachers of primary science. It provides good practical advice to support science teaching at KS 1 and 2 for several years into a teaching career. Like many ASE publications, it is written both by experts in the field and by experienced teachers.

# CHAPTER 12

# Personal and moral development

PAMELA THOMAS

Education has for its object the formation of character.

(Herbert Spencer)

In recent years there has been a great deal of discussion about standards in education. Concerns expressed reflect anxieties about whether children are achieving certain basic levels of skills and competence. The level of intellectual attainment achieved by pupils is causing general disquiet as national projects on literacy and numeracy are launched in primary schools. The concern about standards also encompasses behaviour and conduct. It is argued that young people generally do not seem to know the difference between right and wrong. In many people's minds 'modern society is becoming increasingly more lawless, violent, undisciplined and permissive and this trend is most apparent among the younger generation. Statistics show that vandalism, violent crime and drug taking have risen and are rising among teenagers' (Straughan, 1988, p. 1).

The decline in respect for authority is almost tangible in certain sections of society. Certainly society seems to be in a state of flux at the present time. Rapid social change currently characterizes our society. We live in an increasingly secular society, which appears to be fragmented in terms of its community life. The growing concerns about values and morality in our society are now too great to be ignored, since many feel that we have now reached an all-time low and a radical rethink is essential. There is certainly a strong undercurrent of feeling expressed via the media that society needs to 'teach children not only to be knowledgeable but also to be good, responsible citizens' (Straughan, 1988, p. 1). In a secular, pluralist society it is difficult to see how best we can educate people in accordance with high standards of morality.

In this chapter we will be examining the role which parents and schools can play in trying to impart the right values and ensure that children's behaviour is socially acceptable, and reaches the desired standard. We will look at some of the issues relating to the personal and moral development of the young. We will also examine some of the ways in which schools, together with parents, can provide a firm moral basis for education in the training of future citizens.

The task of preparing the young for the duties of citizenship is a complex one. Society has to invest the time and give the necessary commitment to helping its future citizens to become responsible, self-disciplined individuals. In the future we need individuals who can integrate successfully into society and help to shape its future development in an active and constructive way. As a society we need individuals who will be able to function effectively as workers, as parents and as citizens.

Schools cannot be expected to bear all the responsibility for the personal and moral development of children. Schools already do a great deal of work in this area. However, schools need the help and support of all sections of society if they are to produce effective citizens. All of us must share the responsibility for nurturing the young and working towards the development of a greater sense of continuity between home and school experiences in the transmission of shared values. Therefore a close working relationship between school and the wider community is vitally important if there is to be an effective partnership between schools and parents in educating for personal and moral growth.

In order for young people to acquire the skills to act responsibly, they need a clear set of basic principles and values. Those responsible for educating young people have to try to agree upon these basic principles and values in order for the young to acquire the qualities of citizenship essential for successful integration into society. This is not to say that reaching a consensus about principles and values is easy. We live in a society characterized by diversity, and our society tolerates a range of opposing viewpoints in many areas of both public and private life. As a society we would want to celebrate the richness and variety of our cultural heritage and take pride in our own upbringing that is characterized by differing individual and group experiences.

However, there are values which we all share. For example, most of us would agree that it is wrong to tell lies, to cheat, to bully and to steal from others. Indeed, much of our lives involves obeying generally accepted rules and principles based upon a set of shared values and agreed codes of conduct. The level of agreement between people about what constitutes acceptable behaviour is probably much higher than we often suppose. Therefore schools and parents, together with other sectors of society need to give firm guidance to the young, based on an agreed set of guidelines. Young people need the assurance of a consistent, clear framework in order to learn the accepted ways of behaving.

First of all we have to remember that we are born into a bewildering world and have to adapt to it. Each one of us has to adapt to family life, to school and to wider society generally. We have to learn many things, including the ability to communicate with others. We have to develop appropriate mental, physical and social skills in order to meet the challenges of everyday life. We have to learn the appropriate norms and values of society so that we can adopt the accepted ways of behaving characteristic of that society. In all of this we have to learn to be both flexible and adaptable if we are to negotiate a successful route through the various key stages in our lives, from childhood, through adolescence to adulthood. By the time we reach adulthood we should have acquired some awareness of what it might mean to participate as responsible citizens within the community and society. We cannot achieve any of this without help, guidance and encouragement from others.

In the course of our upbringing we are influenced by experiences from a variety of sources. In adapting to the world around us we are influenced at the outset by our parents. It is normally our parents who mediate between us and the outside world, transmitting their beliefs, attitudes and values to us and influencing our behaviour and our general development. It is during the early stages of infancy that the foundations of our character are laid. The way we are treated by significant others, such as parents (or other major carers), can have profound effects on the ways in which we view ourselves and the ways in which we conduct our lives later on.

Parents and carers begin the process of moulding children into civilized beings. Our experiences within the home can provide a firm basis upon which later experiences build. The manner in which we are treated early on influences our view, not only of ourselves but also of the world. If we grow up in an atmosphere of mutual trust and respect, this is likely to benefit us in later life as we encounter further new experiences. Children whose parents provide a supportive and secure home background are more likely to develop into confident, capable and well-adjusted adults. There do, then, appear to be particular aspects of parental behaviour which are likely to contribute to successful outcomes in the upbringing of children. Such behaviours include not only treating children with respect but also using a consistent approach in meting out praise and punishment. Parents who are consistent in praising or disciplining their children are more likely to engender desirable behaviours in their children, compared with parents whose methods are inconsistent. If children receive conflicting messages about their behaviour, they may well experience difficulty in learning how to behave appropriately. Such inconsistency in treatment can have deleterious effects upon a child's self-image and his or her ability, later on, to integrate successfully with others.

Children learn in a whole variety of ways, but they certainly learn by imitating the actions of their parents. Children very often take their cue from the ways in which their parents behave. If children witness aggressive behaviour in parents they may well learn to respond to their own experiences in similar fashion.

During their early, impressionable years, children identify with their parents and internalize ways of behaving which they have observed. In this way children are storing up a repertoire of learned patterns of response to external events and they will draw upon this pool of learned responses when they encounter similar events in their own lives. The importance of positive role models for children cannot be over-emphasized when discussing the formation of character. There is an increased chance that children who see others behaving with courage, compassion and tolerance will themselves display such strengths in their natures in the future.

It is likely that a child who experiences a positive parental role model will be guided and encouraged towards appropriate ways of behaving. In other words, it is within the family that children begin to distinguish between right and wrong. They begin to appreciate the consequences which their actions may have not only for themselves but also for others. Therefore children learn, very early on, that their actions have unavoidable consequences.

In the normal course of events, if our behaviour results in some form of penalty or punishment, we learn not to repeat that behaviour if we do not wish to face the same painful consequences again. Parents need to be consistent in disciplining children, who will then be suitably equipped with a set of behavioural guidelines that will stand them in good stead for the future. Parents who ignore bad behaviour and do not signal their disapproval contingent upon the behaviour occurring are doing their child a disservice in the long term.

In their early years children are learning the appropriate social rules and conventions that form part of the customs and traditions of society. Telling the truth, keeping promises, caring for property, tidiness, punctuality, politeness, are only some of the socially acceptable values which children need to learn if they are to fit into the fabric of everyday society. Learning the rules which apply to such aspects of behaviour is essential if children are to progress successfully to the stage when they can question rules critically and determine whether or not such rules are in fact justifiable. Only when children know what is expected of them will they have the confidence to develop their own set of values as their ability for rational thought emerges.

During the early stages of moral development children are not fully capable of rational thought. Kohlberg's (1976) description of moral development includes an outline of stages through which children must pass in our society. In the early stages of moral development children's behaviour is very much *rule governed*. These early stages are characterized by the practice of rules that apply to behaviour if the child is to progress to a more formal understanding of the need for rules and conventions governing behaviour. Children cannot be expected to learn the appropriate ways of behaving if they are not taught, by example, to abide by the relevant basic rules.

If children are not given any clues as to the boundaries of behaviour, they cannot be expected to develop into autonomous moral agents later on (eventually reaching Kohlberg's highest, mature adult, stage of developing and following one's own thought-out ethical principles).

Children need to be trained to deal with society's demands, since as they go outside the home they will find that others react to their behaviour in favourable or unfavourable ways. When children start playgroup or attend nursery schools they are soon reminded that actions have consequences and if they misbehave, if they hit someone, if they throw toys around the room, such actions will have consequences. For example, other children will not want to play with them, adults will reprimand them and parents, wanting their children to be socially accepted, will show disappointment. For most children, then, it is normal to want to be accepted by others. If the home background has been encouraging and supportive, they will begin to conform to the standards imposed by external agencies that now begin to form an important bridge between the children's home life and the wider world.

When the child starts school it is important for the school to build positively upon their early experiences in the home. The home forms an important backdrop to the educational system, but it would be difficult to imagine how society would adequately prepare the young for citizenship without the help of schooling. Schools must not only play their part in transmitting basic skills and fostering pupils' academic and intellectual abilities, they must also contribute to pupils' personal development and behaviour generally.

If we consider the complex social, economic and political structure of our society we can see that young people need to be given help and guidance in school which will prepare them for their future roles. Young people need to be both flexible and adaptable if they are to cope with the rapidly changing technological advances in the twenty-first century. They need the necessary interpersonal skills so that they can relate to others and work co-operatively with them. They need to be able to handle pressure and conflict, make decisions and manage change. They need to be willing to meet the challenges posed by day-to-day problems, whether these are personal and social or work related. They need to be trained to make informed, rational judgements on a whole range of moral and social issues that may affect their own well-being and that of others.

Schools provide the wider arena for developing the necessary skills, knowledge and understanding required by the young in order for them to fit into society as responsible and active citizens. A well-rounded, broad education, which helps young people to prepare for adult life and its experiences, will benefit them immensely in the future.

The school has a great deal to offer in preparing pupils for life in the next century. The Education Reform Act of 1988 reaffirmed the important role of education in developing pupils' full potential. The Act places a statutory responsibility upon schools to provide 'a broad and balanced curriculum' which:

> (a) promotes the spiritual, moral, cultural, mental and physical development of pupils in schools and in society; and
> (b) prepares pupils for the opportunities, responsibilities and experiences of adult life.
>
> (DES, 1989, p. 1)

The Act underlines the importance of an holistic approach to a pupil's develop-ment. This means that due regard must be paid not only to intellectual development but also to personal development generally.

The DES Circular 5/89 reflected some of these concerns and outlined some of the intentions of the school curriculum:

> It is intended that the school curriculum should reflect the culturally diverse society to which pupils belong and of which they will become adult members. It should benefit them as they grow in maturity and help prepare them for adult life and experience – home life and parenthood; responsibilities as a citizen towards the community and society, nationally and internationally; enterprise, employment and other work.
>
> (*ibid.*, p. 7)

It seems clear that young people require a carefully planned curriculum with defined aims relating not only to academic qualifications but also to personal growth and development if they are to adapt to the changing needs of the twenty-first century. The 1992 White Paper talked about new 'imperatives':

> Regular attendance at school and taking advantage of a good education within a strong moral, spiritual and cultural context, are not only essential to becoming well-qualified and to growing up well-balanced, they are also one of the best deterrents against criminality. A good school is a bulwark against pressures, which undermine individual and community values.
>
> (DFE, 1992, p. 6)

The rapid nature of social change requires that institutions such as schools should help young people to navigate a way through the often stormy and tempestuous waters surrounding the adjustment required between values and attitudes learned in the home and the new societal demands resulting from rapid social change. By the time children reach the end of the primary school years the tensions between the generations are apparent as children begin to question their parents' advice. The 'generation gap' is nothing new. Even back in the 1960s, Bob Dylan sang about how times were 'a-changin' and that people's sons and daughters were beyond their command.

However, the generation gap poses a range of complex difficulties for society. Young people even now accuse their parents of talking 'a different language', and this may literally be true as children explain to their parents the implications of the terminology accompanying new technology. If we are to grasp the role of schools in preparing young people for their future participation in society we have to be aware that differences in outlook between one generation and the next will be more marked following periods of rapid social change.

The school has to try to offer young people support as they experience pressures exerted by parents, the peer group, the media and wider society generally. Schools can provide learning experiences which strengthen children's ability to think for themselves and allow them time to think about and discuss important issues relating to their own personal and moral development.

In schools, some of the aspects of personal and moral development can be taught as part of the explicit, formal timetable through the subjects of the National Curriculum and religious education (defined by the 1988 Act as *the basic curriculum*). Children can learn about themselves and their communities through the whole range of subjects offered in the primary school curriculum. In thinking about pupils' personal and moral development a certain degree of planning is necessary across the whole curriculum, both at school and classroom level. Schools can build into their methods of teaching opportunities for pupils to work co-operatively together. Teachers can structure lessons in order for children to be given time to explore their own experience, feelings and emotions. For example, we can try to bring out the best in a child during a drama lesson or ask children to work together on a scientific experiment and praise the ways in which they help one another. In managing the everyday curriculum there is a great deal that can be planned in terms of skills, attitudes and knowledge which helps to promote personal growth.

Personal and social education in primary schools encompasses a range of activities which may be beneficial to a pupil's self-confidence and self-image. These activities can range from anti-bullying strategies to developing a child's self-esteem, from a planned lesson on sex education to group discussions on environmental issues. A certain degree of planning is required in order to include preparation for citizenship skills and the whole range of subjects offered in the primary school should be seen as playing a significant role in the personal and moral education of pupils in school. Aspects of personal, social and moral development can be encouraged by the prevailing code of conduct within the school. In the normal course of events within the primary school, issues relating to personal and moral development will arise spontaneously. An element of spontaneity should pervade all primary classrooms and teachers need to exploit situations that occur in the classroom context.

For example, if children are being unkind, there may be a need to gather them together in order to reinforce an important classroom rule. We have to build in time in order to encourage children to listen to others and help them to manage conflict and negative emotions. All this can have a significant impact upon pupils' self-esteem as well as helping to promote productive classroom relationships. If we are to be successful in teaching children anything we have to consider pupils' well-being at all times and uphold as best we can the quality of the context in which their learning experiences take place.

Jenny Mosley's (1994) work has been very influential as a means of enhancing children's self-esteem and enabling them to begin to achieve their potential in all aspects of development. In her book, she describes a circle-time approach to the development of self-esteem and positive behaviour in the classroom. Regular circle-time can help to promote understanding, improve listening skills, solve problems, share ideas, build friendships, develop empathy and personal integrity and promote better behaviour within the classroom and school generally. In this way the learning opportunities provided by the school can be viewed as useful staging posts in alerting the young to various exigencies in life which they may well face in the future. In recognition of this, schools need to have a firm moral framework in order to guide young people into the future.

Nagel (1990) has argued that there can be 'no just democracy without a deeply ingrained moral culture' that 'leads us to impose upon ourselves limits to the pursuit of our own interest, limits we believe everyone ought to observe' (p. 169). In other words, we want pupils to leave school with an acceptable set of personal qualities that will help to enrich any public domain in which they may operate. Our educational system must continue to reflect a strong moral dimension in its promotion of good, active, participative citizens.

Ofsted (1994) states that, with regard to certain issues, 'it is right to stand up and be counted'. An NCC (1993) discussion paper argues as follows:

> Children need to be introduced from an early age to concepts of right and wrong so that moral behaviour becomes an instinctive habit. ... Personal morality combines the beliefs and values of individuals, those of the social, cultural and religious groups to which they belong, and the laws and customs of the wider society. Schools should be expected to uphold those values that contain moral absolutes.

The document goes on:

> School values should include:
> - telling the truth;
> - keeping promises;
> - respecting the rights and property of others;
> - acting considerately towards others;
> - helping those less fortunate and weaker than ourselves;
> - taking personal responsibility for one's actions;
> - self-discipline.
>
> School values should reject:
> - bullying;
> - cheating;
> - deceit;
> - cruelty;
> - irresponsibility;
> - dishonesty.

(p. 4)

In the Ofsted (1994) paper, it was stated that:

> If teachers do not take a clear and consistent stand on questions of morality schools can lack the necessary strengths of a strong ethos and tone, with damaging effects.
>
> (pp. 11–12)

At this point it is only fair to say that schools should not be held responsible for all of society's ills. As Bernstein once wrote, 'Education cannot compensate for society.' However, it is important for us to recognize the key role which schools play in promoting society's welfare. They need to build a positive school atmosphere in which pupils know what is expected of them and learn to recognize the boundaries which demarcate acceptable from unacceptable standards of behaviour.

Good schools have been very effective in transmitting appropriate codes of conduct and Ofsted (1995) makes it very clear that schools should have a 'code of practice' based on 'personal qualities founded on a moral code'.

When an Ofsted Inspection takes place in a school, the Inspectors are required to report on:

> The quality of the education provided by the school;
> the educational standards achieved in the school;
> whether the financial resources made available to the school are managed efficiently;
> and the spiritual, moral, social and cultural development of pupils at the school.
>
> (Ofsted, 1995)

Inspectors' reports contain information about the attitudes, behaviour and personal development of pupils at the school and judgements are based on the extent to which pupils, for example, 'show respect for other people's feelings, values and beliefs' and 'show initiative and are willing to take responsibility'. In relation to the spiritual, moral, social and cultural development of pupils, the school will be judged in relation to a number of areas, including the extent to which it 'teaches the principles which distinguish right from wrong' and the ways in which it 'encourages pupils to relate positively to others, take responsibility, participate fully in the community, and develop an understanding of citizenship' ('Guidance on the inspection of nursery and primary schools', in Ofsted, 1995).

During an inspection, the organization of the curriculum together with the general life of the school comes under close scrutiny. The effectiveness of a school's curriculum will be judged by the ways in which all the various elements interact – from the basic curriculum through to other elements such as the aims, attitudes, values and procedures which contribute to the school's overall ethos. Evidence will be collected from the whole curriculum and the day-to-day life of the school, including the examples set by adults. All this will influence the inspectors' report concerning the personal and moral development of pupils at the school.

The debate about values and the curriculum of schools is continuing. Dr Nick Tate, Chief Executive of SCAA, set up a National Forum for Values in Education and the Community in 1996. The Forum was set up to make recommendations on:

> ways in which schools might be supported in making their contribution to pupils' spiritual, moral, social and cultural development;
> to what extent there is any agreement on the values, attitudes and behaviour that schools should promote on society's behalf.
> (SCAA, 1996, p. 1)

The SCAA document 'recognizes that schools already do much good work in this area' and also realizes 'that schools cannot achieve changes in social behaviour on their own'. As we discussed earlier, education cannot compensate for all the ills within society and the SCAA document suggests that 'the initiative is a way of gaining wider social acceptance of shared values to which all can subscribe'.

The forum drafted several value statements relating to ways in which we might understand our own responsibilities to society as future citizens, the ways in which we ought to relate to others and the value we should place upon the environment generally. The value statements produced provide an invaluable reference point for consultation. It is intended that the document will seek responses from 'the general public, leading national organizations, parents, governors, and a large sample of schools'.

The Forum on Values indicated clearly that schools do not operate in a moral vacuum. They are not 'value-free zones'. Schools need the help and support of all sections of society if they are to produce effective citizens. The SCAA document stresses the importance of the close working relationship between school and the wider community if there is to be an effective partnership between schools and parents in educating pupils for personal and moral growth.

Parents can and do offer their support to schools in many ways. The governing bodies of schools have parent representatives who can support the school and tell other parents about the ways in which the school wishes to move forward. Parent governors have a say in helping schools to uphold their discipline code and it is important for other parents to know that they are responsible for ensuring the good behaviour of their child while he or she is at school. Most parents are very supportive of the school. However, the idea of a written 'contract' between parents and school which has been floated recently is a useful one, since the idea of a contract upholds the right of teachers to teach and reinforces the legal requirement that children attend school primarily to learn.

Schools which involve parents in setting out the boundaries of acceptable behaviour within a clearly defined framework appear to gain the respect of parents and the wider community. Children need a secure, clearly defined structure in which they can operate. While at school, children will test the territory in order to find out where the boundaries lie. If children are not able to discover where the boundaries lie they will keep on testing. There is a need for a clearly defined Code of Practice which the school, the parents and the governors can agree upon and which will provide a moral basis underpinning the work of the school as a whole. Pupils, given a firm structure, can begin to develop their potential and prepare for life within the wider society.

A booklet produced by Highfield Junior School in Plymouth in 1997 provides an excellent example of the ways in which a school set about promoting a positive school ethos. The booklet represents a useful case study of a school which decided to change its practices, and work together to establish a clearer framework that suited all those involved in the life of the school community. The Chair of the School Governors wrote:

> This is a story of a school whose life has been one of considerable change. It is the story of a process, which is worthy of inclusion in any training programme where people are gathered to explore their full potential to be mature and responsible citizens.
>
> (Highfield Junior School, 1997, p. 6)

The story suggests that change can be effected within a school given the collective will and perseverance of those involved. Certainly the school endeavoured to reach its own consensus of shared values such that the resulting code of practice was suitable for the school and realistic in terms of the demands such a code imposed upon all staff, pupils and the wider community. The school stresses the fact that it tries 'to make moral development a two-way home/school experience' (p. 72).

Highfield School decided to change for a number of reasons. This is how they say it all began:

> Once there was a school with lots of problems.
> There were fights and rows.
> Some people broke things, they messed about in class,
> and did not listen to the teachers.
>
> School was not always a happy place to be.
> Sometimes we did not feel safe.
> This book is about how we changed our school.
> Everyone had to help, not just the few people at the top.
> We could only succeed by working together.

The school started to use assertive discipline techniques. They also used circle-time throughout the school. Circle-time was used to enhance self-esteem, consider rules, rewards and sanctions, sort out problems, change behaviour and talk with parents. The school also has a School Council. This meets and uses a whole school circle-time in order to discuss not only successes but also needs, problems and issues relating to responsibility. Many schools are using circle-time but Highfield describes, in useful detail, how it can be used with a whole range of other methods in order to promote a positive school atmosphere in which pupils are learning the rules of morality and good citizenship in a safe and secure context.

Change does not occur overnight. Highfield tells us how they have tried to manage change over the past five years. The work has not always been easy but the book suggests that the efforts have been very rewarding and certainly worthwhile for all concerned. By adopting a whole school approach and involving everyone in the school, they describe a developing ethos which provides children with a safe, secure and caring learning environment in which they will thrive.

The following is an extract from the school's policy statement on spiritual and moral developments, in which the school indicates the ways in which it hopes to develop its pupils as responsible citizens:

> The aim of Highfield Junior School is to encourage the development of pupils as honest, informed and honourable citizens. It therefore promotes healthy spiritual and moral development:
>
> - through its curriculum
>
> - its ethos of care and respect for others
>
> - its firm, fair, negotiated ground rules for behaviour
>
> - its democratic shared approach to school management
>
> - its shared vision of raising standards of self esteem, self awareness and achievement
>
> - and its sensitivity to both the long term and sporadic needs of the individual.
>
> (Highfield Junior School, 1997, p. 72)

The management of schools is a difficult task, particularly as we move into the twenty-first century. However, there is a great deal about which we should feel proud when we see the heroic efforts of schools to promote the effective learning of all pupils in their care. The role of parents in nurturing young children before and during their time at school is also a vital part of the educative process. The mutual benefits of a 'two-way home/school experience' for the moral development of the young cannot be over-emphasized. If we accept that young people will challenge their parents' generation, this does not have to lead to the rejection by the young of all the values which society regards as important. Parents and schools should reaffirm for young people the shared values of society. In working together, the home and the school can provide a healthy territory in which children can test the boundaries of behaviour so that when they leave school they will have the confidence and the necessary survival strategies to become responsible citizens of the twenty-first century.

## REFERENCES

DES (1989) *The Education Reform Act 1988: The School Curriculum and Assessment* (Circular 5/89). London: HMSO.

DFE (1992) *Choice and Diversity: A New Framework for Schools*. London: HMSO.

Highfield Junior School (1997) *Changing Our School: Promoting Positive Behaviour*. Plymouth: Highfield Junior School/London University Institute of Education.

Kohlberg, L.S. (1976) Moral stages and moralization: the cognitive-developmental approach. In T. Lickona (ed.) *Moral Development and Behavior: Theory, Research and Social Issues*. New York: Holt, Rinehart & Winston.

Mosley, J. (1994) *Turn Your School Around*. Cambridge: LDA.

Nagel, T. (1990) Freedom within bounds. *Times Literary Supplement*, 16 February, p. 169.

National Curriculum Council (NCC) (1993) *Spiritual and Moral Development – A Discussion Paper*. London: NCC.

Ofsted (1994) *Spiritual, Moral, Social and Cultural Development: An Ofsted Discussion Paper*. London: Ofsted.

Ofsted (1995) *Framework for the Inspection of Schools*. London: HMSO.

SCAA (1996) *National Forum for Values in Education: Consultation on Values in Education and the Community*. London: SCAA.

Straughan, R. (1988, new edn) *Can we Teach Children to be Good?* Milton Keynes: Open University Press.

## SOME SUGGESTIONS FOR FURTHER READING

The Highfield Junior School (1997) booklet and the book by Straughan (1988), both listed above, provide useful further reading.

# CHAPTER 13

# Teaching the foundation subjects – geography and history

ALISON RYAN AND JOAN JONES

## INTRODUCTION

As former primary teachers we are well aware of the pressures on teachers to plan for English, maths and science in detail and then see what time is left over for the foundation subjects. The National Curriculum, however, aims to satisfy the entitlement of all children to a broad, balanced and relevant curriculum. It is our belief that the foundation subjects have distinctive contributions to make to children's learning. They should be valued and planned for as rigorously as the core subjects. In this chapter we will outline briefly how the foundation subjects might be incorporated into school curriculum planning. However, it is beyond the scope of this book to examine in detail the teaching of every school subject. So, having devoted a chapter each to the three core subjects, we propose now to focus on just two of the foundation subjects in this chapter: geography and history.

Although every subject has its own knowledge base, and each demands different skills and understandings, we nevertheless feel that there is a common thread running through all of them. This includes, for example, the teacher's preparation and approach and his or her decisions about whether to integrate subjects in a topic or to deliver them separately. Thus many of the issues discussed in this chapter are relevant to the teaching of any school subject. Our focus will be on our respective interests in history and geography, where we will detail their essential features at primary level, provide examples of good practice and suggest how they can contribute to children's learning in the twenty-first century.

## AN INTEGRATED OR A SUBJECT-BASED CURRICULUM?

As a student or recently qualified teacher, you may encounter a bewildering variety of curriculum planning methods as schools attempt to combine their own aims and priorities with effective coverage of the National Curriculum. A school should be able to provide broad guidelines on what aspects of subjects and themes should be taught and when, in order that it can provide for balance, continuity and progression as well as coverage of the National Curriculum. However, you will need to use your professional judgement, especially outside the core subjects, to decide on the amount of depth given to each subject and the most effective way of teaching it.

In order to meet the demands of the National Curriculum, there has been a move towards more subject-focused teaching. The foundation subjects can be taught as single subjects, as is often the case with PE and music. However, the curriculum does not have to be delivered in subject packages, an approach that might appear to give priority to the acquisition of knowledge rather than to the processes of learning. Subjects can also be incorporated into topic work, which may have a single- or multi-subject focus.

Topic work in its various guises has attracted considerable criticism. It is claimed, for example, that it can be undemanding and lack progression and that subjects lose their identity and characteristics within it. Those in favour of topic work would argue that a well-planned, carefully structured, integrated approach reflects the holistic way in which children view the world and allows them to construct their own meanings.

There does appear to be a move towards designing topics which are more focused on a single subject and it is important that these have a central and easily identifiable core rather than vague or contrived links with a large number of curriculum areas. There are, however, sound reasons for linking a limited number of subjects or other aspects of the curriculum in certain circumstances.

Common or complementary knowledge, understanding and skills would link, for example, work on weather in science and geography. Skills in one area could be applied in another; for example, the use of co-ordinates in maths and grid references in geography. Work in one subject could provide a stimulus for work in another; for instance, painting in response to listening to a piece of music.

In our experience, the most effective curriculum is one that is flexibly managed and combines teaching both through separate subjects and through topics, exploiting the advantages of both approaches. Whichever approach you take, you need to plan rigorously – clearly identify a subject's basic concepts and skills and incorporate these into activities. You should also ensure that children are able to progress from one level of knowledge, understanding and skill in a subject to the next.

Most class teachers are expected to cover the entire curriculum with equal confidence and effectiveness – a challenging task! The introduction of the National Curriculum has made heavy demands on subject knowledge and there is a growing body of evidence to suggest that a teacher's subject knowledge and understanding are directly related to the quality of the children's learning. For a beginning teacher, curriculum co-ordinators are a useful source of information as to appropriate content, teaching approaches and available resources.

Exchanging classes with a colleague is an effective way of using staff expertise. For example, if your interest lies in history, you could undertake to teach it across a year group. A musically proficient colleague could do likewise. The workload is lightened and the children benefit from the confidence and enthusiasm of knowledgeable teachers.

## APPROACHES TO TEACHING AND LEARNING GEOGRAPHY AND HISTORY

We believe that good teaching in both geography and history is characterized by clear, detailed planning, well-focused learning objectives, thorough preparation and sound subject knowledge. By using a range of teaching approaches and providing a variety of learning experiences, you can also present geography and history as interesting and exciting subjects. You might begin by reading a story, watching a video or asking children to use maps or documentary evidence. Children should be encouraged to ask and answer questions in groups as well as individually, and to respond in a variety of ways, such as through role-play, discussion, using ICT and making models, as well as more conventional graphical and written presentations.

As an extension of their classwork, children must undertake fieldwork; that is, active learning outside the classroom, which includes investigating their school and its grounds. Visits further afield, say to a museum or river, are also usually essential. These are demanding in terms of cost and organization, so it is important to make a thorough assessment of the local area's potential for teaching and learning geography and history. Any fieldwork needs to have clear learning objectives, of which the children are aware, and you must clearly identify any potential hazards.

## PRIMARY GEOGRAPHY

### What is primary geography?

Primary geography involves studying real places, the people who live there and how they are influenced by and affect their environment. Through geography, children are introduced to knowledge, skills and concepts specific to the subject, but it also makes a more general contribution to their learning by helping them to:

- develop a sense of place and to understand how they fit into the wider world

- understand more about the environment and the issues which affect it

- understand and appreciate different cultures and lifestyles.

## Planning

You can teach geography as a single subject focused on a place, such as a village in India or on a theme, like rivers. It can also be taught in conjunction with other subjects in an integrated topic, such as transport, although Ofsted Inspectors have noted that it rarely flourishes unless it is the subject receiving most attention. There are three elements of geography that need to be taught. These are often combined in what is called the geographical cube (see Figure 13.1).

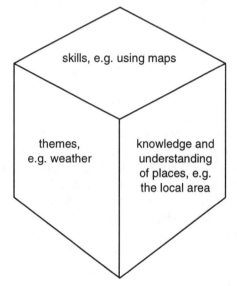

**Figure 13.1** The geographical cube

This means that geographical investigations should feature all three elements. You should normally avoid teaching geographical skills such as drawing plans and using an atlas separately, as these should help to develop children's understanding about places and themes. Skills and themes should be taught by reference to real places. For example, a unit of work on rivers (rivers theme) might involve fieldwork and mapwork (skills) while investigating a local river and a European river (places) and perhaps finding out about measures being taken to improve water quality (environmental change theme). You need to include the human element in any theme:

How does the climate affect people's way of life in this village?

How do people use that river?

It is also important that you recognize continuing opportunities to develop children's geographical understanding by referring to events in the news, discussing family links and holidays and using literature with a geographical setting, such as Mairi Hedderwick's Katie Morag stories. Above all, you need to remember that all children come to school with some geographical knowledge – from experiencing different kinds of weather to going to the local shops – which can be built upon. By drawing on their local knowledge and looking at topical issues, you can make geography interesting and relevant.

## Enquiry

Geographical work should involve children in enquiry; that is, asking and responding to questions. There are seven key questions that should be used to structure geographical investigations in order to build up a framework of knowledge and help children to understand geographical concepts.

> Where is it?
>
> What's it like?
>
> Why is it like it is?
>
> How is it connected to other places?
>
> How is it changing?
>
> What would it feel like to be in this place?
>
> How is this place similar to/different from another place?

Initially, you will be asking the questions. However, as the children become more experienced in using key questions, they will be able to work more independently and devise their own questions. Enquiries can last for a single lesson or may involve several weeks' work. 'How can we improve our school grounds?' 'Where would be the best site for a new zebra crossing?' 'How are visitors to this beauty spot affecting it?' All these are examples of extended enquiries that will involve children in asking relevant questions, finding and recording appropriate information, presenting it and reviewing their findings. As children are involved in their own learning and the focus is local and relevant to them, this way of working is invariably highly motivating and successful. The case study at the end of this section demonstrates the enquiry process in action.

## Knowledge, skills and understanding

In terms of teaching and learning about places, the emphasis should be on small localities, and, especially at KS 1, the local area, rather than a superficial view of a whole country. By choosing contrasting localities of a similar size, the areas can be studied in depth and comparisons made. It is important to put places into context. For example, an enquiry into a village in India should include locating it within the country, seeing how it is connected to other places and also looking at life in a city. Children do not learn about places in a concentric way and, as they move through KS 2, they should be investigating a range of places and themes at a variety of scales from local to global. Some schools choose to bring a European dimension to their curriculum through cross-curricular work as well as studying specific localities in geography. Through their investigations, children should be acquiring the idea of a 'sense of place' that is, what physical features, such as the weather and the natural landscape, and human features, like buildings and transport, make a place distinctive. You should also be encouraging them to look for patterns – how are the streets arranged in this town? And to identify processes – why is the course of that river changing?

It is important that you plan activities which develop children's geographical skills, particularly mapwork, as they learn about places and themes. You need to appreciate that understanding maps is a complex process involving many elements, such as: Where? How big? How shall I show it? Which way round? – all of which require practice. Some of these skills, such as planning a journey and following a map, will be invaluable later in life.

However, geography also involves cross-curricular skills, from making models to using reference books, and you will find it an invaluable subject for reinforcing literacy, numeracy and ICT skills. You will be introducing children to a wide range of vocabulary as well as developing language skills through, for example, role-play and reading about other places. Undertaking investigations such as traffic surveys and reporting the weather will involve them in recording and analysing data. Geography also provides numerous opportunities for children to use ICT: the World Wide Web (WWW) for information; mapping packages and databases; weather loggers and environmental sensors. You can also make children aware of the impact of ICT on daily life, by looking at its role in areas such as traffic control and weather forecasting.

As well as learning skills and acquiring knowledge, geography also provides the ideal opportunity for children to begin to look at issues and appreciate people's differing attitudes and values. At local level, this may involve investigating proposals for developing the park. On a global level, this could be some of the issues surrounding deforestation.

Through this work, children should be developing informed concern about the quality of the environment and a sense of responsibility for it. It is, of course, vital that you present a balanced picture, so that children have a sound basis for examining their own and others' values and that you handle issues sensitively, especially if they have a direct impact on the children's lives. Studies of other localities will also give you the opportunity to challenge children's stereotypes and preconceptions about people and places. Does everyone in Africa live in mud huts? Are they all starving? The image of the Eskimo and his (sic) igloo also remains a powerful one!

## Resources

Geography teachers need a wide range of up-to-date resources. Some resources are essential, such as a globe, reference books, aerial photographs and a selection of maps (perhaps of the London Underground and a local shopping centre, as well as Ordnance Survey maps) at a variety of scales. It is well worth taking a set of photographs of human and physical features of the local area, and many schools have aerial photographs of the school and its immediate locality. For investigating other localities, good quality photographs are essential, showing a variety of people (especially children and ideally named), lifestyles and environments. It is important that these are supported with as much material as possible – maps, videos, artefacts, etc.

The resources available often restrict the choice of localities studied. You could overcome this by compiling your own 'locality pack' while on holiday, including photographs, maps, timetables, brochures from estate agents, local newspapers, samples of local rocks and so on. Links can also be made with schools in other localities using e-mail or the WWW. As a beginning teacher, it is tempting to use published schemes and photocopiable worksheets, but these should be used with discretion: they can be useful as a source of ideas and information, but are not tailored to your school's locality and rarely provide for differentiation.

In the following case study, geography provides the central core to a topic on shopping. The work was undertaken over half a term by Year 2s at Norfolk Primary School in Sheffield, although it would work equally well with other age groups.

## What shall we put on that empty site?

The topic began with a general discussion on shops: What is a shop? Why do we need shops? Where do we find shops? Are there different kinds of shops? The children then began work focused on a local parade of shops and used a large-scale plan and aerial photographs to identify its location. They worked out different routes to the shops using a computer-mapping package and tested these out on each other. Their initial fieldwork involved following a map to the shops, looking at the different use of land and buildings in the area, completing a plan (for which they had previously designed symbols), sketching, taking photographs and considering the environmental quality of the area in terms of, for example, smells and sounds. Back in the classroom, the children matched photographs of the shops to a plan of the site, wrote descriptions of individual shops and expressed their likes and dislikes of the parade (litter, pollution from traffic, bright displays, etc.). A link was made with history when children used photographs of the shops in the past for tasks involving sequencing and making comparisons.

The children had noticed a 'To Let' sign: What should go there? What's missing? How shall we find out? They compiled a questionnaire for parents and children and produced graphs of the results. As the most popular choice was a café, the children went to a modern shopping centre where they looked at environmental quality and investigated features such as design, people's jobs and the use of ICT in three different cafés. They returned to school full of ideas for their café and suggestions for improving the local shops.

The focus changed to technology, as designs for the café, uniforms and promotional material were drawn up. A classroom café gave opportunities for practical activities involving measuring and handling money. Numerous other questions – Where do goods in shops come from? How do they get there? Where do the shoppers come from? – could have been raised to extend the topic.

In this case, the children used a variety of skills to investigate economic activity and environmental quality in the local area. They were well motivated through the use of different teaching and learning approaches to a relevant, locally based enquiry and achieved work of a high quality.

## PRIMARY HISTORY

### The nature of history

The nature of history has exercised the minds of professional historians for centuries and that debate continues. In essence it is the study of the human past. It is about people – individuals and real people – who lived in a variety of situations in different times and in different places. It is about their ideas, beliefs, aspirations, feelings, reactions, decisions and skills. It is about what they said, wrote, built, made, discovered and destroyed. It is about how they lived and died. Besides the special contribution that history makes to the primary curriculum in the areas of knowledge, concepts, skills and values, it shares with other subjects a number of general contributions to the curriculum.

### The aims of history in the primary school

The aims of history in the primary school are many and varied and fully justify the place of the subject in the primary curriculum. The following list offers a selection compiled from various DES/DfEE documents published in the last ten years. The history curriculum in the primary years should be designed to:

- contribute to pupils' knowledge and understanding of the past through a concentric approach from their own families' past, or that of their locality, to a study of world perspectives

- develop an understanding of chronology within which children can organize their understanding of the past

- show children the nature of primary historical evidence and develop a range of skills required to interpret that evidence

- explain to children that events have usually many causes and that explanation is provisional, always debatable and sometimes controversial

- contribute towards developing certain attitudes and values; for example, a respect for evidence and tolerance of a range of opinions

- develop an awareness of cultural diversity, traditions and heritage.

History also acts as a vehicle for other areas of the curriculum. Many of the skills listed above are vital to the study of history, but are also generic skills vital to life in general. We all need to examine the reliability of statistics, detect bias in written prose, distinguish between fact and opinion and ask relevant questions.

## The National Curriculum

Prior to August 1991, when the first statutory orders for history came into force (initially in respect of pupils in the first year of KS 1, 2 and 3), there had been fierce debate over the content and delivery of history. At one end of the spectrum were those who advocated a 'traditional' approach where the acquisition of facts and knowledge was deemed to be of greatest importance. At the other extreme were those who believed that children ought to be primarily developing their skills of historical enquiry. The compromise, modified in 1995, is embraced in the current programmes of study for history. These are divided into two sections: areas of study/study units (the content), and key elements (the skills and concepts).

Details about the content of each study unit are given in KS 1 and 2 of the National Curriculum (DfEE, 1995). The choice about when to study each unit remains with the school. Similarly there is freedom for the school to decide how to deliver the subject material. When policy statements and long-term plans are being devised, a school is also at liberty to decide on whether to deliver its curriculum in subject areas or to integrate in a topic.

There are five key elements in KS 1 and 2. These need to be developed through the areas of study/study units although not all key elements need to be developed in each history theme.

The key elements are concerned with:

- chronology, the understanding of time – an appreciation of time develops slowly in children and is liable to remain rudimentary unless a coherent approach is adopted

- the range and depth of historical knowledge and understanding, in which children study characteristic features of particular periods, look for continuity and change and reasons for any change

- the interpretations of history, where pupils look at how the past is represented

- historical enquiry, in which evidence is examined

- organization and communication, where children learn how to recall, select and organize information and communicate their historical understanding.

## The raw material of history: evidence

The historian uses primary evidence, the traces and clues left behind by people in the past. These sources, often incomplete, are examined and analysed in an attempt to piece together the 'jigsaw of life'. There should be opportunities for pupils to be made aware that as evidence is re-examined hypotheses may need revising. Primary sources come in many forms: artefacts, photographs, buildings, oral recollections, memorials, school log-books, census data – even contemporary songs. The use of real evidence brings history to life.

### *Artefacts*

Visible, tangible sources are excellent to use with primary-aged children. Examining artefacts (objects made by someone) is a form of active learning and can really make children think. By using objects, children can learn to observe carefully, describe precisely, draw for recording (by adding labels, scale, measurements, etc.), ask relevant questions, classify, use fragments and formulate and test hypotheses. Artefacts can be borrowed from some museums for classroom use and children can be taken to museums for 'handling sessions'. Many parents will lend family items (but stress care when handling family treasures and discuss the sentimental value of objects, as well as their monetary value). Begin your own collection – raid your grandparents' kitchen cupboards and visit a car boot sale. Limited to a period in time, artefacts may begin to give a feel for a past period.

### *The importance of visual evidence*

Using photographs with children is equally stimulating. Armed with a magnifying lens, a child can adopt the role of Sherlock Holmes examining evidence. Set the children the task of describing, noting details and looking for change. If the photograph is of someone known to you or the children, or if they know the area, this adds a special element.

When studying more recent history, local film or video material may be available to view. The use of portraits and paintings can develop in children the skill of interpreting what the sitter was trying to reveal about themselves. The clothing being worn and the pose and expression may be an attempt to look wealthy, threatening or powerful. The inclusion of the sitter's family, house and garden may be a further statement of their perceived success. Incorporating the family coat-of-arms or crest was a ploy to announce aristocratic membership. Encourage children to consider the reliability of portraits as evidence. Wouldn't artists seeking to earn favour and perhaps further commissions conceal deformity or accentuate a fashionable trait? Ideally, visit the National Portrait Gallery to view the originals, but transparencies, A4 laminated copies and postcards are easily available for classroom use.

Gravestones and memorials can give a useful insight into past times. Inscriptions may give details about a person's life (and death) and effigies indicate the fashions of the day and perhaps the status of the deceased, from the jewellery, armour or chains of office being worn. Gravestones and memorials may tell of disasters, victories or a life dedicated to the service of the community, and might encourage the onlooker to search for supplementary evidence to paint a fuller picture.

## Site visits

The use of buildings and sites is a requirement of the National Curriculum. Nothing can rival the tranquillity created by sitting among the ruins of an abbey, gazing from the top of a keep in a Norman castle, marvelling at the skill of the medieval stone mason in a church, or absorbing the atmosphere in a timber-framed manor house. It is interesting to plan story-telling sessions in the grounds or building about an episode or person connected to the site. A large number of places encourage role-play or participation in episodes where the children dress up in period costume and take on the role of an occupant, performing activities from that time. Memorable occasions spring to mind but any re-enactment needs to be based on evidence and not merely flights of imagination.

Encourage pupils to search for clues about past use, changes, signs of damage or details of decoration. They should be encouraged to record using observational drawings with captions or labels, to tape thoughts on to cassette, make notes or take photographs. Visiting the remains of a Roman villa can introduce children to the work of an archaeologist and allow them to appreciate the need for meticulous recording of finds when attempting to interpret a site.

### Oral history

Children also need to be aware that people are primary sources. A visitor could be invited into school to talk about their younger days. The visitor would need to be briefed about the aims of the lesson and how long to speak. It is useful if children have thought about any questions they want to ask before the visit. Taped interviews are also very useful and can be edited if necessary. Questionnaires to gather information about the past from family or friends can be devised for children to take home, accompanied by an explanatory letter. Since memories are not always totally reliable, the use of oral recollections can be an introduction for children to consider bias, perspective, reliability and the need to use more than one source.

## Written sources

Written sources offer a wealth of information and range from personal letters to government reports, from the Greek alphabet and fifteenth-century inventories to a 1980 diary. Government records (Parliamentary papers, Acts of Parliament, reports of government commissions, census data and maps) and local records (parish registers, school log-books, street and place names, trade directories) used selectively and with imagination can provide exciting, meaningful sessions. Nineteenth-century government commissions on child labour give an insight into the hardships suffered by named individuals and are guaranteed to capture the imagination of children. There is evidence from every part of the country, from agricultural labourers and chimney-sweeps to cocklers in Morecambe Bay and brick-makers. Similarly, using evidence from school log-books about the lessons taught in Victorian schools, the reasons why children were absent, how and why they were punished and what they regarded as treats, is an excellent preparation before embarking on a living history exercise, where children re-enact a morning in a way similar to Victorian times. Dressed in suitable attire, the children can chant numbers and tables, attempt dictation on their slates, practise copperplate writing with dip pens and ink, sing 'All Things Bright and Beautiful' for the Inspector, while keeping an eye on the dunce's cap and cane! Newspaper accounts can provide useful evidence, but children should be encouraged to check details (errors have been known to occur!). Contemporary literature and music are also worth considering.

Selective use of secondary sources (the books, films, songs and stories of the past written or made after the time they describe) ought not to be overlooked and can add yet another dimension to history teaching. There are some excellent broadcasts produced for children in primary schools, with useful teachers' notes and resources, for example, BBC's *Landmarks, Zig-Zag* and *Watch* programmes and Channel 4's *Eureka* and *How we Used to Live* series.

Similarly, some very good materials have been produced recently, such as children's texts, teachers' resource ideas, packs of photographs, tapes, facsimile documents and software. Using historical fiction can be recommended, especially if the story is well researched and makes use of historical detail. Books such as those by Theresa Tomlinson, Jane Hissey, Martin Waddell and Rosemary Sutcliff can make a real contribution to the teaching of history.

**Table 13.1** Example of a plan for a study unit

STUDY UNIT 3a: VICTORIAN BRITAIN                                    Class Year 4
Sub-theme: The lives of people at different levels of society in town and country (at work)

Learning intention 1:
Children will gain knowledge and understanding of factory life in the Victorian period by using primary evidence (Key Element 4a)

| Evidence | Activity |
| --- | --- |
| • Children examine an advertisement placed in the *Derby Mercury* by Messrs Arkwright and Co for men, women and children to work in their cotton mill  **Newspaper evidence** | • Children in pairs read and discuss advert:<br>What jobs might the men have?<br>What jobs might the women have?<br>What jobs might the children have?<br>How can we find out more? |
| • Children then examine evidence from the *Report on the Select Committee on Factory Children's Labour (1831–32)* to find out about factory life, in particular child labour  **Documentary evidence** | • Children working individually using a handout with selected extracts from the Report empathize and write 'A Day in the Life of . . .' (key elements 5a and 5c are being addressed) |
| • Children visit Styal Mill, Cheshire  **Built environment** | • Children complete questionnaire |
| • Re-cap on visit, note observations/ feelings, watch *How we Used to Live, The Victorians Programme 4: Fatal Mixture* in which a family moves to town to find factory work and lodgings  **Secondary evidence** | • Children design and make a leaflet for visitors to Styal Mill describing the evidence to be found there and conditions for the labourers |

Learning intention 2:
Children will learn about Lord Shaftesbury and the need for factory reform. They will come to realize the range of values and attitudes of various members of Victorian society (Key Element 2a)

| | |
| --- | --- |
| • In groups, children will note the views of different individuals (Lord Shaftesbury, millowners, parents, children) using selected extracts from the Select Committee Report  **Documentary evidence** | • A representative from each group will argue the case for the various individuals studied. The teacher will act as scribe noting the views for and against reform and will inform class of the reforms that were implemented and their impact (key elements 2a and 2b) |

Having been told a story of a historical event, children can be asked to consider why people did things, why events happened and the results of those events. Children need to be aware that in past times people had different values and beliefs from people today. Eyewitness accounts and fictional stories set in the past are useful for getting children to imagine others' perspectives.

## Good practice in history

In summary, good practice hinges around good planning. Lessons need to provide challenge and to build on pupils' existing capabilities and experiences. The use of primary historical sources is essential. Teachers need to interweave content, concepts and skills and to provide balance between them. The acquisition of facts and historical detail is important – many children enjoy learning dates and devouring information. Of equal importance are the concepts and skills (the key elements) associated with the study of the human past. Across the key stages history needs to be viewed from a variety of perspectives – political, economic, technological and scientific, social, religious, cultural and aesthetic. The delivery needs to be varied. Table 13.1 shows how content, concepts and skills acquisition might be incorporated.

## REFERENCE

DfEE (1995) *Key Stages 1 and 2 of the National Curriculum*. London: HMSO.

## SOME SUGGESTIONS FOR FURTHER READING

Foley, M. and Janikoun, J. (1996) *The Really Practical Guide to Primary Geography*. Cheltenham: Stanley Thornes.
Pluckrose, H. (1991) *Children Learning History*. Oxford: Blackwell.
Weigand, P. (1993) *Children and Primary Geography*. London: Cassell.
Wright, M. (1992) *The Really Practical Guide to Primary History*. Cheltenham: Stanley Thornes.

# PART 4

# Relationships in school and with the community

# CHAPTER 14

# A code in the head: special educational needs in the mainstream classroom

JOHN STIRTON AND CHRIS GLOVER

The whole area of special educational needs has changed dramatically over the last few years. Moves towards the inclusion of children with a range of difficulties have meant that most mainstream classes are likely to have a number of children with a diversity of needs.

Such changes were prefigured in the Warnock Report (DES, 1978). This key document proposed the abolition of the statutory categories of handicap and introduced the notion of special educational needs. Such needs were seen to exist on a continuum and this thinking led the committee chaired by Mary Warnock to estimate that up to one-fifth of children would have special needs at some time in their school careers. Of this 20 per cent, 2 per cent were traditionally catered for within special education. The remaining 18 per cent have always been and continue to be in mainstream schools. Thus, the vast majority of these children will be found where they have always been – in mainstream classes.

A number of recommendations from the Warnock Report were given legal status in the 1981 Education Act. This legislation was seen as enabling local education authorities to develop provision appropriate to the needs of the children in their schools. It took from Warnock the basic underlying concept of the 'statement' of special educational needs. A statement emerging from a multi-disciplinary assessment and cognizant of parental views outlined the child's needs and specified how these needs would be met. Statements were to be reviewed at least annually and all statemented children would be reassessed before leaving secondary school, so that appropriate decisions might be made about their future.

The adoption of the procedures devolving from the 1981 legislation was both dramatic and far-reaching. The structure of special education in many authorities altered significantly. Further changes within the area of special educational needs accrued as a result of the 1988 Education Reform Act. This legislation reinforced the notion of the inclusion of children with special educational needs by stressing their curriculum entitlement. Children with special educational needs were to follow the National Curriculum unless specifically exempted from aspects of it within the provisions of their statement. Thus, by the early 1990s, children with special educational needs were increasingly being taught alongside other, more able children and increasingly following the same programmes of study. It is worth stressing at this juncture that this degree of integration would have been very uncommon fifteen years earlier.

Change in special needs was to continue as the 1990s progressed. This change was born of a perception that the 1981 legislation was not working as it should have been. Concern was widespread as to the time it was taking to raise statements and such concern was amplified by the difference in the time taken between different local education authorities. A statement that took one authority six months to raise could take a neighbouring authority some fifteen months to complete. Not least among those expressing concern was Lady Warnock herself, who came to feel that the legislation she had influenced was, in practice, tending to ignore the needs of 18 per cent of children in mainstream schools.

The result of such concern was the 1993 Education Act. This is a key piece of legislation, which determines current practice in respect of children with special educational needs wherever they may be educated. It was designed to address the difficulties that had arisen after 1981 and it provides common guidance as to what schools and authorities need to be doing.

Such knowledge is important for all teachers, and not just headteachers or special educational needs co-ordinators. Everybody needs to be aware of the five-stage process, and to be particularly familiar with the first three school-based phases. What follows is a summary of the main features of the Code and is intended as an introduction to the Code, not as a substitute for it.

Warnock said that the aims for education were the same for all children. The aims for those children with special educational needs are no different from those for any other child. From this it follows that special educational needs are no different from the educational needs of all children. Special educational needs are additional. Children with special educational needs need the same as other children but they need other things too. The Code of Practice attempts to outline how these additional needs can be met.

Under the provisions of the Code, a whole range of agencies and individuals within the school have clearly defined responsibilities. The governors, the head and the special educational needs co-ordinator all have specific respon-sibilities. So too does every class teacher. The first of these is that every individual class teacher has a responsibility 'to be fully aware' of the pro-cedures in existence within the school for identifying, assessing and making provision for pupils with special educational needs.

It is appropriate to remind ourselves just how much this might involve. A new teacher taking over a class is likely to have children already identified within the Code of Practice. It is highly likely, for example, that a number of children within the class will have concerns about their special educational needs registered. Some of these children will continue to have their progress monitored. They will continue to have their work appropriately differentiated. Some of the children will have individual education plans drawn up for them. Some will have access to specialist help from outside the school. Some may have formal statements raised to ensure that their special educational needs are met. All of these groups have distinct requirements within the Code.

Yet the remit is broader still. The incoming teacher needs to consider that all the children within the class have needs. Some of these needs may become so pressing that the teacher will be the one to initiate the registration of concern.

Thus, it would be useful for any new teacher to become familiar with all the stages involved in the Code of Practice. Irrespective of how well the progress of all children is monitored, or how detailed planning for all areas of the National Curriculum is responsive to individual needs, children within the Code must have their individual progress monitored in a particular way. The way this needs to be done is described within the Code itself. Further prescription is likely to derive from specific local education authority directives concerning the administration of the procedures. Finally, the school itself will have an individually tailored response to those local education authority directives. The teacher needs to be aware of each of these and to monitor progress and undertake curriculum planning in the light of all of them.

The Code itself lays down requirements and specifications for both the school-based and authority-based stages of assessment and provision. It outlines in precise terms each separate stage and itemizes the responsibilities at each of these stages. In the course of this it describes the relationship between stages and the mechanisms for progression.

The local education authority response to the Code will be distinct and will take into account existing services and provision. As a result, the responses of different authorities will vary in important details.

The school's specific response to the local authority's guidelines will be unique. It will reflect a range of factors particular to that school. The response will be couched in terms of a policy statement. The special educational needs policy of the school will detail the school's provision for special educational needs, its policies for identification, assessment and provision, and will specify the school's staffing policies and the arrangements for partnership with the external bodies.

Despite the individuality of local educational authority and school policies, it is possible nevertheless to identify a common denominator of knowledge which the class teacher might find useful. It is important to have access as early as possible to the school's policy statement. It is also important to identify the special educational needs co-ordinator. The school's policy should clearly specify who this is. It is important:

- to obtain an authoritative and up-to-date list of the children in the class who are on the special needs register

- to identify at which of the five stages within the Code each of the registered children is located

- to obtain copies of the individual education plans for all registered children

- to obtain statements for any children at Stage 5.

Such information is the minimum that the incoming class teacher needs to have. Beyond this are a whole range of skills and strategies the teacher needs in order to operate effectively on behalf of children with special educational needs within the Code. A number of these skills have been selected as being particularly appropriate at Stage 1 of the Code. It is at this stage that teachers may feel themselves to be particularly exposed. They may feel under-supported and that they are being left to fend for themselves.

The first skill is one of identification. The teacher feeling under-supported may be faced with a dilemma. Many of the children in the class may cause concern. Many may not be successfully performing basic tasks. The dilemma resides in knowing which of these children should be placed on the register. Should it all be of them? If that is the case, then why not put all the children in the class on the register to be on the safe side?

The key point to bear in mind is not what the children know but what they may find difficult to learn. Let us take an example. A number of children in Year 5 may not be able to tell the time to a quarter of an hour. As a class teacher, one would be somewhat surprised and perhaps a touch anxious about this lack of ability. Children may be unable to tell the time for a variety of reasons. Of more significance in deciding on a future course of action is determining which of the children remain incapable of telling the time to the required level after suitably differentiated and focused teaching has taken place within the normal classroom environment.

If, after an appropriate sequence of instruction, an individual child remains incapable of telling the time, the teacher is likely to experience concern. At this juncture, that concern could be shared with colleagues. The concern should be voiced to the special educational needs co-ordinator and a discussion needs to take place as to whether that child ought to be placed on the register of educational concern.

Whatever the outcome of such a discussion, the class teacher will need to undertake a critical survey of the child's overall performance. Is the difficulty in telling the time isolated? Is it part of a pattern? Is it directly impinging upon other learning? Answers to such questions lead to the next two significant questions: 'What might be the cause of the difficulty?' and 'What are the consequences for my teaching?'

Before going on to make some suggestions as to how the second of these questions might be answered, a point has to be made about identification. Identification means much more than having access to a norm-referenced test score. Such data are at best partial and in some circumstances of limited import. A child with a physical handicap will challenge the class teacher to provide maximum access to the curriculum. The nature of the challenge is not dramatically altered by the discovery that the child may be six months behind his or her chronological age in reading. Even when the needs result from mild to moderate learning difficulties, test scores will provide only part of the picture and they should always be considered in the context of classroom practice. An apparently aberrant test result may alert the teacher to a learning delay which can be explored in teaching. A test result which contradicts the teacher's perception of a child's difficulty could form the basis of a discussion with the special educational needs co-ordinator, not a ditching of the teacher's emerging model of the child's needs.

What, then, are the consequences for teaching? How might these be addressed? The key concept here is that of differentiation. Differentiation is not the exclusive preserve of special educational needs. It is part and parcel of normal classroom practice. For children with special educational needs differentiation needs to be both focused and flexible. It needs to be focused, to target the particular difficulties the child might encounter in respect of an activity or task. What the child needs should be considered within an overall structure. The structure should be concerned to:

- present the appropriate degree of challenge
- present the child with small, achievable steps
- present the child with success
- present the child with reinforcement.

Differentiation needs to be flexible. For the child with complex needs the teacher may need to undertake radical revisions in planning the work. It may be that the child with complex needs should have a different outcome to his or her work. The outcome may be the same but the approach may differ. At the simplest level, the resources may be modified. Differentiation is unlikely to be one-dimensional and a complex interplay is likely to occur between altering outcomes, tasks and materials. The answer is unlikely to lie in tinkering with just one.

In relation to differentiation, three additional factors need to be borne in mind. The first is that differentiation encompasses more than the mere simplification of text. Readability has its place in the teacher's repertoire, but in a number of circumstances, like patriotism, it is not enough. It will help with children whose mild learning difficulties result in marginal difficulties in their reading. For them, modifying the text is likely to be advantageous. For others, it is clearly insufficient and may even have a pejorative effect, limiting their exposure to more mature language registers. All children benefit from well-thought out, clearly designed and appropriately written materials. Text modification is again not an issue that is the exclusive preserve of special educational needs.

The second factor that needs to be considered is one of sensitivity. In a Year 4 maths lesson some children with difficulties are likely to need their work differentiating by continued access to structured apparatus. Without it, they may be unable to complete the modified task. With it, the task becomes achievable. A difficulty may arise because the children so supported may view the apparatus as babyish. For example, a 9-year-old working at a 7-year-old level in a Year 4 class could be very embarrassed at being asked to use structured apparatus. To such children this apparatus is associated with their years in the infant department. They may feel stigmatized by having to work with materials that their peers have long since grown out of. This is clearly a situation which requires sensitivity.

One solution might reside in identifying situations in which other, more competent children need to have recourse to such apparatus. Might it be appropriate, for instance, to allow the most able children in the class access to structured apparatus to undertake investigative work? What is being done with the materials is not the issue. Their undisputed adoption within the class as a whole may be the key to reassuring the child with special educational needs about their acceptability.

The final factor needing consideration is realism. Not all the work for all children in all circumstances can be differentiated. Nobody has everything differentiated and nobody ever will. Every teacher, however much experience he or she may have, struggles to get differentiation right. You have to move towards it at a pace that is sustainable in the long term. Differentiation as a problem is never completely solved; the variables are so infinitely complex. Perfection is never an option, but progressive improvement is.

A third crucial skill for the class teacher in relation to the Code of Practice is liaison. There is a range of individuals and agencies with which the class teacher must liaise in order to be effective in terms of the Code. Prime among these are the special educational needs co-ordinator, external agencies, parents and school-based colleagues.

The co-ordinator has a vital function, and is an essential resource in terms of the Code. Good liaison is critically important because there is a dichotomy within the Code between the person charged with formal responsibility for its operation and the person who, in practice, has day-to-day involvement with the children engaged in the process. The special educational needs co-ordinator at Stage 1 of the Code inducts children on to the register. Beyond that, the co-ordinator is required to offer advice and support as necessary. In essence, they have a monitoring function in checking that a record of action is initiated and appropriate information is collated. The class-based teacher is the person who initiates the record of action and is largely responsible for the collection of the required information.

Decisions as to whether a child remains on the register at Stage 1 or moves to Stage 2 are taken as a result of consultation between the class teacher and the special educational needs co-ordinator. If the decision is to move the child to Stage 2, the co-ordinator takes the lead. It is the co-ordinator's task to draw up the individual education plan, and it is the class teacher's task to put that plan into operation. The smooth running of the process can only be ensured if effective liaison takes place and if formal structures exist to plan, monitor and review the special educational needs provision for the child involved. It needs stressing that, although at Stage 2 the co-ordinator takes the lead in these areas, it is the class teacher who will undertake those duties on a day-to-day basis.

Along with the co-ordinator, liaison with parents is an essential feature of the Code from Stage 1 onwards. The views of parents have been a facet of the world of special educational needs since Warnock spoke of the need for professionals to forge a partnership with parents. The subsequent 1981 legislation accorded parents crucial powers of veto in developing provision for their child. The Code has the consideration of parental views at its very centre.

For example, at Stage 1, parents must be informed if their child is being considered for inclusion on the register of educational concern. The class teacher is normally the person who initiates such a liaison, explaining the procedures to the parents. It is important to consider how this might be done so as to cause least alarm or offence. Would a formal parents' evening or afternoon be the appropriate forum? Could one of the parents be contacted at the gate? Should a home visit be specially organized? The school may have a policy. The co-ordinator may have advice. Be aware that the communication of concern may come as a shock to some parents. It may well, of course, come as a relief to others. Parents are likely to need substantial reassurance and support in coming to terms with the fact that, for whatever reason, their child is considered to be educationally at risk.

Handling this first communication of concern with sensitivity is essential to secure the continuing involvement of parents. Unlike the 1981 legislation, under the Code, parents do not merely license the professionals to move to subsequent steps within a process, but are actively involved in contributing to the process in which their child is engaged. At Stage 1 the teacher must solicit parental views on the child's health and development, the child's performance and progress, the child's behaviour at school and at home, factors contributing to any difficulty and, importantly, other agencies or individuals the parents would like to be involved.

Throughout Stages 1 and 2 of the Code parents have to be consulted and informed as to what is happening. If the provisions of Stage 2 are felt to be inadequate and there is a sense that the child ought to be moved to Stage 3, a meeting with parents should be held so that appropriate action at this next stage can be agreed. If liaison has been effective up to this point, parental support is likely to be forthcoming. If liaison has not been well handled, difficulties may present themselves at this juncture, making progression to Stage 3 problematic and future relations fraught.

At Stage 3 the remit for liaison broadens substantially to include agencies and individuals external to the school. Although the co-ordinator is the person from within the school who calls in appropriate specialists from the supporting services, it is again the class teacher who will share with the co-ordinator the task of liaising with these agencies. It is the class teacher, too, who will bear the brunt of responding to the advice and suggestions proffered. This is a delicate situation and one which teachers, irrespective of the extent of their service, may find threatening. Any suggestion as to what might be done in future may be construed as a criticism of what has occurred in the past and teachers may be tempted to respond defensively. Furthermore, there may be a sense of resentment on the teacher's part that brief expert visits leave them with more work, but appear to place no onus whatsoever upon the person offering the advice.

Perhaps the most appropriate way to respond to such feelings is to view the advice for precisely what it is – advice. Accept that it is likely to be finely focused upon the child. Acknowledge that no visitor to a classroom can understand the nuances of that context as well as the class teacher. Take the advice in that spirit and be prepared to ask. Seek clarification as to how the advice might be implemented without detriment to the other children in the group. Involve the co-ordinator. Try to use the support agencies to identify other teachers within the authority dealing with similar problems whose experiences may be of value.

The final group of people with whom the class teacher is likely to need to liaise are colleagues in school working with the children. Many of these colleagues will not be qualified teachers and will operate to support individuals or groups of children who may have special educational needs. Such colleagues operate under a range of titles. They may be non-teaching assistants, educational care officers, child care assistants, curriculum support assistants or nursery nurses. Such colleagues come from a range of backgrounds. A number have extensive, high-quality training. Some have had little opportunity to undertake such training since coming into post. All of them are a potentially invaluable source of help both to the teacher of and the child with special educational needs. Their contribution is frequently under-acknowledged. The Code itself is an example of this. It makes sense to maximize the contribution that this group of professional colleagues might make.

In order to do this it is essential to value their contribution. The classroom assistant may spend more time working more intensively with the individual child with special educational needs than either the teacher or anyone else involved with the child. The classroom assistant has a unique opportunity to gain insight into the child's learning processes and attendant difficulties. The assistant is not just an extra pair of hands, and only comes to operate in this way if their contribution is undervalued.

The involvement of classroom assistants needs to be planned for. They need to be involved in the planning, to understand their role in a lesson and to feel comfortable with that role. Their deployment needs to be considered and integrated into the overall scheme for the whole class. Statements such as: 'When I am doing X, the assistant will be doing Y' should permeate the thinking that underpins the planning process.

Children will be quick to pick up the relationships involved in the roles of teacher and assistant. Assistants need to be supported. For instance, it may be appropriate to tell the child to show his or her work to the assistant because they are the person the child is supposed to be working with during this session. Under these circumstances it is not appropriate for the child to show the work to you. It is better for that work to be shown to the assistant.

Teachers may have two problems in working with assistants. One is to undervalue their contribution, both internally, in terms of the teachers' thinking, and externally, in terms of their public behaviour in front of the children. The second, paradoxically, is to be reluctant to lead. The teacher, after all, is the person with the ultimate responsibility for the class. The assistant works under their guidance. It is simply unprofessional to let the assistant drift without clear direction or purpose. It is equally unprofessional to allow the assistant to assume, by default, responsibility for the education of a child with special educational needs. Liaising with assistants to secure their maximum involvement on behalf of the children with special needs is not an easy skill to learn, but it is an essential one.

## CONCLUSION

This cursory introduction to the wide and complex field of special educational needs is brief and may appear intimidating. There is knowledge to acquire and there are skills to develop. A class teacher with a statemented child in their class, along with other children operating within the Code, will have to organize individual education plans, to test, monitor and assess, and to collect data in order to do this. Non-teaching assistant help will have to be planned for, timetabled and led. Annual reviews will have to be serviced and reports produced. A differentiated curriculum for children with special educational needs will have to be generated. All this is additional to being a good all-round classroom teacher.

At first glance, the task may appear impossible. The key to success is to ensure that forward planning is thorough, and that structures are in place as early as possible. This should ensure that children can work within a structure which gives them all the entitlement that is their due. It should also ensure that all staff involved have the confidence to know that it is going to be a straightforward process. If the children work within a well-organized environment and staff feel that the environment *has* been well organized, the process begins on a positive spiral. Nobody would pretend the task is easy, but it is possible. Importantly for the teacher, it is immensely worthwhile.

## REFERENCES

DES (1978) *Special Educational Needs* (The Warnock Report). London: HMSO.
DfEE (1994) *Code of Practice on the Identification and Assessment of Special Educational Needs* (Circular 61/94). London: DfEE.

## SOME SUGGESTIONS FOR FURTHER READING

For those wishing to undertake further reading within this field, the following three books are recommended. The book by Richard Stakes constitutes an excellent, well-written and easily accessible introduction to the area. Rob Ashdown, Barry Carpenter and Keith Bovair have a number of interesting suggestions to make on how different areas of the curriculum may be accessed by pupils with a range of learning difficulties. Those with an interest in issues relating to special educational needs will find the book by Garry Hornby, Mary Atkinson and Jean Howard a valuable source of insight.

Ashdown, R., Carpenter, B. and Bovair, K. (1991) *The Curriculum Challenge: Access to the National Curriculum for Pupils with Learning Difficulties*. London: Falmer Press.
Hornby, G., Atkinson, M. and Howard, J. (1997) *Controversial Issues in Special Education*. London: David Fulton.
Stakes, R. (1996) *Meeting Special Needs in Mainstream Schools: A Practical Guide for Teachers*. London: David Fulton.

# CHAPTER 15

# Assessment in the primary classroom

MARGARET NOBLE

In this chapter I have concentrated upon assessment as part of the everyday activities in the classroom. I have not addressed the national requirements for assessment, recording and reporting, as these are readily available. Instead I have focused upon the development of the knowledge and skills that will help you to become more proficient at assessing your pupils. Teachers who use assessment as a normal part of their everyday practice can easily respond to requests from outside agencies for assessment evidence and information.

This chapter is based on work I have done with pupils in my own classes and with student teachers and teachers. I have included what assessment is, the different types we use, the methods of collecting information, and the benefits of assessment for teachers, pupils, parents and schools. I have also included some suggestions for making formal assessment part of your everyday practice, as well as ways of recording and reporting on the information you gather.

## WHAT IS ASSESSMENT?

Assessment is an integral part of the daily activity in the classroom. Think of times when you praised children in recognition of their actions, told them to work more quietly, gave support to those having difficulties, marked work, or planned the next step for children who had successfully completed an activity. Your action in each case was in response to assessments you made about those children. As a teacher you are good at 'knowing', or assessing, your children. You make use of assessment daily to find out about your pupils' characters, needs and abilities.

## WHY USE ASSESSMENT?

There are many reasons for including assessment as part of normal classroom practice. You can use it to help you to be more effective in your teaching, to improve your practice and to become a better planner and a better manager.

You can use it to give feedback to your pupils about their progress, and to plan what you are going to teach next. You can use it to support your pupils to become independent learners, by teaching them the skills and knowledge they require to assess their own work. You can use it to develop your own understanding of the subjects and areas of the curriculum in relation to your pupils. You can use it to compile records for your own use and to inform the pupils' subsequent teachers. You can use the evidence it provides when reporting to parents. You can use to it to evaluate your own practice in the classroom and to evaluate new initiatives within the school. You can also use it to provide information for outside agencies such as Ofsted.

Before I discuss the different types of assessment, there are some points you should consider. If you want to improve your practice in this area you should 'think big and act small'. If your ultimate goal is to be able to assess each of your pupils in every subject, begin this process by taking small, safe steps with which you feel confident and comfortable and which will bring you success. If you are successful, you are more likely to have another go. Begin with one lesson and assess three or four children who you think will be easy to assess, who will provide good evidence and will communicate easily with you and with their peers. As your skills and confidence grow, you will become more adventurous. Do not underestimate the ability you already have to make judgements about your pupils. Improving your ability to assess means building upon the skills and knowledge you already possess. Assessment is not yet another thing to do. Assessment is an integral part of teaching and learning for both teacher and pupil.

## WHAT ARE THE MAIN TYPES OF ASSESSMENT?

Most of the assessment done in the classroom is *informal assessment*, the daily business of looking at what pupils are doing, assessing what they need and then responding with, for example, a frown, a smile, an explanation, praise, an admonishment or a suggestion. It is an integral part of teaching. We constantly make informal assessments and take action in response to what we see or hear. We do not plan for these informal assessments, but they form the basis of the constant interaction between teacher and class, and between teacher and individual child.

When making informal assessments we gather information as it arises from the situation and the moment, we do not plan for it in advance; instead we react at the time and look back at what happened. Unless something significant occurs we do not usually record informal assessments. When, however, we are making *formal assessments* we establish in advance the purpose for the assessment and the criteria against which we will measure the outcomes. We also plan in advance for the ways we are going to collect the evidence and, if required, how we will record it.

Both types of assessment, the informal and the formal, are equally valuable and you should develop skills in each area. The two are not exclusive. Both provide information you can use for a variety of purposes. In some situations you will find one more appropriate to use than the other, and in other situations you will find it better to use both types. In planning a lesson, for example, you will have a formal assessment framework, planned in advance, but during the lesson you will make many informal assessments that were unplanned but which deal with unexpected incidents and the general smooth running of the activities.

Having established that there are two main types of assessment, informal and formal, we can now look at the categories that apply to both types. These include *formative, diagnostic, summative* and *evaluative* assessment. It is important, however, that you understand the purpose of each type of assessment rather than become too concerned with its name. The purpose of formative assessment is to identify the positive achievements and progress of your pupils in order to inform the next step in your teaching and their learning. Diagnostic assessment is used to diagnose learning difficulties. It can also be used neutrally to find out all the characteristics of a pupil's learning or achievement. Summative assessment is done to establish markers showing the stages in a child's achievement; for example, at the end of a block of work, a term or a year. Evaluative assessment is carried out for evaluation purposes, when attempting to give a value to an initiative; for example, a new discipline policy, or to aspects of your own practice. As this is an introduction to assessment, I have focused in this chapter upon formative assessment. As your ability to assess develops, you may wish to look at the other three in more depth.

## FORMATIVE ASSESSMENT

Formative assessment is one of the most frequently used types of assessment. When doing formative assessment, either informally or formally, your purpose is to identify the positive achievements of your pupils in order to form or shape the next stages in your teaching and their learning. Progress, for your children, is about building up a repertoire of things they know or can do. When formatively assessing, look for *positive* achievement. Do not confuse this with diagnostic assessment (see above) in which you look at learning difficulties. As teachers we help children to add to their lists of achievements that have been lengthening rapidly since they were born. We do this by identifying suitable and appropriate information or skills, and the right time to introduce them. Formative assessment helps us to do both.

You already make use of formative assessment during the course of any lesson. You see or hear evidence which demonstrates children now know, or can do, something that they could not do or did not know before. You recognize their achievements and take steps to move them on, often immediately. Much of this you may not plan for. However, to make your lessons more productive and more focused you should use formal formative assessment as an integral part of your lesson planning. Plan for it in advance, making it formal rather than informal. The information you gather will give you a clearer idea of what your children are capable of now and what they need to learn next. This will help you to plan the subsequent stages in your teaching programme more confidently and effectively. You will also find that it will be easier for you to provide differentiated work.

## How do I make formative assessments?

Formative assessment is concerned with answering five basic questions:

1. What do I intend to teach the children? – the purposes of the lesson (known also as learning objectives, learning outcomes, learning intentions or curriculum outcomes).

2. How will I know if the pupils have learned anything? – the criteria against which you will judge the pupils' achievements.

3. How am I going to collect the evidence? – the mode, or method, of assessment.

4. What activity shall I use to achieve the purposes of the lesson? – the appropriate strategy for your class.

5. Am I going to record the information? If so, how shall I record it and share it? – record keeping and reporting.

## WHAT DO I INTEND TO TEACH THE CHILDREN? SETTING PURPOSES

There are a number of expressions used to describe what you intend to teach the children (see above). Here I will use 'purposes' to cover these.

To plan for formal assessment within the lesson or activity you should set specific and realistic purposes. Your purposes will be translations of the National Curriculum programmes of study and the parts of the cross-curricular elements, such as health education or personal and social education, that appear on the schemes of work for your class. The national programmes of study are quite general; make them more specific for your lessons.

When children are learning something new, purposes usually begin with 'To teach the pupils ...'. If the activity is about consolidation it is appropriate to use 'The pupils will practise ...'.

**A Purposes of the lesson**   (Example of a D&T lesson at KS 1)

---

*Subject: D&T*        *Focus: Designing skills*

**A  Purposes: To teach the pupils**

**a. to clarify their ideas through discussion with the teacher** (D&T 3 Designing skills b)

**b. to develop their design ideas by modelling their ideas in card and paper** (D&T 3 Designing skills c)

---

| B  Criteria for success: the pupil can ... | C  Method of assessment |
| --- | --- |
|  |  |

---

Share the purposes of the lesson with the pupils. If you tell them in advance what you expect them to learn they are more likely to succeed (see also criteria below). Also, encourage and support them to set their own individual learning purposes for the activities, as part of their development as independent learners.

## HOW WILL I KNOW IF THEY HAVE LEARNED ANYTHING? SETTING CRITERIA

The purposes of the lesson are concerned with what you are going to teach your pupils. Criteria help you to decide whether or not they have learned anything. Use criteria to look at what children now know or can do. Criteria must be specific. If they are vague, you will find it difficult to decide if pupils have achieved. Criteria begin with such phrases as 'The pupil knows. ...', 'The pupil can ...', 'The pupil makes use of ...', or 'The pupil is able to ...'. Criteria provide information that children can add to their lists of things they know or can do.

Share the criteria with your pupils. If the children know what it is you are expecting from them, they are more likely to demonstrate their abilities. Wynne Harlen (Pack B, p. 28) illustrates this with an example. The teacher asked the pupils to produce a poster. They produced a beautifully drawn and illustrated poster, but the detail was so small that it could only be seen close to.

The children did not demonstrate their ability to make a poster, because the teacher had not told them that a poster has to be seen easily from a reasonable distance. If the teacher had told them this they would have taken it into consideration. Criteria supply children with information that guides them through a task and teaches them what counts as a successful outcome.

Children often have problems when attempting work because they are not sure what you want from them. As a student teacher now, or in the past, you will empathize with this if you remember trying to work out how a tutor was going to mark your essay. Make the criteria clear and achievable and share these with your pupils. Put the purposes and criteria for the lesson on the board or on the wall for the pupils to refer to during the lesson. Use the criteria at the end of the lesson when reporting back to the pupils, or for your pupils to use when assessing themselves or their peers.

Criteria setting is another requirement for independent learning. Teach pupils to set their own criteria. Begin by setting the criteria for them, then provide short lists to which they can add. Follow this with a varied diet in which the criteria are set either by you or the pupils, or by both of you.

**B Criteria for assessment**    (Example of a D&T lesson at KS 1, continued)

---

*Subject: D&T          Focus: Designing skills*

A.  Purposes: To teach the pupils

a.  to clarify their ideas through discussion with the teacher (D&T 3 Designing skills b)

b.  to develop their design ideas by modelling their ideas in card and paper (D&T 3 Designing skills c)

| B  **Criteria for success: The pupil can** | C Method of assessment |
|---|---|
| • **discuss design ideas with the teacher** | |
| • **design using ready-cut shapes in card and paper** | |
| • **give an explanation for his/her design choice** | |
| • **design for a specific person or event** | |

---

As you set the criteria, you will find that they influence the content and the way in which you plan to run the lesson. Purposes and criteria are essential elements in effective lesson planning.

## HOW AM I GOING TO COLLECT THE EVIDENCE?
## MODE OR METHOD OF ASSESSMENT

There are different ways of collecting evidence. Which you will choose will depend on whether you are assessing what your pupils produce, things they have written, made or drawn, or the processes of learning; for example, their abilities to discuss their ideas with others. You can assess the former without the child necessarily being present, but the latter requires you to be there at the time to see it or to hear it. Many of the National Curriculum programmes of study require you to assess work in progress, not just the 'hard copy' outcomes of that work.

## Assessing the product

This is easier to do if you have set purposes and criteria for the product. Discuss these with your children so that they are clear about what you expect them to produce and how you will judge the outcomes. This will improve the quality of their products and will help them to set their own purposes and criteria when assessing their own products or those of their peers.

## Assessment through observation

Observation involves listening and watching. Plan how you are going to do this and which children you will be observing. Plan to observe for only a few minutes. Observation does not mean sitting for hours beside a child. Do the assessment openly and make it non-threatening. Tell the pupils what you intend to do and what you are looking for. Tell them that it is a chance for them to demonstrate their capabilities and achievements, and make it celebratory. Teach your pupils that being an assessor is yet another role you play in the classroom, an important role. By doing this you are also providing a model they can use in their own assessments.

When doing observations, use a clipboard or notepad that signals to the class that you are in 'assessor' role. Tell the children not to approach you for those few minutes when you are assessing a child or a group. You will find that you still get interruptions followed by quick apologies but your pupils will quickly accept this as a normal part of classroom life. Show the children what you have written on your clipboard or notepad and say that at the end of the session you will use the information to tell them what progress they have made. When observing, place yourself at a little distance from the group or the child. If you sit with the group they will use you as an easy source of help. Do a series of short and focused observations. You will find that the more you do the better and quicker you will become at making well-judged assessments.

When planning the lesson, think about the best times in that lesson to observe. Plan, for example, to do three observations in the lesson for a few minutes each time. At first you may find that you collect too much information, too much to use. Avoid this by having specific criteria and using a grid and tick system with space for a few notes if needed. Do not collect evidence about anything other than the child's achievement against the criteria. Keep your formal assessment clearly focused.

Report only *positive* achievements to the child, group or class, adding to their lists of things they can do and know. Do not report learning problems and difficulties. If children are having difficulties you can do some diagnostic assessment (see above) and take action at the time. If they have not achieved at the end of the session, plan to remedy this in subsequent lessons. When giving positive feedback, focus upon the purposes and criteria you gave at the start of the lesson. Do not give them too much information; keep the feedback focused and short.

## Questioning

This is an effective way of finding out why children carried out particular actions, or the extent of their knowledge. By questioning, you can help children to reconstruct events that you were unable to observe. Plan basic questions in advance and be prepared to ask supplementary questions if required.

## Discussion

You can conduct a discussion with a group of children at the beginning, during, or at the end of a lesson. This will give you an insight into the learning that is taking place. It will also provide evidence about children's ability to communicate with you and with their peers. Again, you must plan for this. Make a note of the points and questions you will use in the discussion. Tell the children the purpose of the discussion and what you are looking for. This will help them to demonstrate their capabilities.

## Presentations

Your pupils can make presentations individually or in groups. Tell them that the purpose of such presentations is to inform you and others of their new knowledge and skills. Presentations also allow you to assess your pupils' organizational, planning and communication skills. If you do use this method of assessment, provide pupils with guidance, setting out purposes and criteria for good presentations.

## Concept mapping

Using concept mapping (see p. 62), you can find out how children's knowledge or attitudes have changed over time. There are different ways of doing this, some quite sophisticated. One simple way is to ask them to write or draw what they already know or feel about the topic you are about to teach. Repeat this at the end of the lesson. You and the children can then compare the two responses and note the changes. You can also use this at the beginning and the end of a programme of work done, for example, over a term.

## Pupils' own assessments

Once your children are able to set purposes and criteria, introduce them to the ways of collecting evidence to gather information about their own progress. Pupils' self-assessments will also provide you with evidence.

**C Method** (or mode) **of assessment** (Example of a D&T lesson at KS 1, continued)

---

*Subject: D&T*        *Focus: Designing skills*

A   Purposes: To teach the pupils

a.   to clarify their ideas through discussion with the teacher (D&T 3 Designing skills b)

b.   to develop their design ideas by modelling their ideas in card and paper (D&T 3 Designing skills c)

| B   Criteria for success: The pupil can | C **Method of assessment:** |
|---|---|
| • discuss design ideas with the teacher | • **discussion** |
| • design using ready-cut shapes in card and paper | • **observation** |
| | • **product** |
| • give an explanation for his/her design choice | |
| • design for a specific person or event | |

---

Use the positive information you gather for feedback to the children about their individual progress, so that they can add to their 'list'. Use the information to discuss with each of them, or with the group, the next step they need to take in their learning. This will help children to set their own personal learning goals, essential if a child is to become an independent learner. Children need not only to learn about the subjects of the curriculum, they also need to learn how to learn. Teach them the vocabulary they need to discuss their learning, and how to examine and improve the ways in which they learn. Formative assessment, focused upon the things they produce and the ways in which they work, helps them to do this.

When planning a lesson, provide some time for pupils to reflect on the content of the lesson and on their own progress. Contribute to this by feeding back your observations of the individuals' and the group's progress. Over the week, or term, decide which lessons you might use for such reflection and discussion.

## WHAT ACTIVITY SHALL I USE TO ACHIEVE THE PURPOSES OF THE LESSON? THE STRATEGY

When you begin the year with a new class, or if you are fairly new to assessment, you will usually plan your lessons by deciding what you are going to do with the children and focusing upon the activity. As you begin to make assessments, and begin to know your children, the starting point will change. You will more usually begin by deciding upon the purposes and criteria for the lesson and only then will you choose a suitable activity for achieving those purposes. For any one purpose, there are many strategies you might use to teach it effectively. If you look at the purposes given in the example above you will be able to think of many ways in which you might do this. The activity you choose will suit your purposes and will be appropriate for your pupils. When planning the activity, use the assessment information you have collected to plan for a balance of progression and continuity. The purpose of the lesson, the new learning, is the *progression*; it is the next stage in the children's learning.

Progression provides the focus and the challenge in the activity, the 'hard bit'. In the case of the example lesson, the progression is about designing; more specifically, designing a) through discussion and b) by making. Therefore, make the rest of the activity as easy as possible for the children by making use of *continuity*, their previously acquired skills and knowledge. Do not give your pupils too much to learn in one lesson; build up their skills and knowledge gradually, using a proper balance of progression and continuity.

Examples 1 and 2 opposite illustrate how changing the purposes alters the strategy for running the activity. Note how this affects both 'progression' and 'continuity'.

By focusing on what you are going to teach and upon what you want children to learn, you can shape the activity to give you the most effective strategy to help your pupils to achieve.

**Example 1**

---

**Activity**: The pupils will make cards for Mother's Day

*Purposes* for the lesson:   The pupils will be taught
a) to clarify their ideas through discussion with the teacher (D&T 3 Designing skills b.)

b) to develop their design ideas by modelling their ideas in card and paper (D&T 3 Designing skills c)

*Strategy* for this activity
- *Progression* – the new skills and knowledge are about designing. I will prepare questions to help them discuss their ideas with me. I will record their ideas and put these up on the wall for them to discuss during and at the end of the activity. I will teach them to design by making, using the shapes. This part of the activity, *designing*, will provide the focus and the challenge.

- *Continuity* – making use of skills and knowledge they already have. As the focus is on designing, not on making, they will work with materials and tools they have used before. To make more time for designing, I will give them prepared cards and a variety of shapes in a choice of colours. This part of the activity, *making*, will be as easy as possible.

---

**Example 2**

---

**Activity**: The pupils will make cards for Mother's Day

*Purposes* for the lesson: The pupils will be taught
a) to use scissors to cut card (KS 1 D&T 4 Making skills a)

b) to use glue to join card (KS 1 D&T 4 Making skills c)

*Strategy* for this activity
- *Progression* – to learn how to use scissors and apply glue properly. I will demonstrate both techniques and give them time to practise before they make the cards. I will check that they are doing this properly as the activity progresses. This part of the activity, *making*, will provide the focus and the challenge.

- *Continuity* – as the focus is upon making, and not on designing, I will provide an option of three pre-designed cards and samples for them to copy. I will also prepare pre-drawn shapes for them to cut round and assemble. This part of the activity, *designing*, will be as easy as possible.

---

## RECORD KEEPING AND REPORTING

### Recording the information

Much of the assessment you make in the classroom is informal and you would not normally record the information arising from it, unless you thought it was significant. You would, however, usually record the results of formal assessments. Most schools already have recording systems. If yours does not, then a simple matrix is a good starting point for your own records (see Figure 15.1). For some subjects, such as reading, you may wish to use more detailed records. You will develop your own preferred way of recording to meet your needs.

**Figure 15.1** An example of the top few lines of an assessment recording sheet

**Design & Technology** (Making Mother's Day Cards   2 March 1998)

*The pupil can/knows how to:*

| discuss design ideas with teacher | design using ready-cut paper shapes | explain his/her design choice | design for specific person or event | | | Pupils' names |
|---|---|---|---|---|---|---|
| √ | √ | √ | √ | | | Anne B. |
| × | √ | × | √ | | | Sarah C. |
| √ | ○ | ○ | ○ | | | James D. |
| | | | | | | |
| | | | | | | |

Notes: √ – has achieved    × – has not achieved    ○ – partially achieved    A – absent

Use a ring binder to which you can add pages. Attach a list of your pupils to the inside of the back cover and trim the pages so that you can see the list of names. You will need a page for each subject (add more as required). When planning lessons, write the criteria you are using for the lesson along the top row of the matrix. At the end of the lesson, record the progress of the pupils using a simple format - a tick if they have achieved, a cross if they have not, a circle for partially achieved and an A if the child was absent. Tick these when they eventually do demonstrate achievement. You may leave a space at the bottom of the sheet for notes on particular pupils or activities. Over the term, or the year, these records will provide detailed profiles of the pupils' achievements.

## Using the information

If you have included regular formal assessment as part of your lesson planning, you will have a useful amount of objective information. The profiles will show the children's progress over the year. You will be able to identify the children with particular strengths or difficulties in certain areas of the curriculum. The records will alert you to those children who are not being challenged by your lessons or who are finding that your lessons are pitched at too high a level. The records will also be useful for colleagues who share the class or who subsequently teach them.

Use the profiles to produce individual reports for the children based on their *positive* achievements over the term, or over the year – 'I know ... and I can ...' sheets. These are the lists of what each child can now do and now knows. Compile these from the criteria at the top of the record matrix. For younger children, modify the wording of these criteria by using more appropriate language. Use the subject headings to group the criteria. Design the sheet to be suitable for the age group. Use balloons, clouds or other shapes for the youngest children; for older pupils use a generous border and a suitable font.

The reports are about positive achievements and should not list things a child cannot yet do – those belong to the list of things you have still to teach the child. Do not use a tick list, as this would include unticked boxes. Do not include anything you have not formally assessed, and, unless you have a formally assessed PSE programme, do not include comments about the children's characters. Keep these sheets focused upon curriculum achievements. By providing these for your children you are modelling good assessment practice for them to adopt. Encourage your pupils to compile their own sheets, charting their progress and achievements.

Use the profiles when deciding on a child's National Curriculum level of attainment. Look at the criteria in your matrix and at the level descriptions. Look for a 'best fit', not a perfect match. Do not break down the level descriptions into individual phrases or sentences but use the descriptions holistically. The major part of the child's profile should match the level description. If you find that the child is halfway between two levels then they are still at the lower one. Having identified the level, enter it in a column on your record matrix, along with the date.

Use the information in your records as a basis for your discussions with parents and for writing more informative and objective reports. List all the positive things their children can do or know, but do not include any subjective comments. Reports based on regular and formal assessments provide parents with a clear and objective picture of their children's progress and abilities. Ask pupils to write a report for their parents based on their own assessments over the term or the year. This helps the children to identify their achievements and provides their parents with yet more useful information.

## CONCLUSION

Assessment is an essential part of good practice. We acknowledge that one of the things which makes teachers excellent practitioners is their ability to get to know the children and to act effectively upon that knowledge. A good practitioner is also a good assessor. Make assessment, both formal and informal, a regular part of your normal classroom practice. By developing your skills in these areas you will become more effective in your teaching and planning, and will be able to support your pupils to become independent learners. You will be able to provide parents with more valid and objective information, and you will find it easier to respond to the demands for evidence from outside agencies. Finally, you will feel more in control of what you do and be more aware of your own achievements.

## REFERENCE

Harlen, W. (undated, *c.* 1990) *A Guide to Teacher Assessment: Packs A, B and C.* London: Heinemann/School Examination and Assessment Council.

## SOME SUGGESTIONS FOR FURTHER READING

Drummond, M.J. (1993) *Assessing Children's Learning.* London: David Fulton.
Harlen, W. *A Guide to Teacher Assessment*, as above.

# CHAPTER 16

# Managing children's learning and behaviour

LYN OVERALL

## INTRODUCTION

As a basic competence by which both student teachers and those newly qualified (NQTs) are judged is the extent to which they achieve a good standard of discipline and classroom organization, this chapter is about managing the classroom so that children can learn. One analogy of teaching is that of a pie with a rich filling. The rich filling is the curriculum and its delivery. In the pastry crust are those things that go towards creating an environment in which each child has the opportunity to be successful, learning how to learn and how to work to potential. The point is that it is the whole pie which needs to be given attention so as to make each child's experience of school distinctive. Having a perfect crust with excellent discipline and class management is not enough. The pie filling needs to be nutritious and imaginative as well.

Teaching has to enable each child to learn. This means that as well as knowing how to put the content across and providing accurate information, teachers need to work with the children to establish a classroom environment that promotes a feeling of self-worth, and to make the learning as easy as possible by having routines that help to find the time needed to be able to teach. Clearly, children also need to understand how to behave so that they can learn. There needs to be an agreed framework of rules that makes the learning possible. The first part of this chapter is about organizing teaching, the second part is about managing behaviour; the objective for both is to 'maintain a safe and a purposeful working environment' (TTA, 1997, p. 12).

## CLASSROOM MANAGEMENT

Teaching is telling the tale and making sure that the tale is understood. Teachers spend each moment of the teaching day listening and responding so that each child understands what is being taught. These conversations between teachers and children are a starting point for thinking about managing learning. Teachers must be able to use questions well. This means hearing what children say and mean when they answer. The teacher then has to respond appropriately, often by providing explanations. Both explaining and questioning take place in a wide variety of sessions. In many lessons the teacher will pose carefully prepared key questions. A good deal of thought will have been put into the content and wording. In lessons which are driven by questions, the pattern is for the teacher to ask the question very clearly, quite slowly and carefully; there is then a pause while the children think and the teacher waits to listen carefully to the answers given. The teacher will then move the learning forward by offering a thoughtful response. The lesson will then proceed to the next question and subsequently from question to question, following the same cycle.

Another type of lesson is in the form of highly regulated discussion. Here the conversation between the teacher and the pupils moves back and forth and around a topic. While the way forward may be controlled by the use of key questions, the use of other devices will also be appropriate. For example, the teacher may make a statement related to what was said, there may be a review of what has been said, or the children may be required to ask their own questions. In discussion lessons, if children are to be actively involved, the teacher needs to be very encouraging, summarizing and extending the thoughts that the children offer.

Other lessons require that the skill to be taught is analysed and demonstrated. In these, the children need time to practise and to be given feedback. For example, think about teaching handwriting. Here children will be offered a model; that is, they are shown how the finished letter can be written, given the opportunity to try under close supervision and then allowed time to practise. In lessons where investigative learning is required, the teacher needs to recognize where children are having difficulty, then to ask questions to clarify understanding and guide pupils towards the right solution. Of course, it also hugely important to know when to withhold support, to recognize that very often children will reach a correct solution without extra explanation or questioning.

Within each lesson type, the pacing and timing used by the teacher to drive the learning forward is important. If the pace is too slow, children get bored; if it is rushed, they get frustrated and may not understand what is being taught. In both cases the result will often be that order may break down, and then teaching time will need to be spent on re-establishing control. Thus the time that needs to be devoted to the preparation of questions and explanations should not be underestimated. It is always better to be over-prepared.

Much too can be learned from carefully observing experienced teachers, especially those who handle questioning and explanation skilfully. Student teachers should note how the skilled teacher moves lessons along, the pace and timing of questions and the use of explanation, as well as how they use the responses of the children in their teaching.

If learning conversations, the questions and explanations that teachers use day by day are important, so too is careful planning to provide children with activities that are at the right level to take them forward. One of the frequent anxieties expressed by student teachers is 'Will I know enough?' Children, rightly, expect teachers to know and understand what they are teaching. In teacher training, great emphasis is placed on planning for teaching. For student teachers this enables them to deal with the curriculum when on school placement. Once qualified, their planning will be developed and refined. A major aspect of National Curriculum planning is devising tasks and work which are just right for the children. Setting work with the right amount of challenge so that the child will learn the next piece of the puzzle is one of the most intellectually challenging aspects of teaching.

The teacher's job is to choose worthwhile tasks that meet learning purposes for each child in the class. She or he then has to choose how to deliver the session. Essentially this means deciding how to use the time available. Decisions have to be made about when to work with all the children at once, which children to group together for which task and when to work with individuals. Decisions about where children sit are under the teacher's control and it is worth exploiting this advantage. The teacher needs to know which children need to have teaching time during any session and which tasks children can undertake without detailed teaching.

During the session, the teacher will be finding out who is learning, who is stuck, who needs encouragement and who is finding the work at the right level. At the end of sessions, checking on what has been understood and what has been misunderstood or ignored by children is another part of the job. This cycle of managing learning goes on against the knowledge the teacher has about what has to be taught and how children learn. An example may help to illustrate how a teacher may use the lesson time.

> Year 3 children are working with their teacher, learning to read information text. In the previous session the class identified the key words they needed. In this session they will be working with the teacher, using enlarged text which all the children can see. The teacher's first objective in this session is to start to look for the key words. Having grouped them round the text, she asks them where they could look up the key words. Various answers are taken; the ones that are accepted reinforce the task. In a moment or two all the children are clear that what they are doing is learning to look for key words in information text. After this ten-minute introduction where contents list, index and its relationship to the text have been explored, children move off to undertake related group and individual tasks. Again, the teacher makes what the children have to do very clear by telling them and then by writing the instructions with the children, checking with questions to individuals as she goes.
>
> The children move off to where the teacher has asked them to sit. She has carefully selected which children will work together. On the

tables are all the things they will need for the task. The children quickly settle to the work. The teacher circulates to make sure that everyone is clear on what to do. She then moves to work with one group. For about ten minutes she gives them her undivided attention. She then circulates again, this time checking with each group for progress and errors. Children who need help know that she is available to them now that she is moving round the room, so one or two put their hands up. She deals with these children promptly and quickly, then moves away to spend some more time with the first group. About ten minutes before the end of the session the children are asked to stop what they are doing and the tasks they have undertaken are reported upon, with the teacher reinforcing relevant learning points.

The teacher made sure that the learning was effective not just by knowing what to teach but by making sure that the session was effectively managed. The classroom layout had been designed so that the children could all see the enlarged text clearly; when they were working in groups the teacher could move easily to each child. She chose how the session should be managed: a whole class activity followed by group and individual tasks. She made sure that the children knew what they were supposed to do by checking and providing a written list. When she circulated she was checking for errors and progress. It was then possible for her to give one group her attention because the children knew that their turn would come and that interruptions at this stage should only be for dire emergencies.

In this class, children are given a clear understanding about the difference between individual and collaborative work. After working with one group, the teacher helps by dealing with specific requests, but this did not become an opportunity for any one child to get the teacher to do the work and so monopolize her time.

The children knew and used established routines. They knew what to do if their pencil broke, where materials were kept and whether they could just fetch them or whether permission should be sought. The way the work was to be laid out on the page was taught to the children early in the year. The teacher had done everything possible to ensure that the children could be autonomous and get on with learning. Simple routines carefully thought out and taught to the class made classroom life much easier for both children and teacher. The children in this class have a clear understanding of how the teacher will give help and attention.

When an organization system is being set up in the classroom, many children like to be the teacher's assistant. Helping in the classroom can be a powerful reward for most children. If the teacher makes sure that each child regards being chosen to help as a reward too, and they all have an opportunity so to do, then even the least helpful child may co-operate. Obviously this can be used for classroom jobs; for example, watering the plants, taking the register to the office, tidying the books; but it should also be exploited in the establishment of routines. The importance of routines that leave children to work, freeing the children to learn and the teacher to teach, should not be underestimated. Efficient teachers work with children to establish classroom routines, by discussing with them the regular events that take place and how routines can make life simpler. Routines will work better if there is a shared and agreed understanding about them. They also seem to work better if the children have helped to set them up.

An example of a routine that avoids wasting any classroom time is when work is set out before the children leave the classroom at break, so work can begin immediately upon their return. A way of spotting good practice is to observe what the children do while the register is taken. Examples of positive activities include reading a book, looking at picture story-books, practising spellings, writing in a diary, table squares, quiet play with construction toys, craft work, in fact any quiet task that has an educational value.

Another way of sharing the responsibility is to encourage the children to be alarm clocks, so that routine and special events in the school day are not forgotten. They will understand that when everything is new, at the start of a school term or a school placement, it is easy for the teacher or the student teacher to forget some things that happen. For example, while you may forget that some have swimming on a Wednesday the children will not, so make sure they know that it is helpful to remind you about this. Having routines in place which reduce the need for children to ask the teacher for help are also important. For example, when a word needs to be checked for spelling children need to know what they can do to help themselves. In the example above, the routines for help with spelling included: look on a wall chart, look in a word book, ask another child, use a dictionary, or put the first letter and a line for words about which they are not sure. Only when all these had been tried could they ask the teacher.

Children can help to maintain a working ethos by co-operating with their teacher to decide clearing up routines at the end of sessions; they will know where to put finished work, whether to put pencils and rulers away, and what to do with wet paintings. Another area where routines can save time and effort is in the use of materials. Consider the following list. In your class, what happens if a child

- breaks a pencil?
- needs to use the scissors?
- needs a rubber?

If the answer is that they do not have to ask the teacher, the routine is sound. If the need is met without disruption, the classroom is probably arranged to maximize the effective use of space.

By explaining what a learning task requires them to do, children begin to understand how where they sit is determined. For example, the children can help to decide how tables are arranged so that everyone can work well. While children may want to sit with their friends, they will recognize that this may lead them to talk rather than work, so the teacher's plans for who should sit where are more likely to be accepted with a good grace. In the management of the classroom, the aim is to give children responsibility and some autonomy.

## MANAGING BEHAVIOUR

You will notice that effective teaching is being defined as the teacher deciding how to spend his or her time. We each have to decide what our actions are in the classroom in terms of the values we hold. In part, the actions that we take will be determined by the need to be aware of the pupils as individuals. Some may need extra care and more of the teacher's time, for a variety of reasons. It is a mistake to assume that children will know how to learn and how to behave; many children have to be taught both. The discipline within each school and each classroom is clearly a key factor. For student teachers the key question is 'Will the children do as I ask?'

Misbehaviour is behaviour that can be considered to be inappropriate in the context in which it occurs. It will include:

- aggression, both physical and verbal; this includes bullying

- immorality – lying, stealing, cheating

- defiance

- most commonly, class disruptions, where children either talk out of turn or hinder each other

- what Americans classify as 'goofing off' – what we would call day-dreaming.

Discipline is what teachers do to help children to behave acceptably in schools (where there is no misbehaviour, no discipline is required). Discipline is intended to repress and redirect misbehaviour. Its goal is to reduce the need for teacher intervention over time, so that pupils learn to control their own behaviour. Discipline is about the way in which children behave towards each other and to their teachers and the way the teachers behave towards the children. It is important to acknowledge that the word discipline should not be used to imply punishment. The suggestions made here are based on the principle that prevention is better than cure, but also that where there is misbehaviour this has to be dealt with.

There is a view that the behaviour of children is worse than it used to be. Teachers often say this, and it is something that Ofsted comments upon in reports on schools. To investigate this, a major government research project was carried out into discipline in schools. The evidence from the Elton Report (DES, 1989) concluded that minor disruptions – children talking when they should be quiet, interference with other children – were more common than serious incidents. The consistent view from Ofsted reports on primary schools is that classrooms are generally well ordered. The Elton Report (DES, 1989) suggested that schools should have policies in place to deal with children's behaviour. Policies, designed and developed within the school, can provide a framework within which to work for teachers, adult assistants and children.

The school discipline and behaviour policies will be the starting point for teachers to work out with the children how appropriate social behaviour can be achieved in the classroom and around the school. Policies need to address ways in which children can be taught to find non-aggressive solutions to incidents that arise. This is especially important when dealing with both potential victims and bullies. School may be where the child becomes aware of the differences and similarities between values at home and those outside the home. The code that the teachers choose to implement will reflect their knowledge and understanding about issues such as social justice, of the need to develop children's moral understandings and children's self-concepts and their self-esteem. The rules that will be implemented must take account of the needs of the whole child, and the needs of society, as well as the essential need for good order in the school.

The establishment of an agreed school policy on behaviour is never going to be easy. The values held by school staff may conflict with those held by the children's parents. Because of this there is a very strong case to be made for involving a wide constituency in the establishment and implementation of the policy. Perhaps this can best be illustrated by considering one of the most challenging aspects; that is, how an anti-bullying policy is best embedded.

Bullying is an extreme form of aggressive behaviour. Whitney and Smith (1993) researched bullying in primary schools in Sheffield. They found that over a quarter of the sample of children reported that they had been bullied at some time, while 10 per cent were bullied once a week or more frequently. Twelve per cent of children admitted to being bullies. As children got older, the amount of bullying declined. The survey led to an anti-bullying project in a number of Sheffield primary schools and a follow-up survey demonstrated that the action taken to reduce bullying was effective.

The first step means spending a considerable amount of time exploring with all staff, pupils and parents what constitutes bullying. Agreement on whether or not one child pushing another is bullying will vary from school to school. Is it bullying when a child teases another without intending to cause distress? Is it bullying when a child is always excluded from a playground game? Is spreading spiteful stories, making faces, acceptable or not? Clearly the intention and frequency of the action is at the root of the definition, as is the relative strength of the children involved. As Smith and Sharp (1994, p. 13) suggest, 'it is not bullying when two children or young people of about the same strength have the odd fight or quarrel'.

Working with children to establish what is and what is not acceptable behaviour has a special significance when considering bullying. It is worth remembering that for some children even one unpleasant incident is enough to blight their life. Time spent working through actual incidents or teacher-created scenarios is a powerful tool, both in creating the agreed definition for the policy and in starting to work out acceptable ways of dealing with bullies and their victims. Creating a climate where it is all right to tell is clearly vital. Jenny Mosley (1994) is one of many advocates for the use of quality circles (QCs) as a way of implementing policies that enable children to learn to deal with aggression. Her book provides a useful introduction to QCs.

This way of policy making may well be used as a model for other aspects of the school's discipline and behaviour policy. It is clearly helpful to encourage the widest possible involvement at every stage. This will be important as agreements between parents and teachers about behaviour come to be more widely used.

Applying school policy in the classroom needs to be carefully thought through. In each classroom, the regime is new for the child each time a new teacher is encountered. Teachers, especially student teachers on block school experience, need to be aware of this and to plan for this aspect of classroom management and control. They will have to work out how to support both learning how to learn and learning how to behave. Thorough preparation, by knowing what the curriculum is and how to deliver it, is unavoidable. For experienced teachers the workload may be less because they have taught the curriculum before. For student teachers time spent in preparation is never wasted. For all teachers the rules established within the school need careful translation to work well within each classroom.

Children need time to learn how the new teacher expects them to behave. This means that the rules have to be taught to them. It also means that positive steps have to be taken to establish *esprit de corps*. One way of doing this will be to use public audit – for example, by asking a specific child how he or she is getting on with the task by saying, 'Owen, I'm hoping you'll have finished all those sums before break.' This establishes the teacher's expectation about work habits for the whole class. Praise can be used in this way as well; for example, by remarking to one child about his obvious readiness: 'Well done, Owen, I can see that you are ready to listen.' Every effort needs to be made to create a positive working environment.

Rules in schools are very interesting. Children usually like the security that rules bring, but they are not easy to teach. Take for example, the list below, designed by Reception children following a series of incidents in the playground.

- Do not hit people
- Play nicely with your friends
- Do not play on the steps
- Do not play on the field when it is wet

- Do not play on the bank
- Do not go on the juniors' grass
- Do not pick up glass. Tell the grown-ups
- Put your sweet papers in the bin
- Do not throw sticks or stones
- Do not climb on the walls.

Note first that even Reception children can start to work out what is acceptable social behaviour. They tend to phrase many rules as prohibitions. 'Do not' seems to be a favoured injunction, but this gives a useful starting point to their teacher for working through how they should behave in the playground and gives the children the skills and strategies they are going to need to keep to the rules.

The best advice when working out rules with children is usually to keep them few in number and phrase them positively. Perhaps the children and teacher would work towards a version of the rules something like this:

- Play nicely with your friends
- Keep your hands and feet to yourself
- Stay in the infant yard
- Put your sweet papers in the bin
- Only throw balls
- Stay on the ground.

These rules are much more complex than those which the children suggested, but they are ultimately more effective. However, rules are not useful until they are understood. Each rule would need to be thoroughly taught, working out with children what was meant. So 'Play nicely with your friends' might be taught through role-play, using real or imaginary scenarios. The teacher would make sure that each child understood. I can imagine the list describing what 'play nicely' means being expanded and expanded until the rule itself was so well understood that it became redundant. This would make a really valuable topic for QCs.

While the above example deals with behaviour in the playground, the rules for working in the classroom and around the school need to be well understood in order to be successfully enforced. This is part of the teacher's role in establishing socially acceptable behaviour.

There are many models for how to achieve the well-ordered classroom. Kounin (1970) used the following terms in his model: *withitness*, *momentum*, *smoothness*, *group alerting*, and *accountability*. Perhaps the most important of these is withitness. This is about knowing what is happening in the classroom at all times. Teachers do not have eyes in the backs of their heads, but the children need to think that they do! This is about referring a child back to the task in hand before that child leaves his or her seat to wander over to a friend for a chat. It is dealing with more than one thing at once. It is about dealing with the person who is misbehaving. It is about keeping children focused on what they should be doing both by what the teacher says and more often by subtle actions he or she takes.

In the example where Year 3 children are working with their teacher learning to read information text, the teacher had taken great pains to make sure that the children knew what was expected in terms of how to behave. She was constantly praising individual children for appropriate behaviour, clearly aware of what children were doing, moving children through tasks, reminding them of the time remaining and the amount to be finished. To prevent misbehaviour, she moved to the potential miscreants to encourage, to clarify and to refer them back to the work in hand. However, the regime created was not at all repressive; rather, it was based on a mutual respect and an agreed understanding of the need for order, so that the tasks set could be successfully completed.

One way to achieve this satisfactory state is to adopt a systematic approach to dealing with misbehaviour in the classroom. In the A B C framework that Wheldall and Merrett (1984) propose, the explanation of the behaviour is not an issue; rather, teachers are encouraged to prevent misbehaviour by focusing on what the children actually do.

The B stands for Behaviour, so instead of labelling a child disruptive, the teacher has to record exactly what happens; for example, that the child left his place on five occasions during the session, did not finish the task set, broke his pencil twice, asked to go to the toilet twice, came to the teacher with a tale of 'them ganging up on me' and all the other things some children can learn to do to disrupt teaching.

The A stands for Antecedents: having identified what the child actually does, the teacher is asked to look for what leads up to the behaviour. The observations involve looking carefully at what happens immediately before the child leaves his place and immediately before he deliberately breaks his pencil. 'Did the others in the group gang up on him?', 'Was the work too easy or too hard so that the child was not making progress?' The method encourages the teacher to intervene before the child leaves his place, and to take control over events. The teacher is encouraged to reinforce with the children those behaviours that are acceptable, rather than drawing attention to those that are not.

C, the Consequences, defines consistent ways of dealing with misbehaviour. Wheldall and Merrett (1984) use the phrase 'desist strategies' for what to do. They emphasize the need to stay calm, quiet, implacable but brief in interventions. This is what the teacher does in the above example. The intervention is kept positive; the child is praised for the work achieved and reminded of the next step.

Positive approaches mean using praise more than blame in dealing with children. Using praise effectively is a major skill for teachers. Typically, teachers find it easier to praise work than conduct. Praise tends to be used more lavishly with infants and decreases in the junior years. Up to the age of about 7, children have an insatiable appetite for praise, but after this age some children become embarrassed by the use of public praise in front of their peers. It is wise to avoid negating praise, for example: 'Well done Owen, shame about the hair cut'.

There are some important rules for giving praise:

- Praise delayed is praise denied; it is important to be alert and 'catch the child good'.

- Praise should be for something specific: 'Well done Gary, that is a kind act', 'Good, everyone is sitting'; to pass kind remarks on: 'Samantha, Mrs X told me how you helped her.' It should carry information about the accomplishment: 'That is a really good drawing because I can see exactly what the spaceship looks like' – and it must be genuine.

- Praise should refer to an internal attribution (to the effort made, or to ability and achievement), but with older juniors care should be taken when praising for encouragement rather than achievement, as they do not trust it or value it in the way that younger children do.

- It should be given sensitively, recognizing that some children need more praise than others.

Written praise should follow the same rules – 'good' and a tick signifies nothing. Something that responds to the task, shows that the teacher has read with care, will be far more rewarding. Praise thoughtfully and appropriately given for both encouragement and achievement is one of the most powerful rewards the teacher can use.

As part of the school's behaviour policy, there should be plans for rewarding children. While most infant children will work hard and behave well almost on the teacher's smile alone, in KS 2 the rewards may need to be considerably more sophisticated. Especially in junior schools, there is a real need for a reward system that takes account of what the children regard as rewards and to involve them in choices. Suggestions for useful ways of praising both work and conduct include:

- a letter home to parents about good work, conduct or effort

- negotiating a reward

- privilege time, earned for the whole class

- stickers, certificates

- seeing the head

- 'good work' assemblies

The use of rewards to modify child behaviour can be open to criticism. It can certainly be misunderstood in a number of ways. Those who use them will claim that behaviourist approaches are open, that they deal with the observable and the outcomes can be predicted. Those who criticize may be confusing rewards with bribes. However, rewards are always given as a consequence of action. Positive reinforcement is given after, and only if, the appropriate behaviour has occurred. It is important to make the distinction between bribery; for example, 'I will give you ... provided that ...' and reward: 'When you do this, then ...'.

Another issue is the difference between equality and equity. In behaviourist approaches some children will get special attention. All children expect to be treated fairly, but they do not equate this with equality of treatment. They are realists who are part of the group. In fact, there is considerable value in involving peers in support of a programme. Thus, the reward for one child behaving better may reward the whole class with an extra benefit. The other way is to reward the child quietly and unobtrusively. The judgement of whether the reward is open or surreptitious may well depend on what works best for that child. Either way, the reward system used needs to be clearly understood and kept under review.

Sanctions and punishments also form part of the package for dealing with misbehaviour. Work by Kohlberg (1968) suggests that the way in which children develop a sense of right and wrong should have an influence on the choices made. Younger children may not understand why one child is punished for an offence while another is let off, but if the teacher takes the trouble to explain, by between the ages of 6 and 7 most children will start to grasp the reasons. The teacher needs to be simple and direct; for example, paint thrown = punishment, paint spilled by accident = no punishment. The younger the child the more time and care is needed in explanations; this is part of the infant teacher's role. Children need to be clear that the punishment is for the consequences of a rule broken or of an act the child committed – never because of the person the child is.

Children must know that a consequence of misbehaviour is a punishment. The teacher should act firmly, without fuss, and the punishment should be unambiguous. The justice of the punishment must be understood by the child who is being punished and by the other children in the class. The punishment must be one that takes account of the circumstances of the act. The message to the child should be 'You have broken our rules and you have not thought about the feelings and needs of others', not 'You have upset me'.

There are some rules that must never be broken. For example, children are not allowed beyond the school gate unaccompanied. This is a safety rule and children will have to know that to break it is never acceptable. Quite often, though, children are in the process of learning socially acceptable rules. In these cases punishment is carried out after a warning; for example, 'John, you have been asked not to interfere with Tom on three occasions. Do not do it again, or you will be sitting next to me for the rest of the lesson'. Here the warning is accompanied by a specific punishment. But note that sitting near the teacher to support learning is not a punishment!

Effective punishments need to be specific and real punishments, not some sort of reward for the child. So if the rule is 'Put your hand up for attention', how is the child who yells 'Miss, miss' across the classroom treated? Some cunning is needed here, because if the teacher responds in almost any way to the yelling child this will reinforce the unwanted behaviour. Several things probably need attention to reinforce the rule. As hard as this is to do, the teacher needs to ignore the child who yells out until he or she is quiet, at which point the child is reminded about the rule and invited to put a hand up and then asked for the answer or the response required.

More work with the children on what the rule means and why it is there then needs to be undertaken. The children who keep the rule need to be very heavily rewarded. If rules are being broken, it may well be that they have not been fully understood. It may be that the rule is not one that really matters. It is a useful exercise to review classroom rules when they are broken to see if they are useful.

Some school policies encourage teachers to use segregation or 'time out' as punishment. This can work very well if it is, say, five minutes of good behaviour and then back to one's place. However, children can manipulate this for their own ends. For example, a child may choose to commit an act of disobedience in order to miss the rest of a lesson. Once again, this is an example of the punishment becoming a reward and therefore reinforcing the unwanted behaviour. The use of this punishment in these cases can also have the effect of creating for the children concerned a certain amount of 'street cred' with their peers. This will not contribute to good order in the classroom.

Alternatively, the punishment may cause the child to become alienated and to feel unwanted. The segregation may be more effective if it involves sitting in a different place rather than leaving the room for another classroom. In this case this needs to be clearly distinguished for all in the class from the occasions when the teacher moves children to another area of the classroom to give them more support.

Many punishments involve loss of privileges. These are also quite tricky to work out. The loss of privilege cannot deny the individual any part of that child's curriculum entitlement. It is also important to avoid depriving the child of something that is really enjoyed. The child should acknowledge the punishment as just, but the punishment must not allow that child to build up strong feelings of resentment. For example, not allowing the child to take part in a football match could cause more problems than it solves, especially if he or she is the top goal scorer! Losing an outing, too, would be seen as unjust and would also deny the child part of the curriculum. One way forward is to use loss of negotiated privilege time. In this, the child would have a behavioural contract which sets out privileges that could be earned. Popular privileges include the right to be indoors when other children are out, extra playtime, use of special games equipment and time on the computer.

Other punishment options include a severe telling off, going beyond a mild reprimand of the 'Don't do that' kind. This has to be carried out privately (but where the teacher/student teacher can be observed to be behaving correctly). The telling off is the result of the child breaking a well-understood rule. Who carries out the punishment will be important, as this is a punishment that uses position power. Thus it may have more effect if it comes from a class teacher than a student teacher. For a class teacher this punishment may be better delivered by the head. The telling off is often more effective if it is carefully scripted. It should be carried out quietly and calmly. Demeaning remarks that personalize the 'crime' should be avoided.

More serious repeated offences need to be dealt with within school policy. The use of the head to discuss with the child some form of support to improve behaviour and the help of parents in the working out of these plans is well worth considering. Behaviour contracts between the child, parents and teachers are becoming increasingly popular. These attempt to tackle one or two problem areas at a time. The level of demand on the child increases over time; for example, staying in place may rise from five minutes to an hour in five-minute intervals. It is usual to ignore inappropriate behaviour while improvement is systematically reinforced through praise and real rewards.

For student teachers it is important to know what is being done with children who have more than the usual difficulties in controlling their own behaviour. The expectation would be that the approaches the teacher has chosen should be understood and used by the student teacher. However, while student teachers should expect to have some success with these and an increased understanding of how to deal with children with more long-term behaviour difficulties, they should not expect to work miracles. It may be necessary to enlist the help and support of the class teacher to prevent school placement time from being dominated by one or two problem children.

Finally, a reminder that the use of punishment in school has to be within the law. It has to be moderate and carried out without malice. It must also be acceptable to parents and what teachers might usually do. Corporal punishment is illegal, for example, so not only must teachers not smack children, but also they must not throw chalk at them. Detention needs to be used with caution; normally this is not an option for student teachers. Punishments are never a substitute for establishing the need for socially acceptable behaviour and teaching children how this can be achieved.

## CONCLUSION

Good teaching means recognizing the need for good order. The order created in the classroom and the school has a wider significance than just enabling the curriculum to be delivered. The business of the school is to help children to learn more than the content of the National Curriculum; teachers have a unique opportunity to develop self-esteem and the child's self-concept. Teachers have a role in creating a just and fair society. The discipline policy in any school, how children behave towards each other and how teachers behave towards children, is not static, but will need to develop and change over time. Democracy, in the sense of sharing the power with the children, needs to be coupled with clear leadership by the teacher. By working out the rules of behaviour with the children, teachers are involved in their moral and social development.

If the discipline in the school is to have positive effects, careful thought needs to be given to devising genuine rewards and just punishments. Teachers who are successful have a determination that children will reach their potential. The trick is to prevent misbehaviour where possible. Good teachers also deal with issues as they arise. When they make a mistake they make changes, when they have success they capitalize upon this. Their vision is coupled with an ability to work hard to get the details right, so that children can succeed. This means that the work which the children are required to do is carefully prepared, so that each child is working appropriately and everything is done to make this possible – the pencils are sharp, the scissors are out and the paper is there! In such classes there is a positive atmosphere and children will be successful learners.

## REFERENCES

DES (1989) *Discipline in Schools*. London: HMSO.

Kohlberg, L. (1968) The child as moral philosopher. *Psychology Today*, **2**, 25–30.

Kounin, J.S. (1970) *Discipline and Group Management in Classrooms*. Holt, Rinehart and Winston.

Mosley, J. (1994) *Turn Your School Around*. Cambridge: LDA.

Smith, P.K. and Sharp, S. (eds) (1994) *School Bullying: Insights and Perspectives*. London: Routledge.

TTA (1997) *Framework for the Assessment of Quality and Standards in Initial Teacher Training 1997/98*. London: Ofsted.

Wheldall, K. and Merrett, F. (1984) *Positive Teaching, The Behavioural Approach*. London: Unwin.

Whitney, I. and Smith, P.K. (1993) A survey of the nature and extent of bully/victim problems in junior/middle and secondary schools. *Educational Research*, **35**, 3–25.

## SOME SUGGESTIONS FOR FURTHER READING

Docking, J. (1996, 2nd edn) *Managing Behaviour in the Primary School.* London: David Fulton.
Croll, P. and Hastings, N. (eds) (1996) *Effective Primary Teaching: Research-based Classroom Strategies.* London: David Fulton.
Mosely, J. (1994) *Turn Your School Around*, as above.

CHAPTER 17

# Accountability: a practical guide

BRIAN TAYLOR

## ACCOUNTABILITY TO THE LOCAL COMMUNITY

I firmly believe that schools belong to the communities we serve. My experience has always been within Sheffield's urban corridor which stretches right across our city, and I have constantly been aware of the generations-deep mistrust of schools as partners, in a disabling process which keeps the underprivileged where they are, as opposed to using schools as agents of empowerment.

For thirteen years I worked as a member of staff responsible for community links within a purpose-built community school in the East End of Sheffield. The school was open for extended hours and adopted very much a partnership stance with parents and carers.

Much of our work was concerned with extra-curricular opportunities, many of which were sports-based. Consequently, a great deal of support for the school was generated throughout the whole community which, in turn, generated great enthusiasm regarding our work in general.

This spirit has been a lasting one, and even now, some twenty years later, I am able to draw upon a substantial network of ex-pupils and colleagues who appreciate the value of mutual support, to help me with my current work within the Wybourn community.

Recently, Wybourn Primary School was inspected by an Ofsted team from Barnsley and, while there is plenty of work to do in several areas, the team described our links with the local community as 'the best we have ever seen', high praise considering the fact that they had inspected approximately sixty schools.

Much of this is due to our Parents as Partners project, which enables parents to support and influence the work of their school. The LEA, the Workers' Education Association and various more 'fragile' sponsors fund the project. It is the first of its kind in Sheffield and is now in its fourth year.

The project has been instrumental in developing a constructive and open atmosphere within our school but, more importantly, this atmosphere has adopted a learning context which is showing proven signs of raised achievement for parents and pupils alike and is beginning to re-awaken a belief in the power of education throughout our community.

Our experience has shown that increased attainment by pupils is not sustainable without the ongoing trust and active support of parents. We have achieved this support by opening up classrooms, entering into debate with parents and giving them a real voice regarding their school.

Alongside this approach we have also adopted the role of a satellite site for adult education as well as providing numerous opportunities, on a daily basis, for parent/pupil workshops. A member of staff has been appointed with an extra responsibility point for community education links and she works very closely with our partners to maintain these developments.

Recently, the Parents as Partners project has run a college-accredited course, 'Helping in Schools', which required a two-day commitment per-week for a period of twelve weeks. Ten of our parents graduated and, just as importantly, the course attracted two further candidates from other schools. The costs of this course have been met by European funding gained by LEA colleagues.

Many of these activities take place within Wybourn Basement, a fifth corridor in our school, which is dedicated primarily for community use. Throughout the last five years we have been able to draw together a multi-agency team of workers who support our community. These include a development worker and further workers from family and community services, the Youth Service, Sheffield College, the Workers' Education Association, the Youth Association of South Yorkshire and community police officers, to name but a few.

The direction which this corporate work takes is to a large extent shaped by the Wybourn Action Group which is a conglomeration of these workers, local councillors, housing and cleansing services, and, most importantly, Wybourn residents. Together we have formulated a five-year community action plan with key multi-agency targets for community improvements. Through our co-ordinated efforts, different representatives have been enormously successful in gaining funding to enable ideas to become reality.

Quite recently, one of our members, the Youth Association of South Yorkshire, made a successful lottery bid for £250,000 to form a trust to renovate and reopen a derelict building as a Youth Training Centre for young adults in order to claw back educational opportunities which had been missed previously through more formal channels.

More recently still, our community action plan has been adopted as part of a successful Single Regeneration Budget bid for Wybourn and its neighbouring communities to the value of £17,000,000. This should provide approximately one thousand jobs over the next seven years.

Now the cycle of deprivation and underachievement will be broken!

In summary, therefore:

- Schools belong to the communities they serve.

- To regenerate our schools we need to regenerate our communities.

## ACCOUNTABILITY TO COLLEAGUES AND GOVERNORS

The days when individual teachers, even if they wanted to, could close their classroom door and teach what and how they liked, have gone. Education is now right at the centre of the political arena and there is great pressure from the government downwards, together with far too much accountability and local competition to allow this to happen.

Now, the curriculum has to deliver specifically in terms of input regarding curriculum breadth, balance, continuity and progression and in terms of output regarding SAT results. Thus, too much idiosyncratic teaching can short-circuit the work of colleagues and damage the reputation of the school.

In addition, there is an increasing propensity for Ofsted to report back regarding the quality of teaching that they observe. Apparently, many thousands of us are succeeding, but fifteen thousand of us are failing and need to be replaced. What an encouraging thought!

This is a sign of the times; but through links with other schools, LEAs and communities I hope we can acquire an extra skin to protect us.

In the current system the teacher is the classroom deliverer, the headteacher is in day-to day control with plenty of responsibility but very little power. This is because, in theory at least, general accountability lies with the governing body, which is an awesome responsibility for unpaid laypeople. In practical terms, it is almost without exception the headteacher who carries the can.

In such circumstances, recruitment and active involvement of school governors can be a real problem, but a strong, supportive and effective governing body can considerably enhance the performance of a school. Due to rising pupil numbers our governing body numbers have recently been increased from twelve to sixteen members by boosting the number of parent governors as a formal acknowledgement of parents in our school. Alongside this we have some 'key players' insofar as the city is concerned, who can help to place our developments strategically in line with developments throughout Sheffield.

This has been particularly true regarding our ongoing school improvement initiative which, in partnership with Sheffield city as a whole, has received much local, national and international publicity, thus adding to the 'feel-good' factor within our school community as well as to the belief that our school is beginning to make a difference.

In summary, therefore:

- Teachers are accountable to each other.

- Governors are accountable for the performance of their schools.

- Headteachers are accountable to their governors.

## ACCOUNTABILITY TO THE LOCAL EDUCATION AUTHORITY AND GOVERNMENT

Since the 1988 Education Act the balance in terms of external accountability for teachers and schools has changed completely.

Prior to the Act, local authorities reigned supreme but as a result of the Act the then Secretary of State for Education gained 163 new powers to drive the country's education agenda from the centre.

The introduction of local financial management largely removed the facility of LEAs to set their own frameworks for funding, through circumnavigating their role almost completely by the devolution of budgets to individual schools. Further regulations added yet more momentum to this shift.

These changes, alongside the introduction of the National Curriculum and its subsequent testing, have changed the face and the climate of education almost beyond recognition throughout the last decade.

The publishing of the test results for individual schools and local authorities alongside the Ofsted inspection process and the apparent climate of choice provided by open enrolment have also added substantial pressure on everyone from the centre and thus greater accountability for everyone except, apparently, the centre itself. However, the 1997 General Election ousted a government whose key approach was one of pressure in terms of their expectation that achievement must be raised, despite the fact that appropriate support in terms of resources would not be forthcoming.

As part of this process, local education authorities had been reduced to the role of passive spectators of a game which they once controlled. Such little power they were left with lay in their advisory role and partnership with schools by consent, for if schools were not happy they could opt out of their control.

However, with the advent of New Labour it appears that while, if anything, there is likely to be even more pressure from above in respect of the ensuring of 'Excellence for All' as a basic entitlement as well as the continuation of league tables and Ofsted, there do at least appear to be some limited improvements insofar as support in the form of resources is concerned and a spirit of partnership seems to be slowly re-emerging.

These developments are aimed at ensuring effective organization and delivery of education – particularly, it seems, for the underprivileged. However, major questions still remain regarding whether adequate resources will in fact be made available and whether a true constructive partnership will emerge. Until this partnership does emerge, schools will continue to feel threatened by the current climate and those who are weak and/or desperate will, at the very least, be unable to resist the temptation of teaching to the tests and narrowing their curriculum accordingly. Whatever your opinion, there continues to be plenty of demand for accountability, which means individual teachers and local education authorities are definitely not setting the agenda.

In summary, therefore:

- Schools have to prove their improvement.

- Those who fail are named and shamed.

- The government is still very much in the driving seat.

- LEAs are still very much passengers at this stage.

## ACCOUNTABILITY TO THE PUBLIC

Teachers and schools are, in general, at the mercy of the public. I have lost count of the thousands of times in my career when people have commented on the length of school holidays! Even though I usually work throughout most of my holidays I now avoid at all costs stating what my job is unless I absolutely have to, since the cause of and antidote to every single ailment in society seem to lie at my personal doorstep:

- 'Standards are dropping!'

- 'There's no discipline!'

- 'There's not enough education!'

Education certainly does have a massive role to play in these major issues. None the less, broad sweeping statements such as those given above still cut us to the quick, especially since these opinions seem at times to be so widespread. The reality is that almost every person will be, or has been, a beneficiary of the state education system so their value-judgements should be given due regard.

However, it sometimes seems as if the impossible is expected of individual teachers and schools. If a child achieves, he or she is a good pupil. If a child fails to achieve, he or she has a bad teacher. It can be a thankless task and it clearly has something to do with encouraging our clients to take a broader, more detached view. But it is only by engaging in effective dialogue with them that we can raise their awareness. Parents wanting pupils to achieve excellence is clearly desirable; but there needs to be an acknowledgement that there are other pupils in school in addition to their own. The only way forward seems to be to continue to build a true partnership with parents by opening up and engaging parents in the decision-making process.

For inspections, Ofsted largely measures success in this area through a behind-closed-doors meeting for parents and a questionnaire. In Wybourn's inspection, Inspectors were initially concerned when over fifty parents turned up for the meeting, fearing for some reason that there might be a lot of anger. They needn't have worried – it was just enthusiasm!

The results of the questionnaire were stunning. First, the response was adjudged to be a full return, with over 280 written replies. From these replies it emerged that:

- Ninety-eight per cent of all parents felt that they had an active part to play in the school.

- Ninety-seven per cent of all parents were happy with the education the school provided.

- Eighty-eight per cent of all parents said their child was happy at school.

There is room for improvement in all these areas, but what an encouraging start!

As educators, we should constantly strive to provide as near to a personalized menu of learning experiences for each pupil as possible. The recent statutory guidelines for pupils with special educational needs is a good way to ensure quality entitlements for these pupils, particularly since individual education plans are required (see Chapter 14). We are now in the process of adopting the same approach for our more able pupils.

This degree of differentiation is necessary to meet the needs of all pupils, and I certainly believe that the acid test is the question 'Is this good enough for my own child?' If the answer is 'No', we need to improve it. In addition, I firmly believe that schools should be as open as it is safely possible for them to be. If we are confident and believe in what we are doing this policy will raise awareness and enlist parents as partners in the continuing process of improvement. A by-product of this might just be that teachers will get the resources and credit which most of them so richly deserve.

In summary therefore:

- It is desirable for everyone to have an informed view regarding education.

- School won't always be positive, but that should be our aim.

- Don't take general criticisms personally.

- Nurture your belief that you personally can change things.

- Be open about what you are doing.

- Be proud of what you are doing.

## ACCOUNTABILITY TO PUPILS

Learn about your children for surely you do not know them.

(Rousseau)

Every teacher needs to ask her- or himself the fundamental question regarding whom schools are supposed to benefit – and for every teacher the answer needs to be: every individual pupil.

While it is true that, as institutions, schools and the education system as a whole are valuable providers of training for employment, unless we meet the needs of each and every pupil we are living a lie. In any event, the current market forces approach is that schools that fail to deliver for pupils will eventually die through lack of numbers, or be put to sleep by Ofsted. All this points to the same conclusion: either out of idealism or necessity, the school, and therefore every teacher, needs to aim to meet the needs of every pupil.

Every child is a unique individual who may well get only one chance insofar as formal education is concerned. To use a gardening analogy, each one needs to grow to maximum height and strength, but each one may need slightly different conditions in which to flourish. Slightly less favourable conditions will still produce some growth, but it will not be as good as it could be. If the teacher is the only gardener we have, he or she may well have to struggle to create such a varied learning environment, so what we need are more gardeners. Pupils and parents can help us by developing the learning environment from which we all benefit. Parents as Partners is one application of this theory, as are the regular school assemblies, parts of which are often dedicated to raising the awareness of pupils regarding school development plans.

Further to this, though, we underestimate the power of our pupils at our peril. Both teacher and school need to enlist all partners in every aspect of the whole school development process as well as enabling them to develop independence by offering choices. If pupil independence can be developed within a strong and challenging learning ethos, the value added to achievement can be considerable.

Alternatively, pupils who do not engage with the learning process often exhibit behavioural difficulties which is when the real difficulties start. Good behaviour results from good teaching; therefore, to avoid this, pupils need to be at the heart of all our considerations and be totally valued by all concerned. We need to both encourage and equip them as true partners, thus enabling them to walk alongside or even lead us on the journey towards the fulfilment of potential, in this way offering maximum opportunities for the future, both in terms of employment and of life in general.

In summary, therefore:

- Good schools are accountable to pupils in terms of process and outcome.
- Schools need to be child-centred.
- Pupils can comfortably manage many aspects of their own learning.
- Pupils can be leaders.
- Pupils are 100 per cent of the future.

## SELF-ACCOUNTABILITY

> ... to thine own self be true,
> and it must follow, as the night the day,
> thou canst not then be false to any man.
>
> (From Shakespeare's *Hamlet*)

When interviewing candidates for teaching posts, a key quality I am looking for is someone who is driven by a clear educational vision and philosophy. Teachers who do not have this inner drive and belief leave themselves vulnerable to outside pressures which may well sway them away from their own vision. Of course, newly appointed staff need to be flexible, but they also need to be strong. If you have done your best, no one can blame you for not trying.

As the years go by your philosophy will be subjected to many onslaughts resulting from the massive gap between ideals and reality – large classes and lack of free time for preparation are two, which spring to mind. But used constructively, your experiences will enable you to work towards your vision while constantly fine-tuning it. This may sound a bit pious, but at the start of each day I make a list of targets for improvement and at the end of the day I tick off those which have been achieved. It may have been a discussion with an individual teacher, parent or pupil, to agree targets for improvement, or it may be to do with the organization of the school in general which improves its effectiveness. By quietly celebrating your successes on a personal level you will recharge your batteries for future use.

While your philosophy needs to be clear and strong, if you remain open-minded you will never stop learning. Always remember that in choosing to become a teacher you have acknowledged your own responsibility to meet the personal, social and intellectual needs of every pupil in your care, day upon day, year upon year. The pressure is relentless, but when it goes well it is exhilarating. Year upon year you will bask in the reflected glory of the achievements of your pupils as they fly off into the future. All high-flyers had a teacher, as did most of those unfortunate individuals who never took off because their teachers never enabled them to do so!

Certainly at primary level, children in your class may well spend more time with you than any other adult, including their parents. The influence and responsibility you will have is crucial, so you will need to look after yourself. Teaching as a career will be a marathon, not a sprint, but keep your vision constantly in mind and you will get there in the end – and remember, great change only takes place slowly.

In summary, therefore:

- Form your own educational philosophy and keep improving it.

- Pace yourself and celebrate your successes.

- Don't despair ... every day is a new day.

- Learn from your mistakes, and then forget them!

- Look after yourself, you will need to be robust.

- There is no substitute for hard work.

## SOME SUGGESTIONS FOR FURTHER READING

Croll, P. (ed.) (1996) *Teachers, Pupils and Primary Schooling: Continuity and Change*. London: Cassell.
Hayes, D. (1996) *Foundations of Primary Teaching*. London: David Fulton.
Robson, S. and Smedley, S. (1996) *Education in Early Childhood – First things First*. London: David Fulton.

# Index